Liberal Nationalism in Central Europe

After the collapse of communism there was a widespread fear that nationalism would pose a serious threat to the development of liberal democracy in the countries of Central Europe. This book examines the role of nationalism in postcommunist development, focusing in particular on Poland, the Czech Republic and Slovakia. It argues that a certain type of nationalism, that is liberal nationalism, has positively influenced the process of postcommunist transition towards the emerging liberal democratic order.

Stefan Auer is a lecturer in European politics and societies at the Dublin European Institute, University College Dublin. Prior to this, he studied at the University of Melbourne, and at universities in Slovakia and Germany. His research interests include the challenges of postcommunist transition and aspects of political theory.

RoutledgeCurzon contemporary Russia and Eastern Europe series

Liberal Nationalism in Central Europe
Stefan Auer

Liberal Nationalism
in Central Europe

Stefan Auer

RoutledgeCurzon
Taylor & Francis Group

LONDON AND NEW YORK

First published 2004
by RoutledgeCurzon
11 New Fetter Lane, London EC4P 4EE

Simultaneously published in the USA and Canada
by RoutledgeCurzon
29 West 35th Street, New York, NY 10001

RoutledgeCurzon is an imprint of the Taylor & Francis Group

© 2004 Stefan Auer

Typeset in Times by Taylor & Francis Books Ltd
Printed and bound in Great Britain by Biddles Ltd,
King's Lynn

British Library Cataloguing in Publication Data
A catalogue record for this book is available from the British Library

Library of Congress Cataloging in Publication Data
A catalog record for this title has been requested.

ISBN 0–415–31479–8

For Alex, Ben and Dasha

Contents

Preface

The nations of Central and Eastern Europe and their nationalism(s) have been seen in the West as backward and barbaric. One of my favourite examples which illustrates this view comes from the great gothic novel of 1897 by Bram Stoker, *Dracula*. It starts with the impressions of a traveller who has embarked on a long journey to Transylvania. He complains repeatedly about the inconvenience of travelling to the East. Having had to wait for more than an hour for his train to depart from Budapest, for example, he concludes 'that the further East you go the more unpunctual are the trains' (Stoker 2002: 28). And long before arriving in the mountains of Transylvania, which are populated by vampires and other beasts, he sees some truly remarkable creatures:

> The strangest figures we saw were the Slovaks, who are more barbarian than the rest, with their big cowboy hats, great baggy dirty-white trousers, white linen shirts....They are very picturesque, but do not look prepossessing. On the stage they would be set down at once as some old Oriental band of brigands. They are, however, I am told, very harmless and rather wanting in natural self-assertion.
>
> (Stoker 2002: 29)

Not many people would today form their views of Central and Eastern Europe by reading *Dracula*, and not many Slovaks these days wear 'baggy dirty-white trousers'. Yet there are many more sophisticated accounts of different national and political cultures in postcommunist Europe that still rely on a conceptual division between the civilized West and the backward East. This is especially true for Slovakia. Ruled until 1998 by a former boxer, Vladimír Mečiar, the Slovaks have been seen as being trapped in their own history, which in turn is characterized by illiberal regimes and an endless struggle for national survival. Just as Stoker's hero encountered ever more backwardness as he travelled further East, nationalism is assumed to have gained an ever more illiberal character as it moved in the same direction. Many scholars argue that nationalism degenerated as it 'travelled' from the West to the East, changing from its more civilized and progressive forms into barbarity. In line with this, it was assumed that contemporary nationalism in Central and Eastern Europe – extremist by definition – would be a serious impediment to the process of democratic transition. Many scholars also believed that nationalism would undermine the integrationist ambitions of these countries and their keenness to 'return to Europe'.

These fears proved largely unjustified. By the time of the completion of this book, the countries of Central Europe were set to become full members of the European Union. Hence, increasingly, what needs explaining is why nationalism has *not* manifested its destructive potential after the collapse of communism in Central Europe (Krasnodębski 1995; Sunley 1996: 7–8; Brubaker 1998). Considering the economic and political difficulties that accompanied the process of postcommunist transition, one may well ask why the appeal of right-wing extremism in the region has been so limited (Segert 2002: 623). Does it mean that nationalism became irrelevant for the peoples of Central Europe? This book takes a different view. It seeks to demonstrate that certain types of nationalism could, in fact, *contribute* to the success of political transition. Likewise, liberal nationalism could also prove to be conducive to the project of European unification. As a recent comprehensive survey of public opinion in all applicant states (including the Czech Republic, Slovakia and Poland) showed, 'high levels of national pride' did not 'prevent high levels of European pride' (*Eurobarometer*, March 2002). In fact, the survey identified a positive correlation between the two feelings. These findings support the argument that liberal nationalism makes the ambitious project of European unification feasible by allowing for the development of multiple identities (cf. Laffan *et al.* 2000: 31).

The structure of the book is as follows. Chapter 1 presents a survey of the different theories of nationalism which have influenced the perception of the region. It will pay particular attention to the notion of 'two types of nationalism', which distinguishes between a 'Western' nationalism that is by definition conducive to liberal democracy, and an 'Eastern' nationalism that poses a serious threat to it, and was thus used to explain the proclivity of the East (which, at different times, included or excluded the countries of Central Europe) for harbouring illiberal regimes. This view has seriously distorted our understanding of the political developments in Central and Eastern Europe. Nationalism in Central Europe has been used for the legitimation of both left-wing and right-wing dictatorships, but it has also repeatedly been employed as a tool of national liberation (as in 1989) and thus furthered the case of liberal democracy. As theorists of liberal nationalism (e.g. David Miller, Yael Tamir) have demonstrated, certain conceptions of national identity are compatible with basic liberal values. Although this concept is usually thought applicable only to the well established democracies in the West, a balanced view of Central European developments indicates that liberal nationalism can also be supportive of an emerging liberal democratic order.

This is not to say that liberal nationalism can solve all the problems in the ethnically diverse environment of Central Europe. As the second chapter of this book demonstrates, there are no universally valid answers to the conflicting demands of different groups. The question arises, for example, whether the liberal state should actively support and protect various cultural and ethnic identities, or whether it should, rather, be indifferent to any demands for special treatment. The responses of the state to the legitimate needs and aspirations of ethnic minorities must be based on a balanced assessment of the particular situation of the ethnic group in question, and its relationship to the majority group. To illustrate this, Chapter 2 will discuss the position of Romanies in Czech and Slovak societies as well as the situation of the Hungarian minority in Slovakia.

The theoretical discussion of the first two chapters is applied to Poland (Chapter 3), the Czech Republic (Chapter 4) and Slovakia (Chapter 5). Each chapter begins with a short historical survey, which allows for a better understanding of the ongoing debates about the 'right' meaning of their respective national histories. These debates constitute an important part of the various nationalist discourses that compete for dominance within each nation. I will show that in all the three countries it is possible to identify not only the forces of extreme nationalism (as one would expect from the premise of 'two types of nationalism') but also influential liberal nationalist forces. This leads to cautious optimism about the prospects of democratic transition, the success of which is partly predicated on the prevalence of liberal nationalism.

Finally, a remark on the geographic limits of the book is in order. The choice of case studies is the result of a compromise between depth and comparative scope. I believe that the countries chosen are most representative of the different paths that postcommunist development in Central and Eastern Europe has taken, and of the potential for liberal nationalism to play a role in this process. At any rate, the choice of countries was determined more by practical considerations than a judgement about who belongs and does not belong to Central Europe (see also Chapter 1). The methodology employed demands access to primary sources of the various national discourses; thus limits were also set by my linguistic capabilities.[1] This approach is in line with the sound advice of Richard Sakwa, who argued that

> a distinctive type of 'political anthropology' is required [in postcommunist studies] combining 'intimate familiarity' with the subject of study (analysis of the debates in the societies themselves, a thorough study of the books, newspapers and think tank reports, and above all interviews and informal talks with people involved) with macro social and political theory.
>
> (Sakwa 1999a: 717–18)

The book is based on my doctoral dissertation at the University of Melbourne. I wish to express my gratitude to Leslie Holmes for his outstanding supervision and continuous support. Furthermore, I was greatly assisted by Tony Coady, especially in the area of political theory. I owe special thanks to Robert Manne and Robert Horvath from whom I learned about the history of Central Europe. My thanks go also to my friends and colleagues in Melbourne for their interest and ideas: Nick Anson, Krystyna Duszniak, Zoe Knox, Robert Lagerberg, Tim Mehigan, Cezary Milosinski, Carolyn O'Brien, Daniel Ritlewski, Peter Shearman, Charles Sowerwine and David Tucker. I am very thankful for the extensive and encouraging feedback from David Miller (Nuffield College, Oxford), and Robert Pynsent (University College, London), who were the examiners of my thesis.

I could not have finished this book without the support of the Dublin European Institute at University College Dublin. I am grateful to Dolores Burke, Katy Hayward, Brigid Laffan, and especially Ben Tonra, who helped to accommodate my ambitions to travel, research and teach. I also benefited from the support provided by the Contemporary Europe Research Centre at the University of Melbourne. For assisting me in my research in the Czech Republic, Poland and Slovakia, I wish to thank my friends David Vaughan in Prague; Barbora Ertlová in Krakow; Róbert and Zuzana Erby, and Pavel Vilikovský in Bratislava; Ivan and Ivona Janda in Košice; and Róbert Antožy and Peter Konkoly in Kembridž (read Cambridge) for their hospitality and great insights. My thanks go also to my students in Melbourne and Dublin: Dermot Corrigan, Martin Fedor, Inka Fischer, Karen Mulchinock, Derryn Schoenborn and Agnieszka Skolimowska. For extensive comments and constructive criticism, I am indebted to the anonymous reader at Routledge. I am very grateful to Anna Gwiazda, Zdzisław Krasnodębski, Brian Porter and Katharina Stankiewicz, who read and commented on the Polish chapter. Finally, I wish to thank my friend Tobias Theiler, who was very helpful and supportive, especially in the last stage of my work.

Small sections of this book have been published, and I thank the editors for their permission to adapt them for this book. An earlier version of Chapter 1 was published under the title 'Nationalism in Central Europe: A Chance or a Threat for the Emerging Liberal Democratic Order', in *East European Politics and Societies* (University of California Press) vol. 14, no. 2, spring 2000, 213–45; a part of Chapter 2 appeared in Carolyn O'Brien and Linda Hancock (eds) (2000) *Re-writing Rights in Europe*, Aldershot: Ashgate, 69–90; and a modified subsection of Chapter 3 was published under the title 'Church and State in Liberal Theory and Polish Political Practice', in Justyna Miklaszewska (ed.) (1999) *Democracy in Central Europe 1989–99: Comparative and Historical Perspectives*, Krakow: Meritum, 131–49. I am also grateful to Pavel Štecha for the permission to use his photograph of the 1989 revolution in Prague on the cover of this book. Finally, I wish to thank my editor, Peter Sowden, and his dedicated team, particularly Faye Kaliszczak and Andy Soutter, for their assistance, encouragement and continuous support of this project.

Note

1 Unless indicated otherwise, all Czech, German, Polish and Slovak sources quoted have been translated by the author.

1 Nationalism in Central Europe

Some of the worst excesses of political violence in twentieth-century Europe have been attributed to the influence of nationalism. Against this background, it may appear fanciful to argue that a certain type of nationalism — liberal nationalism — can, in fact, play a positive role in the postcommunist transition of Central Europe. The concept of liberal nationalism, which seeks to reconcile the universal demands of liberalism with particularist attachments to a national culture, has gained new credibility in the West owing to recent studies by political theorists (Tamir 1993; Miller 1995; Kymlicka 2001a). However, no significant attempt has been made to show its relevance to the experience of the postcommunist countries of Central and Eastern Europe. It was assumed that owing to the lack of strong democratic traditions, people in these countries were prone to succumb to the lure of ethnocentric nationalism, which would seriously endanger the prospects for a stable liberal democratic order.

This assumption is in line with the old notion of two essentially different forms of nationalism: the enlightened Western, that is supportive of democracy, and the 'backward' Eastern form, that is an obstacle to any genuinely democratic society (Kohn 1944; Plamenatz 1973; Schöpflin 1995). According to this view, people in the West were liberal virtually by definition, in contrast to their eastern neighbours, who were deemed unable to overcome the illiberal legacies of the past. To label the differences between nations and their nationalism(s) with this reference to geography is, however, misleading. As this book seeks to demonstrate, different conceptions of nationalism have been competing for dominance *within* particular countries in both the East and the West.

What is nationalism?

Nationalism is a contentious issue. Analysts cannot agree on its definition or its role in society. Most contend, however, that nationalism is a specifically modern phenomenon, which became salient in the eighteenth (Anderson 1983; Berlin 1979; Hobsbawm 1990) or nineteenth century (Gellner 1983). Ernest Gellner convincingly demonstrated that nationalism, rather than fulfilling some ancient human need, is a specifically modern phenomenon (Gellner 1983). The Industrial Revolution in the West necessitated a radical change in the relationship between polity and culture, which in turn produced nationalism. The salient feature of the preceding agrarian societies was, according to Gellner, cultural diversity and fragmentation into small autonomous sub-communities, each of which lived in its own specific idiom. A peasant had no need to communicate with the elite of high culture who existed beyond his experience (usually limited to the breadth of his valley). The modern industrial and predominantly urban society required mass literacy and a high degree of social mobility, which could only be achieved by nearly universal access to a state-sponsored 'national' educational system. To be successful, such a system needed to use a vernacular accessible to the entire population of the country. Thus a need for cultural homogenization arose and gave birth to the political doctrine of nationalism, 'which holds that the political and the national unit should be congruent' (Gellner 1983: 1). Nations were being 'created' either by turning the 'low', spontaneous and oral cultures into the literate and cultivated ones, or by imposing the existing 'high' culture on the available and diverse idioms of peasants. Nationalism can then be characterized as 'the organisation of human groups into large, centrally educated, culturally homogeneous units' (Gellner 1983: 35). In short, Gellner concludes that modernization leads to nationalism and nationalism engenders nations, and not the other way around. And since ours is the time of a never-ending process of modernization, we live in an 'age of nationalism':

> Nationalism – the principle of homogeneous cultural units as the foundations of political life, and of the obligatory cultural unity of rulers and ruled – is indeed inscribed neither in the nature of things, nor in the hearts of men, nor in the pre-conditions of social life in general, and the contention that it *is* so inscribed is a falsehood which nationalist doctrine has succeeded in presenting as self-evident. But nationalism as a phenomenon, not as a doctrine presented by nationalists, is inherent in a certain set of social conditions; and those conditions, it so happens, are the conditions of our time.
>
> (Gellner 1983: 125)

Gellner's conception has been criticized for being simplistic and historically inaccurate, and many examples seem to refute the assumption that nationalism only became important in the nineteenth century as a result of modernization. Anthony D. Smith challenged this 'modernist fallacy' above all on historical grounds by arguing that 'expressions of fervent attachment to the concept of the nation as a territorial-cultural and political community' go back as far as the fourteenth and fifteenth centuries 'in France, England ... as well as in Poland and Russia' (Smith 1995a: 38; for the Polish case see also Walicki 1997a). Similarly, Czech nationalism can be traced back to the early fourteenth century. Robert P. Pynsent, for example, refers to Dalimil's chronicle as the first instance of the preaching of mass nationalism in the Czech context (Pynsent 1999).

Yet there can be little doubt that the scope and impact of nationalism in pre-modern times was rather limited. The full potential of nationalism as a political force could only develop in modern societies that were characterized by an unprecedented degree of social mobility and the active involvement of ever more citizens in political processes. As Ray Taras observed,

> even if early forms of literary nationalism had made their appearance in the fourteenth century, magnates still went to war against each other and showed no loyalty to the nations from which they originated. In their turn, the masses were still far from experiencing any sense of larger community.
>
> (Taras 2002: 13)

Although the link between the rise of nationalism in the nineteenth century and the process of modernization is not always as straightforward as Gellner's model implies,[1] the theory offers valuable insights into the emergence of modern nationalism in Central Europe.

In fact, the example of 'Ruritania', which Gellner offers as a characteristic scenario of the evolution of nationalism, is based on the historic experience of the people of the Habsburg Empire, where more often than not 'the obligatory cultural unity of rulers and ruled' was lacking. The story proceeds as follows: the multilingual 'Empire of Megalomania' was politically dominated by the elite who communicated in a language very different from that of the common peasants, 'Ruritanians'. With the rapid development of industrial centres, 'Ruritanians' were drawn to seek new employment opportunities in these centres, in the process of which they were forced to assimilate into the existing 'high' culture. Their 'obscure and seldom written or taught language' represented their major obstacle to upward social mobility. Even if many individuals succeeded in fully integrating themselves into the new environment, still others felt disadvantaged and discriminated against because of their 'Ruritanian' origin. This gave birth to a nationalism led by a new group of intellectuals, who reminded their compatriots of 'the famous Ruritanian social bandit' from the eighteenth century who fought against injustices afflicted on the innocent people of Ruritania. The logical alternative to assimilation is the insistence on one's own glorious traditions, which should eventually lead to the creation of an independent nation-state, Ruritania.

This account corresponds rather well with the actual history of the Habsburg Monarchy. The demands of modernization called for the introduction of one common vernacular throughout the whole empire. The Germanizing policies of Joseph II were thus not inspired by any particular national feelings of the ruler but by the practical needs of industrialization (as it happened, the elite spoke German). The attempts to introduce German as a universal language of the empire were met with fierce resistance in Hungary, where Latin remained the language of administration well until the early decades of the nineteenth century. With some delay, Hungarian (rather than German) was introduced as the official language in the Hungarian part of the Empire – a move that strengthened the Hungarian nationalist cause. In turn, the Hungarians, who managed to secure rights for their own national language, tried to impose it on the Slovaks, who reacted as had the Hungarians before. Hungarian nationalism engendered by default the evolution of the Slovak nation, which in turn strove for political autonomy and later even independence (see also Chapter 2).

Gellner's interpretation of the emergence of nationalism has been very influential, but it does not explicitly explore the issues that are arguably more pressing for the present political development of Central Europe: What is the relationship between nationalism and liberal democracy? Why did some forms of nationalism become virulent in the first half of the twentieth century (like German, Italian or even Slovak and Hungarian) and others not? Is nationalism a deadly enemy of liberalism, or its natural ally? Is the best nation no nation?

Nationalism was originally regarded as progressive and supportive of the development of liberal democracy. The two distinguished nineteenth-century liberal thinkers, Alexis de Tocqueville and John Stuart Mill, for example, considered national attachments a valuable source of social solidarity, which would strengthen the political stability of liberal democracy. Conversely, the political creed of the great eighteenth-century German nationalist thinker, Johann Gottfried Herder, was characterized by a liberal and democratic spirit, despite later abuses of his philosophy by extreme nationalists in Germany and elsewhere in Central Europe (Barnard 1965: 154). Herder had maintained that 'a nation based on genuine culture would be peaceful, because it would respect other nations, and that concern for humanity as a whole was more important than concern for one's own nation' (Koepke 1987: x). Echoing this sentiment, the nineteenth-century Italian liberal, Giuseppe Mazzini, believed that 'democratic nationality was the necessary precondition for a peaceful international order' (Urbinati 1996: 203). This has changed dramatically in the twentieth century, with Europe experiencing fanatical nationalism leading to wars, ethnic cleansing and the Holocaust. Hence, despite disagreements about the true nature of nationalism, most analysts today view it as a hindrance to the development of a liberal democracy. Some (like Habermas and Hobsbawm) say that this hindrance must be superseded altogether, while others (like Kymlicka and Tamir) see how democracy and nationalism can be reconciled.

Civic versus ethnic nationalism

Liberal defenders of nationalism are mostly indebted to the original Enlightenment ideal of a nation as an agency of democratic power that was able to challenge the oppressive order of an *ancien régime*. Hence French and American nationalisms have traditionally been regarded as the epitome of civic nationalism, based as they were on the political ideas of revolutionaries who fought for the sovereignty of the people. Membership in the community was thus defined primarily in political terms; civic virtues were more important for the new republic than ethnicity, common culture, or even common language. The only means of exclusion were the territorial boundaries of a country. For that reason, everybody, at least in theory, could become a French or American citizen by acquiring the necessary civic virtues (of which French or English language proficiency was but a part). This voluntaristic notion of national identity is usually contrasted with ethnic nationalism, which tends to be exclusionary, since in that case belonging to a nation is defined by birth, blood and ethnicity. While the former ideally conceives of the nation as a voluntary association, the latter sees it as a community of fate and is thus deterministic.[2] Ethnic nationalism emerged in the late nineteenth century, and it is said to be pertinent to the people of Central and Eastern Europe (Smith 1991: 11; Crawford 1996: 126–8; Eatwell 1997: 238). While civic nationalism is usually associated with liberalism, exclusionary ethnic nationalism has often been conducive to authoritarian regimes.[3] It is the latter that is feared by many critics of nationalism. For liberal nationalists, on the other hand, the distinction between civic and ethnic nationalism has its limitations, as both versions can lead to intolerance, undermining the aims of liberalism. Hence the arguments in this book will rely more on the differentiation between liberal and illiberal forms of nationalism.

The end of nationalism?

The distinguished Marxist historian Eric Hobsbawm argues that, 'in spite of its evident prominence, nationalism is historically less important' in world politics today (Hobsbawm 1990: 181). Given that 'characteristic nationalist movements of the late twentieth century are essentially negative, or rather divisive', Hobsbawm is hopeful that ultimately 'nationalism will decline with the decline of the nation-state' (Hobsbawm 1990: 164, 182). He goes as far as to suggest that ' "nation" and "nationalism" are no longer adequate terms to describe, let alone to analyse, the political entities described as such, or even the sentiments once described by these words' (Hobsbawm 1990: 182). From Gellner's finding that national identities are to a certain extent arbitrary results of nationalism based on myths and half-truths, Hobsbawm infers that their importance should subside with time. This seems to be plausible, considering that citizens in a truly modern (and enlightened) society are expected to act following their reason rather than feelings and attachments connected with some 'imagined communities' (Anderson 1983). Hobsbawm tacitly assumes that by showing that particular national traditions are usually invented and manipulated, the allegiance of the people to their nations can be undermined.[4] But the simple fact that national identities are social constructs and not something inherently 'natural' does not mean that they can be easily abandoned, or replaced by some form of enlightened cosmopolitanism. The term 'imagined communities' should not be confused with imaginary ones (Tamir 1995: 423). As Anthony Smith accurately observed, 'whenever and however national identity is forged, once established, it becomes immensely difficult, if not impossible (short of total genocide) to eradicate' (Smith 1993: 131).

Republican alternative?

Another possible strategy to minimize the political relevance of national identity is to build on the republican tradition, which seeks to bind political communities around an ethnically neutral concept of citizenship. This idea has gained in importance owing to the ambitious project of the European Union, in which national boundaries are being transcended in order to create a new multinational state. Jürgen Habermas, for example, argues that the political unity of European nations cannot be based on the shared traditions, languages and cultures, which lie at the basis of nation-states. What is needed instead is a 'post-national' sense of *Verfassungspatriotismus* (constitutional patriotism), which is based on shared principles of justice and democracy. Only this would make the idea of a federalist European Union, comprised of European rather than national citizens, politically viable (Habermas 1995).

But it is questionable whether it is possible to develop strong attachments to a democratic constitution that is devoid of any references to the particular tradition and culture of a nation (Dahrendorf 1994). In fact, even the Germans, who, as a result of their troubled history, have been more inclined than any other nation to opt for a post-national identity based on constitutional patriotism,[5] are currently re-discovering the importance of national attachments. While the question of national identity had for a long time been almost the exclusive domain of those right-wing political forces which sought to restore the lost pride of the German nation, the situation has changed. Ten years after unification, the heated debate about the German *Leitkultur* has seen a number of politicians and intellectuals from both sides of the political spectrum advocating the need for a 'guiding culture', which would encompass not only political values (including the endorsement of basic liberal principles expressed in the constitution), but also aspects of national culture. For example, Wolfgang Thierse, a Social Democrat leader of the Bundestag, argued that a political community needs a common language and a common set of references, which cannot be attained without reliance on history and culture (Thierse 2000).

Hannah Arendt, who like Habermas was deeply suspicious of nationalist forces, conceded some thirty years earlier that a liberal democratic republic could not be sustained simply by a contract:

Neither compact nor promise upon which compacts rest are sufficient to assure perpetuity, that is, to bestow upon the affairs of men that measure of stability without which they would be unable to build a world for their posterity, destined and designed to outlast their own mortal lives.

(Arendt 1973: 182)

For this reason, even France and the United States (i.e. the republics which are usually regarded as the exemplary manifestations of constitutional patriotism) 'required many of the trappings of nation-states, including founding myths, national symbols, and ideals of historical and quasi-ethnic membership' (Kymlicka and Norman 1995: 315). One of the telling paradoxes of American history is the fact that the founding fathers of the new republic, who as thinkers of the Enlightenment and revolutionary leaders challenged the power of tradition, were soon to be revered as cult figures of the American nation, and became the focal point of a (new) tradition. As Conor Cruise O'Brien noted, 'enlightenment ideas are far more solidly established in America than anywhere else, because there, as nowhere else, they are firmly embedded in the massive edifice of sacral nationalism' (O'Brien 1995: 59). One could hence argue that liberal democracy in America could only be sustained, not against national values, but rather with their support.

Yael Tamir raised further objections against all the contractarian theories that have national values hidden in their liberal agendas. If the liberal state were truly a voluntary association founded on a contract in which citizenship was ideally based on shared principles of justice and democracy (not more and not less), then two problems would arise. First, all those who comply with the criteria of constitutional patriotism would be entitled to become citizens – which is hardly a practical option for virtually all existing states, as no state can fully retreat from controlling migration.[6] Second, whoever questions the values of justice and democracy (like some anarchist groups) should be stripped of their citizenship – which is difficult to reconcile with the liberal ideal of tolerance. Indeed, civic nationalism can, according to Tamir, be more exclusive than culturally based nationalism:

Contrary to widespread perceptions, national communities might, in some respects, be more open and pluralistic than communities in which social bonds rely on a set of shared values....But in a society where social cohesion is based on national, cultural, and historical criteria, holding nonconformist views does not necessarily lead to excommunication.

(Tamir 1993: 90)

Tamir supports her statement with the example of the United States, where communists were marginalized precisely because they did not share the political values of the state. However, many examples from Central Europe demonstrate that a culturally defined nationalism can be at least as damaging and divisive, and can in fact lead to excommunication. Thus Slovak nationalists (including Mečiar) have repeatedly accused their political opponents of 'not being Slovak enough'. Moreover, citizenship in Slovakia – as in any multinational state – cannot be founded solely on a culturally and/or ethnically defined nation, thereby excluding, amongst others, the large Hungarian minority (see also Chapters 2 and 5). It appears that aspects of both ethnic and civic forms of nationalism can undermine the basic principles of liberalism. The age of nationalism is, however, not over yet.

Even scholars who are concerned about the potential dangers of nationalism in Central and Eastern Europe, acknowledge that

> Democracy rests on the strongly cohesive identities provided by nationhood – there is no democratic state that is without this....On its own democracy is not capable of sustaining the vision of past and future that holds communities together politically, because it does little or nothing to generate the affective, symbolic, and ritually reaffirmed ties upon which community rests.
>
> (Schöpflin 1995: 42)

This is in line with the reasoning of the liberal political philosopher David Miller, who highlighted the importance of national identities in creating the sense of solidarity needed in modern societies more than ever before:

> Nationality answers one of the most pressing needs of the modern world, namely how to maintain solidarity among the populations of states that are large and anonymous, such that their citizens cannot possibly enjoy the kind of community that relies on kinship or face-to-face interaction.
>
> (Miller 1993: 9)

Liberal nationalism

A certain form of nationalism is, hence, still needed to support and sustain liberal democracy. Furthermore, not only democratic states, but also most individuals cannot, or do not want to, do without a sense of belonging to a nation. Whether we like it or not, 'features characteristic of a nation – language, history, culture, religion, geography – are among the most substantive components of individual identity' (Tamir 1995: 427). Tamir correctly observed that 'the liberal tendency to overlook the value inherent in nationalism is mistaken', (Tamir 1993: 4) and she explored ways in which nationalism may in fact contribute to liberal thinking. Tamir's liberal nationalism is polycentric; that is, it 'respects the other and sees each nation as enriching a common civilisation', unlike ethnocentric nationalism, 'which sees one's own nation as superior to all others and seeks domination' (Tamir 1995: 430). This conception is considerably more optimistic about the actual potential of nationalism for a modern liberal democracy than most writers on nationalism allow for. 'Nationalism', Tamir argues, 'is not the pathology of the modern age but an answer to its malaise – to the neurosis, alienation, and meaninglessness characteristic of modern times' (Tamir 1995: 432). The proponents of liberalism have more in common with some proponents of nationalist projects than is usually assumed. Both liberals and nationalists concede the importance of seeing individuals in a social context. Tamir suggests that 'the liberal tradition with its respect for personal autonomy, reflection and choice, and the national tradition, with its emphasis on belonging, loyalty and solidarity, although generally seen as mutually exclusive, can indeed accommodate each other' (Tamir 1993: 6).

Politics in the vernacular

In order to make liberal values relevant to a particular political community, they have to be articulated within the specific cultural context of that community. For example, the ideal of democratic citizenship, which can only be achieved through the active participation of the people in the democratic polity, is difficult to realize without a common language that is easily understood. As Will Kymlicka argued, 'democratic politics is politics in the vernacular' (Kymlicka 2001a: 213). This points to the practical limitations of the cosmopolitan ideal of Enlightenment, explored in the eighteenth century by the likes of the Marquis de Condorcet, which was to be achieved through the creation of a universal language. However, if cosmopolitanism is simply 'understood as a state of mind, exhibited in a rejection of xenophobia, a commitment to tolerance, and a concern for the fate of humans in distant lands' (Kymlicka 2001a: 220), then there is no inherent contradiction between cosmopolitan and liberal national values. In this light, liberal nationalism can be seen as offering pragmatic responses to the idealistic demands of cosmopolitanism.

Moreover, if we accept the insights of the early critics of Enlightenment, such as Herder, the limitations of the cosmopolitan project are not only practical. The assumption that ethnic attachments are irrational and hence can (and should) be overcome by the adoption of a purely cosmopolitan perspective is based on false premises about human nature and the role of language in cognitive processes. If humans were purely rational actors – as many Enlightenment philosophers believed – then the role of their particular national cultures in both their self-understanding and their interaction with the world could indeed be ignored. Similarly, if languages were just different 'value-neutral' means of communication, then a universal language could one day be adopted in a 'universal civil society' that would entail the whole of humanity. However, Herder's insights into the origin and nature of human languages pose serious challenges to the Enlightened cosmopolitan ideals. For Herder, 'language was not merely a vehicle for the transmission of ideas, but was – more fundamentally – a constituent of identities' (Poole 1999: 23). The consequence of this is that 'humans both make and are made within language' (Vincent 2002: 183), and are hence, at least to a certain extent, constituted by their national identities.[7]

Nation as a moral community

Since national identities still matter to people in Central Europe, it is important to conceptualize the possibility of a nationalism that is liberal. Nationalism not only satisfies basic psychological needs, but also fulfils important political functions. As noted above, national identity can generate solidarity in a given community and alleviate alienation of individuals in modern societies. Furthermore, it gives a sense of continuity by strengthening the perception of a society as a partnership between 'those who are living, those who are dead, and those who are to be born' (Burke 1968: 195). While imagining themselves as a part of a larger community with a glorious and long-lasting past and a promising future, individuals can transcend their own limits, and even their own mortality (Anderson 1983; Smith 1991: 160). In that way 'membership in a nation promises individuals redemption from personal oblivion' (Tamir 1995: 433). It is tempting to dismiss such 'irrational' feelings and needs and expect that they should be overcome. But the conception of a community with present, past and future also has important political and moral implications. Indeed, without it, we could not meaningfully discuss the historic responsibility of a nation. If Germans were serious about their non-national politics, they could not accept – as a people and as a nation-state – the moral and even practical responsibility for the crimes of the Second World War.

Habermas, however, disputes this connection. He dismisses the attempts to derive the legitimacy of a nation-state based on a community of fate (*Schicksalsgemeinschaft*) from the necessity to come to terms with the heritage of Auschwitz. The Germans have to realize that they cannot rely on the continuity of their history. Hence, they have no other choice but to base their political identity on universalistic civic principles, which do not allow an uncritical acceptance of national traditions. As Habermas puts it: 'the post-traditional identity loses its substantial, uninhibited character; it consists only in the form of an open, discursive dispute about the interpretation of constitutional patriotism within a particular context of our history' (Habermas 1990: 220). Habermas' conception of a post-traditional identity that must be reflective and discursive appears similar to the one proposed by Tamir and Miller (see below). Thus it would seem that liberal nationalism could be equated with *Verfassungspatriotismus*. However, the term 'post-traditional identity' is misleading, since it implies the existence of a traditional, more substantial national identity that is essentially unquestioned and immutable over time. Furthermore, it is not clear why anyone should be involved in the discursive contest for the 'right' meaning of the identity and history of a community that lacks historic continuity. It is inconsistent to claim both a break of continuity and an interest in history paired with a commitment to acknowledge the practical and moral responsibility for its bleak parts.

This does not imply that people should uncritically embrace any conception of a national community. On the contrary, a more ambivalent approach is in fact desired, so that people can cherish, or be ashamed of, different aspects of their histories or identities. But even radical criticism of some aspects of national history presupposes engagement with the fate of a particular national community. If one were to be fully indifferent towards one's own nation, there is little reason to study, let alone criticize, its history. This applies also to present endeavours. 'Emotional involvement with one's country – feelings of intense shame or of glowing pride aroused by various parts of history, and by various present-day national policies – is necessary if political imagination is to be imaginative and productive', argued Richard Rorty, making a strong case for liberal nationalism (Rorty 1998: 3).

Two types of nationalism?

Whether liberal nationalism in Tamir's fashion was possible or not, according to most scholars of postcommunism, it was hardly an option for Central and Eastern Europe (e.g. Brown 1994; Chirot 1995; Greenfeld 1995; Schöpflin 1995; for rare explicit references to liberal nationalism see Tismaneanu 1998: 188; Bader 1998: 207–8; cf. Szacki 2002). While the West was seen as coming to terms with the dangers of nationalism (either by overcoming it, or adapting it to the requirements of a liberal democracy), the postcommunist world of Central and Eastern Europe was expected to succumb to the nationalistic ideologies of ancient ethnic hatred. The war in Yugoslavia appeared to confirm the worst fears analysts had about the end of communist power.[8] The apparent resurgence of nationalism after the end of communist power seemed to have confirmed the proclaimed existence of 'two types of nationalism'. The English historian of ideas John Plamenatz had argued in the 1970s that the Slavic nations of Eastern Europe were doomed to adhere to an Eastern nationalism that is mostly (if not invariably) illiberal.[9] Since the nations of Central and Eastern Europe were modernized considerably later than the West, their people suffered under 'a feeling of inferiority or inadequacy' (Plamenatz 1973: 29) of their cultures. They had to catch up by imitating their more successful European rivals (such as the Germans, the Italians, the French or the English). Nationalism born out of frustration leads, according to Plamenatz, to extremism, as was shown by the ascendance of Nazism in Germany and fascism in Italy after the First World War. The 'true' nature of German and Italian nationalism is, however, Western (i.e. free of frustration), as it was culturally strong and rather liberal already in the nineteenth century.

Thus, according to Plamenatz, while Germany and Italy can be seen as an integral part of the West, – even if their liberal development was interrupted by the historic 'accidents' of fascism and Nazism – the Slavic people to the east of Western Europe had always been backward and impeded in their development by a tradition that was of little help in addressing the needs of modern times. When Germans and Italians fought for the establishment of their modern national states, they were already prepared culturally. The people in the East had to create both: their states as well as their nations! 'Drawn gradually into a civilisation alien to them...they have had, as it were, to make themselves anew, to create national identities for themselves' (Plamenatz 1973: 30). According to Plamenatz these people – forced to adopt *an alien civilization* – were historically marked as Eastern, meaning virtually non-European. Their relationship with the West was ambivalent, characterized by feelings of admiration mixed with envy and *resentment*. There was thus 'Eastern' nationalism that 'is both imitative and hostile to the models it imitates, and is apt to be illiberal' (Plamenatz 1973: 34). In other words, while the West (Germany included) finally found a sane nationalism, Eastern Europe was doomed to remain wild for considerably longer.

More than twenty years later, Schöpflin still subscribed to Plamenatz's dichotomy by averring that nationalism in Central and Eastern Europe showed characteristics that were 'in many respects substantially different than in Western Europe, for both historical and contemporary reasons'. The most important factor influencing postcommunist developments was, according to Schöpflin, the traditional backwardness of these societies, the consequence of which was 'the weakness of civic elements of nationhood' (Schöpflin 1995: 49). Furthermore, in Central and Eastern Europe 'there is a long tradition of using or rather abusing nationalism for political purposes not connected with the definition of nationhood' (Schöpflin 1995: 52). Isaiah Berlin also distinguished between the 'sated nations...of North America, Western Europe, Australia, New Zealand', and those in Eastern Europe and the former Soviet Union, where 'after years of oppression and humiliation, there is liable to occur a violent counteraction' (Gardels 1991: 19). Thus, despite some truly liberal personalities (like Václav Havel or Adam Michnik) who had a positive influence on the political life of Central and Eastern Europe, Berlin was convinced 'that the possibility, unfortunately even the likelihood, of ethnic strife abounds in that part of the world' (Gardels 1991: 21). J. F. Brown similarly noted that while 'nationalist violence had burned itself out in the West', in the East it seemed to be making up for lost time. According to Brown, 'the imprisoning past' endangered the present (Brown 1994: 172). It is the past in which 'nationalism in the East was characterized by its virulent intolerance' (Woolf 1996: 24). Thus all nations of Eastern Europe were – virtually by definition – illiberal.

Differentiation between the two conceptions of nationalism can only be maintained by a one-sided interpretation of European history. While any nationalistic excesses in Eastern Europe were considered by Schöpflin to be fundamental to the tradition of their backward history, both German national socialism as well as Italian fascism were explained away as some temporary aberration resulting from 'loss of faith in building on the existing European tradition' (Schöpflin 1995: 43). Similarly, more recent problems in Northern Ireland, or Basque separatism in Spain, were seen as exceptions to the rule, which states that problems with nationalism are in general limited to Central and Eastern Europe (Schöpflin 1995: 46).[10] It is questionable whether 1920s–1940s German nationalism was any more Western (i.e. liberal) than, for example, the Czech nationalism of the Czechoslovak First Republic. While Germany sought to overcome the economic and political problems of the interwar period with national socialism, Czechoslovakia remained true to some basic principles of liberal democracy for considerably longer. Hence either German nationalism should be seen as traditionally Eastern, or Czech as traditionally Western. Or perhaps the whole dualistic approach generates more questions than answers? Are, indeed, all nationalisms somewhat Eastern?

Nationalism as a 'continental problem': Germany and Central Europe

A positive answer to the last question could be derived from Liah Greenfeld's *Nationalism: Five Roads to Modernity*, which considered the development of the English, French, Russian, German and American nations not only by comparing them, but also each on its own terms. Through the closer study of particular historic cases, it becomes clear that almost all nations evolved with some feelings of inferiority towards their competitors, and their formation was more often than not 'an expression of existential envy, ressentiment' (Greenfeld 1992: 372). In the second half of the eighteenth century, the French saw themselves drawn into competition with England. France was perceived 'as essentially comparable, equal to England, and at the same time was clearly inferior to it' (Greenfeld 1992: 178). The admiration of England for its liberties (for example by Voltaire) was to be replaced with contempt for its lack of liberty. Rousseau, characteristically, advised his Polish contemporaries *not* to follow the English example in their fight for freedom. He averred that England offered 'a lesson to the Poles' on how not to behave: 'Your constitution is superior to Great Britain' (Greenfeld 1992: 179). Feelings of inadequacy and inferiority were even more pervasive in German nationalism. 'Much of German culture in the eighteenth century drew its inspiration from and developed in response to and in imitation of the "advanced" Western nations: France and England' (Greenfeld 1992: 372). Finding their process of modernization extremely difficult and alienating, many Germans grew to hate the West – feelings which found their best expression in the literature of German Romanticism. Thus a point could be made that both the French and the German forms of nationalism were at least originally 'Eastern', in that they both came into existence out of resentment and admiration for their more successful models.

While a 'purely anti-Western type of nationalism' was characteristic of Russia and Germany, 'France ... at least in the days of its national infancy, could be seen as the first anti-Western nation' (Greenfeld 1995: 20). Nevertheless, according to Greenfeld, it was German nationalism that could be held responsible for all the influential totalitarian concepts of the twentieth century. The Romantic's rejection of the West and its rationalistic values led not only to national socialism, but equally, even if only by the way of sublimation, to Marxism and communism. In Marxism the nation was merely substituted by the notion of class, and the much-hated West with 'the Capital'.

Greenfeld acknowledged that the distinction between Western and Eastern types of nationalism makes little sense geographically, because

> if we assigned individual societies to any of these originally geographical categories on the basis of civilizational characteristics, we might have to characterize many Western European societies as 'Eastern Europe', while most of the 'West' or 'Europe' would paradoxically move to another continent [the United States].
>
> (Greenfeld 1995: 18)

She conceded, however, that it was possible to distinguish between 'Western, less Western, and anti-Western nationalism in Europe and elsewhere' (Greenfeld 1995: 22). In that way, any society could be located on an imaginary map that would not need to resemble its actual geographic location. I submit, however, that the terms 'Eastern' and 'Western' types of nationalism are of little use, indeed are misleading, because they can hardly be conceptualized without their geographical connotations. Moreover, some forms of liberal and illiberal nationalism coexist within each European nation and, thus, one should be careful not to 'condemn' a nation, because of its history, to be and remain illiberal in its inclination. Since national identities are constructed, they can change.

Hence the crudely deterministic interpretation of German history, which sees the emergence of twentieth-century virulent nationalism as the inevitable outcome of the nineteenth century nationalist movements, needs to be questioned because it amounts to a backward reading of history. Greenfeld's argument that 'Germany was ready for the Holocaust from the moment German national identity existed' (Greenfeld 1992: 384) cannot be sustained. To see the rise of national socialism in Germany as a mere consequence of the anti-Western tradition of German Romanticism, and the desire of Germans to overcome their feelings of inferiority by offering their salvation to mankind, is simplistic. Clearly, there were many other social, economic and political reasons for these developments. Moreover, German Romanticism cannot be reduced just to those ideas that gave rise to the ideology of extreme nationalism (expressed, for example, in Fichte's *Addresses to the German Nation* of 1808). At any rate, even a nation formed by a 'purely Eastern type of nationalism' was not doomed to end up with a totalitarian regime.

The condemnation of German Romantics as the direct precursors of twentieth-century outbreaks of violence instigated by German Nazism, is in line with a strong tendency in the English-speaking world to see the origins of all nationalist excesses exclusively limited to the European continent, and more specifically to Germany. The earlier theories of two types of nationalism in Europe relied, after all, on the contrast between rational and pragmatic Anglo-Saxon ways of dealing with the challenges of modernity, and the supposedly irrational responses of those German Romantics who rejected the Enlightenment project in favour of the irrational exaltation of pre-modern, tribal communities (Kohn 1944). An instructive illustration of this approach is the classic and highly influential study by Elie Kedourie, *Nationalism*. In Kedourie's account, there is no such thing as British or American nationalism, since nationalism is by definition a comprehensive illiberal ideology of ethnic exclusion and the suppression of individual will (Kedourie 1966: 74). Kedourie traced the intellectual history of (extreme?) nationalism back to the influential German philosopher, Immanuel Kant, German nationalist thinkers like Herder and Fichte, and German romantic writers like Heinrich von Kleist and Heinrich Heine. In his view, the romantic's idealist 'contempt of things as they are, of the world as it is, [which] ultimately becomes a rejection of life, and a love of death' paved the way for the 'nihilist frenzy of Nazism' (Kedourie 1966: 87).

Considering the lasting impact of German romanticism on the nationalist movements in Central Europe (particularly the profound influence of Herder's ideas of linguistic nationalism), the illiberal character of some aspects of these thoughts is a serious cause for concern. Clearly, the romantic view of nations as God-given entities, which have strong moral claims over individuals, can lead to the suppression of individual liberties and the intolerance of outsiders; this problem is most visible in Fichte's nationalist ideology. But the impact of Herder's philosophy was not limited to Fichte (consider, for example, the great liberal theorist Wilhelm von Humboldt). Ironically, Herder's humanistic political ideals found more resonance outside Germany. One of the most influential heirs of Herderian liberal nationalism in Central Europe was the first Czechoslovak president, T. G. Masaryk, whose writings and practical political work 'revealed a remarkable degree of affinity with the democratic and republican sentiments of Herder's political creed' (Barnard 1965: 175).[11]

Mill or Herder?

In fact, the ideals of romantic nationalists can be more conducive to the promotion of liberal tolerance than the Enlightened (and rational) nationalism of the likes of John Stuart Mill, who advocated the absorption of 'inferior' cultures into the dominant nationality of a country. In contrast, most romantic writers stressed the intrinsic value of *all* cultures and their importance for the full development of human potential. Herder, for example, objected to the claims of superiority of certain cultures on the grounds that 'at bottom all comparison [between nations] is out of place. Every nation has its centre of happiness within itself' (Herder 1994: 38–9; Greenfeld 1992: 330). Mill's elaborate defence of British colonialism, which was based on his strong belief in societal progress, certainly appears less progressive today than Herder's views about the inherent value of cultural diversity.[12] Hence, contemporary liberal nationalism can take inspiration from the best aspects of cultural nationalism represented by romantic writers like Herder, who are usually associated with ethnocentric, that is 'Eastern' nationalism. Their celebration of cultural diversity can enrich a liberal discourse that is primarily concerned with the individual rights of citizens (see also Chapter 2).[13]

The role of histories

Will the nations of Central Europe, because of their 'imprisoning past' (Brown 1994: 172), remain prone to an illiberal nationalism – as the various conceptions of Eastern nationalism imply? Not necessarily. First, the historic experiences of the peoples in Central Europe are ambivalent, and cannot be seen as leading to one outcome only (i.e. the dominance of ethnocentric nationalism). Second, and more importantly, the present is not thoroughly dependent on the past.[14] Nations are 'imagined communities', and their histories are always, to a certain extent, created, rather than simply documented by disinterested observers. Open debates about the historical heritage of a nation can turn past events into a valuable source of moral deliberation. In this way the past is ironically dependent on the present rather than the other way round. As Hannah Arendt noted,

> Experiences and even the stories which grow out of what men do and endure, of happenings and events, sink back into the futility inherent in the living word and the living deed unless they are talked about over and over again. What saves the affairs of mortal men from their inherent futility is nothing but this incessant talk about them, which in turn remains futile unless certain concepts, certain guideposts for future remembrance, and even for sheer reference, arise out of it.
>
> (Arendt 1973: 220)

A nation's 'true character' is constantly being reinvented; old symbols can and do attain new meanings. Liberal nationalists should adopt a critical attitude towards their own particular culture; 'they can aspire to change it, develop it, or redefine it' (Tamir 1993: 89). This is not to deny the limits of the 'flexibility of identities and the malleability of group boundaries' (Smith

1993: 129). Despite the fact that national identities are dependent on myths, they are not entirely optional and manipulable. Even if we accept that nations came into existence as a result of modernity, they do, at their core, rely on pre-modern ethnic communities. Through the example of Polish history, Walicki demonstrated

> that nations could be constructed to a certain extent only, that modern nations, like it or not, need a firm ethnic basis, and that ethnic conflict could not be exorcized by inventing or imagining a nonethnic, purely political (let alone spiritual) definition of a nation.
>
> (Walicki 1997a: 252)

These findings highlight the importance of ethnic histories that, whether imagined or not, do somewhat restrict the malleability of national identities. But it does not follow that these identities are immutable. Walicki's study actually shows that the content of Polish national identity *has* changed radically throughout history; only the change did not always correspond with 'the will and imagination of the political and cultural elites' (Walicki 1997a: 252).

Indeed, as David Miller observed, a distinguishing aspect of national identity is that it is an active identity. 'The nation becomes what it does by the decisions that it takes' (Miller 1993: 7). Historic narratives are being reinterpreted in order to fulfil the requirements of the present, and fierce polemics within a nation are often led in order to determine which parts of its history are to be seen as highlights and which as a national shame. What T. G. Masaryk means to the Czechs, Tiso or Štúr to Slovaks, Piłsudski to Poles and Kossuth to Hungarians can and does change with time and has serious implications for current political developments. Through these debates, different conceptions of a nation compete for dominance within one particular national community at any time in its history, and they also change dramatically throughout history. National culture is always a public phenomenon, which means that, though changeable, it is difficult to manipulate or control. Only when public culture is characterized by an open deliberation is it likely to further the case of liberal democracy (Miller 1995: 69, 150). Hence, liberal nationalists stress the importance of critical participation in a nation:

> The assumption of national obligations implies the reflective acceptance of an ongoing commitment to participate in a critical debate about the nature of the national culture, suggesting that individuals have a reason to adhere to their national obligations even after the establishment of a national state.
>
> (Tamir 1993: 89)

The need for critical engagement in nations' formative debates is relevant not only to the experience of the people of Central Europe. A discussion in the 'older' democracies of the world about the 'right meaning' of being a good American, Australian or German can be equally controversial, as it is in the nations that have only recently freed themselves from communism. Furthermore, all nations that pride themselves on being liberal today had illiberal pasts. To label certain national cultures intrinsically illiberal is crudely reductionist. What Kymlicka argued in defence of cultures of national minorities is valid also for independent national cultures:

> To assume that any culture is inherently illiberal, and incapable of reform, is ethnocentric and ahistorical. Moreover, the liberality of a culture is a matter of degree. All cultures have illiberal strands, just as few cultures are entirely repressive of individual liberty. Indeed it is quite misleading to talk of 'liberal' and 'illiberal' cultures, as if the world was divided into completely liberal societies on the one hand, and completely illiberal ones on the other.
>
> (Kymlicka 1995a: 94)[15]

In fact, it is questionable whether one can make meaningful observations about the quality of a particular culture (liberal or otherwise). This kind of assessment is based on essentialist assumptions about the 'true nature' of the culture in question. However, cultures are not entities endowed with essential, distinguishing and never-changing qualities. National cultures are more usefully conceptualized as complex sets of cultural practices, which constantly evolve in response to the changing demands of their own times (cf. Brubaker 1998: 292). While some of those cultural practices may be inimical to the rational demands of liberalism, others can be supportive of them.

Having shown that the (essentially Manichean) distinction between some forms of Eastern (i.e. illiberal) and Western (i.e. liberal) nationalism is not helpful in analysing the processes of postcommunist transition in Central Europe, I am far from suggesting that nationalism poses no challenges for the development of liberal democracy. Nor can I deny that certain historic experiences of the nations of Central Europe can be detrimental to their further advancement. The argument advanced in this book is that different manifestations of nationalism have more complex and ambivalent potentials than any dualistic classification would allow for. The character of a national culture and its history is not one or the other, liberal or illiberal. Nationalism in Central Europe was used to legitimize both left-wing and right-wing dictatorships, but it was also repeatedly employed as a tool of national liberation, and thus furthered the cause of liberal democracy.[16] The end of communism in Central Europe, on the other hand, ultimately revealed the failure of communist leaders to generate popular support for their ideology by presenting it as compatible with the 'best' aspects of their respective national traditions. Their attempt to ally the national allegiances of citizens with loyalty to the socialist homeland failed. The question is whether the forces of nationalism can now be enlisted to support the creation of stable liberal democracies.

Liberal nationalism in Central Europe

If liberal nationalism sounds 'weird' in English (Tamir 1993: ix), it is virtually unthinkable in the languages of Central Europe. Whereas in English nationalism can, but does not necessarily have negative implications, in Polish, Czech, Slovak, or German the term cannot be conceptualized without negative connotations and association with Nazism and fascism. Only patriotism, which is usually contrasted with nationalism, can be seen as a positive value.[17] As Walicki accurately observed, 'in the vocabulary of Polish politics the word "nationalism" is a pejorative term, reserved for the manifestations of intolerant, xenophobic ethnocentricity' (Walicki 1997a: 253). In line with this, David Ost was right to suggest that Michnik's 'nacjonalism' should read 'national-chauvinism' in English (Michnik 1993: ix). Similarly, the definition of nationalism proposed by the Czech historian Miroslav Hroch certainly brings nationalism closer to chauvinism than liberalism. In his understanding, nationalism is 'that state of mind which gives an absolute priority to the values of one's own nation over and above all other values and group interests' (Hroch 1995: 65). This does not mean, however, that the concept of liberal nationalism cannot be usefully applied in Central Europe. Indeed, I contend that many leading intellectuals like Adam Michnik,[18] Miroslav Kusý, or even Václav Havel, who are fierce opponents of (extreme!) nationalism, could be labelled 'liberal nationalists'.

The bias favouring patriotism against nationalism is shared by Western republican tradition (from Arendt to Habermas), which, despite its long-established concern with political solidarity, has in general viewed citizenship as a desirable alternative to nationhood rather than an expression of it. According to this ideal, 'good citizens are patriotic but not nationalistic' (Canovan 1999: 133). However, even the republicanism of Hannah Arendt cannot resolve a basic dilemma of liberal democracy. 'If a republic is to be viable and lasting, it cannot be completely non-national. It still needs the natal bonds of inherited obligation and natural piety to sustain it; it still needs myths that disguise its contingency' (Canovan 1999: 148). Thus the boundary between patriotism and (liberal) nationalism is not as clear-cut as many scholars assume, since the sentiments of belonging needed for the success of the republican project usually tacitly rely on national sentiments.

There can be little doubt, however, that the fears of intellectuals that nationalism can lead to xenophobia and extreme chauvinism are justified. Xenophobic nationalism that is 'based on fear of and rejection of the stranger or foreigner' (Snyder 1990: 427) is to a certain extent a logical – even if extreme – extension of any concept of national identity. Similarly, chauvinism, denoting 'excessive pride in one's own country, and a corresponding contempt for other nations', (Snyder 1990: 52) appears to be just an undesirable aspect of patriotism. The other side of belonging, that is constitutive of all national identities, is always exclusion. Thus, according to Huntington, 'for peoples seeking identity and reinventing ethnicity, enemies are essential'. In that way all identities in effect require animosity, because 'we know who we are only when we know who we are not and often only when we know whom we are against' (Huntington 1996: 20–1). However, there are other ways of basing identities.

Xenophobia accompanied by communal egoism is the result of extreme nationalism and not an inherent aspect of any conception of nationalism. As Walicki observed, 'xenophobia is a much older phenomenon than nationalism and thus cannot be an expression of it' (Walicki 1997b: 35). Tamir derived the distinction between liberal nationalism that knows its limits, and extreme nationalism that gives absolute priority to the needs of its fellow members, from the philosophical differentiation between selfishness and individualism. While the former is 'the pursuit of one's own interests without regard to the interests of others', the latter is 'the doctrine that it is legitimate to pursue one's own interests on the same terms as those on which others are free to pursue theirs' (Tamir 1993: 15). This is close to Kant's categorical imperative that translates into a national context in Mazzini's words:

> You must ask yourself whenever you do an action in the sphere of your country, or your family...if what I am doing were done by all and for all, would it advantage or injure humanity? And if your conscience answers, it would injure humanity, desist; desist, even if it seems to you that an immediate advantage for your country or your family would ensue from your action.
>
> (Mazzini cited in Tamir 1993: 115)

Similar conceptions of 'foreign-friendly' nationalism can also be found amongst some Central European writers. Jan Kollár (1793–1852), despite his antiquated understanding of a nation as a biological community – expressed in his notion 'all Slavs are One Blood, One Body, One People [Ein Blut, Ein Körper, Ein Volk]' – was a strong advocate of the pursuit of Herderian 'Humanität', subordinating the concerns with one's particular nation to universal human values. As he stated unambiguously: 'Consider the nation only as a vessel of humanity and always when you cry "Slav", let the echo of your cry be "human being"' (quoted in Pynsent 1994: 55). František Palacký (1798–1876) could later see himself true to the same tradition, declaring in his famous letter to the Frankfurt Parliament: 'With all my ardent love of my nation, I always esteem more highly the good of mankind and of learning than the good of the nation' (Palacký, in Bannan and Edelyeni 1970: 147). The Poles can proudly recall the heritage of their patriotic poet Kazimierz Brodziński (1791–1835), who claimed primacy for the Polish nation in overcoming the age-old chauvinistic belief according to which each nation had regarded itself as the goal and centre of the universe. As he stated,

> the Polish nation alone (I say it boldly and with patriotic pride) could have a foreboding of the true movement of the moral universe. It has

recognized that every nation is a fragment of the whole and must roll on its orbit and around the centre like the planets around theirs.

(cited in Walicki 1982: 74)

Even the liberal strands of nationalism can, however, drift towards a certain type of chauvinism. People in Central Europe, for example, often seek to set themselves aside from the 'barbaric' East (usually epitomized by Russia, or more recently by the Balkans) by claiming that liberal democratic values constitute an indelible part of their 'superior' culture. Adrian Hyde-Price thus observed the emergence of 'a new nationalistic myth' – the myth of belonging to Europe (Hyde-Price 1996: 60). The notion of Central Europe, as expounded by intellectuals like Milan Kundera and Czesław Miłosz, was also accepted by many Western observers and politicians, which arguably led to special treatment of the region. This was possibly to the detriment of other parts of Eastern Europe, like the Balkans, which did not enjoy the political and economic assistance comparable with the help granted to Czechoslovakia, Poland and Hungary. In fact, Perry Anderson argues that the Western preoccupation with Central Europe, which origi-nated in the late 1980s and found its most vocal spokesman in the British journalist and 'historian of the present' Timothy Garton Ash, was partly responsible for the tragic developments in Yugoslavia, a country that had been largely ignored by the West. This contributed to a dramatic economic decline, which created the backdrop for the ensuing disintegration of the country and violent ethnic conflicts. According to Anderson 'the myth of Central Europe was not just a negative condition of the unfolding of this crisis; it was an active catalyst' (Anderson 1999: 8).

Thus the concept of Central Europe, very much like some liberal tradi-tions within particular nations of the region, can be a double-edged sword. If the concept implies that the people of Central Europe are better than their neighbours in the East, or in the South simply by virtue of belonging to one of the nations of the region, then the notion can lead to complacency and a 'superiority complex' that goes against basic liberal values. In contrast, if the concept rather expresses the ambition of a particular people, who aspire to become more tolerant and liberal, then the notion can be employed as a motivating force.

Once again, this problem is not only restricted to the experiences of the postcommunist world. In fact, the problem is intimately linked with the basic paradox lying at the heart of the liberal democratic project, which is universal in its aspirations, but always particular in its practical implemen-tation. An instructive illustration of this contradiction is the opening sentence of the American Declaration of Independence, which states 'We hold these truths to be self-evident ... '. As Hannah Arendt commented, the formulation is awkward, as truths that are so universal that they are self-evident must be such to everyone (Arendt 1973: 193). Yet the 'we' of the declaration originally only referred to the white, male property-owning

Americans, and even today the notion is practically restricted to American citizens (even if its definition is significantly broader). Thus the traditional project of liberal democracy is burdened by an inherent contradiction between its universalist aspirations, which aim for the political equality of all citizens, and the realities of nation-states, which cannot free themselves from their particularist agenda.

This contradiction is also reflected in liberal nationalism, which seeks to conceptualize universalist ideals within particular contexts of national cultures and histories. When the Czechs, for example, see their traditional maxim, which states that 'věc česká je věc lidská' ('the Czech concern is a human concern' – Havel in *Lidové noviny*, 11 September 1992), as a guardian for morally desirable political behaviour, then their liberal ideal fulfils a positive role. The same idea can, however, lead to complacency, such as when the Czech people simply perceive themselves as the most democratic in the whole of Europe without realizing the need to live up to this image (see Chapter 4). Likewise, a deeply rooted perception of Poland 'as a country of individualists, of a nation which in the past not only kept up with the West but even outpaced it in the development of liberal institutions' (Szacki 1995: 45) can further the cause of liberal democracy, or paradoxically be a source of a peculiar type of chauvinism.

More often than not these conceptions are supported by national 'histories' which are rather free interpretations of the actual past – what does not fit into the desired picture is suppressed, or interpreted as an irregularity caused by external forces (e.g. Russia, Germany, Austria-Hungary). Clearly, all these historic myths can be easily contested; if there were any democratic moments or elements, they could easily have been seen as an exception rather than a rule. (And they were contested – see Chapters 3, 4 and 5). The Polish sociologist Jerzy Jedlicki observed the paradoxical irony that Poland has always been returning to Europe, although it has actually never been there (Jedlicki 1990: 39–45). Thus Stephen Holmes is right to claim that 'if you examine the past closely, you can find foreshadowings of just about anything that comes to pass' (Holmes 1996: 27).

The 'meaning' of history

But this does not necessarily matter, as long as it is possible to highlight some positive moments in the past, and/or to derive lessons from past failings. This is not to advocate a 'noble lie', that is, a deliberate distortion of historic events for commendable political ends. Still, it is worthwhile considering that even the well established democracies of the West are based on many myths, and their histories are not without 'nasty' and illiberal aspects (including imperialism, slavery, etc.). Democratic society can be viewed sceptically as an exception to the whole of human history; or – in the words of Richard Rorty – as 'a lucky accident' in human development (Rorty, in Niżnik and Sanders 1996: 47). The actual establishment of democracy, however, was furthered by the optimistic belief of the Enlightenment that universal human history must lead to human emancipation and democracy. Moreover, it is questionable whether a liberal democratic order can be sustained without the strong belief of *a* people that the implementation of the ideals of freedom is in line with the 'true meaning' of their particular history.

Liberal nationalists are likely to reject Rorty's view of history, which sees the rise of democracy as merely a contingent event, but they need not accept the other extreme either; that is the view that their nation was destined to become free and democratic. Their philosophy of history can be derived from the Kantian understanding of history. Kant, in his 'Idea for a Universal History from a Cosmopolitan Point of View', saw the value of history as a source for moral deliberations. He expected that people

> will naturally value the history of earlier times…only from the point of view of what interests them, i.e., in answer to the question of what the various nations and governments have contributed to the goal of world citizenship, and what they have done to damage it.

Kant believed that 'the greatest problem for the human race, to the solution of which Nature drives man, is the achievement of a universal civil society' which would secure the greatest possible freedom for its members. Kant's view that the ultimate goal of history was the emancipation of all people in a truly just society was normative, rather than teleological. Kant's 'prediction' about the future of humanity was thus prescriptive rather than descriptive; he argued that people should work towards this noble outcome, not that they are destined to attain it.

Similarly, the slogan 'Back to Europe' can prove instrumental in the promotion of universal liberal values in the countries of Central Europe. Even if the assumption that these countries have for a long time been an integral part of the freedom-loving, democratic West is not always accurate, perhaps the immensely popular slogan can turn into a 'self-fulfilling fiction' (Holmes 1996: 65).

Two types of civilization? The West and the rest

It is an historic irony that the West-East contrast that has been employed by scholars of nationalism in order to show why the nations of Central Europe *could not* (or at least not without difficulties) succeed in establishing and/or sustaining liberal democracy, has been successfully used by intellectuals and politicians in these countries to mobilize their people for the fight against communism (that was 'Eastern' and thus illiberal) and for democracy (that was 'Western' and thus liberal). All the nations of Central Europe sought to distance themselves from 'the barbarian Eastern culture', epitomized in Russian Stalinism, by reclaiming their traditional belonging to the West (whether real or imagined). Typical is the confident statement of György Konrád: 'Like it or not, Hungary – together with Central Europe as a whole – is fated to be a democracy' (Konrád 1995: 129). This is a stance very similar (only inverted) to the cultural determinism that characterizes all concepts of 'Eastern', illiberal nationalism. However, though questionable as an analytical tool in social science, these kinds of culturally deterministic views can prove valuable in promoting democracy in actual societies. When people in Central Europe believe that the West and thus democracy is their 'natural' destiny, then they are more likely to succeed in implementing this new political order than if they perceive it as something alien to their national character.

It can be argued that the widespread conviction – voiced memorably by Kundera in 1984 – that the nations of Central Europe were by virtue of their cultural history an inseparable part of the West, and were only deprived of their true identities by an unfavourable accident of history (Yalta), was a catalyst for the end of communist power (Kundera 1984; see also Chapters 3, 4 and 5). Once the detested foreign hegemonic power was removed, and Czechs, Slovaks, Hungarians and Poles asserted their political independence from the communist Soviet Union, a new task followed. Lájos Grendel, a Slovak writer of Hungarian origin and language, stated programmatically that 'the mission of a Central European citizen is the abolition of Central Europe, a region of a transitional period, of ethnic conflicts and of habits of an authoritarian regime' (Grendel 1997). Central Europe needed to be abolished as far as it denoted a territory lying politically in between the West and the East.

This was clearly a continuation of Kundera's conception that considered Russia (especially the historic Russia, not only the Soviet Union) the antithesis to Europe. 'On the eastern border of the West – more than anywhere else – Russia is seen not just as one more European power but as a singular civilisation, an *other* civilisation' (Kundera 1984: 34). While Kundera was careful not to condemn Russian culture as a whole, he stated unambiguously that 'Russian civilisation is the radical negation of the modern West' (Kundera 1984: 37; see also Miłosz 1962: 19). The liberation of the nations of Central Europe from communism was facilitated by strong nationalistic feelings of resentment against the influence of Russian communism that were seen as the political manifestation of the 'barbaric' East (see also Chapters 3, 4 and 5). Although many other factors contributed to the ultimate end of communist power in Central Europe (e.g. economic, global-political), the role of culture should not be underestimated.

Culture's importance to the understanding of political processes has been much debated in response to the publication of Samuel Huntington's *The Clash of Civilizations and the Remaking of World Order* (Huntington 1996). This study challenged the theories of modernization that claim that the logic of capitalism, which led to the end of the ideological conflict between liberalism and communism with a victory for the former, would lead to a universal acceptance of Western values, and of the liberal-democratic political system throughout the world (Fukuyama 1989). Huntington asserted that the West was unique rather than universal and must content itself with sustaining its own success, which can be endangered by six or seven other competing civilizations, rather than trying to export it. This has profound implications not only for the foreign policies of the major Western powers, but also for the countries that have shed their communist regimes. Huntington argued that the success of the reforms is predicated on the suitable (i.e. Western) civilizational background of the country concerned:

> Developments in the postcommunist societies of Eastern Europe and the former Soviet Union are shaped by their civilizational identities. Those with Western Christian heritages are making progress toward economic development and democratic politics; the prospects for economic and political development in the Orthodox countries are uncertain; the prospects in the Muslim republics are bleak.
>
> (Huntington 1996: 29)

One can sympathize with Huntington's warnings against the presumptuous attitude of Westerners towards other civilizations, but it is hardly less condescending to deny peoples and civilizations any chance of economic and political progress, because they have for centuries not taken part in the developments of the unique Western culture. Huntington's cultural pessimism and determinism – according to which certain civilizations are more or less fated to be what they are – does not convince. Democracy can flourish in places lying far beyond the West, however this is defined. Civilizations, like nations, can and do change with time.

Political and economic developments are always influenced, but never fully predetermined by the cultural history of a country, nation, or even civilization. The logic of cultural determinism would not accommodate Japan becoming, after the Second World War, not only a leading economic power, but a remarkably stable Asian democracy. Even Europe or the West was not destined to become democratic and economically successful. Indeed, one could argue that 'fascism is not less European than liberal democracy' (Holmes 1997: 8).[19] None the less, the alleged belonging to Europe, 'imagined' as the embodiment of democracy, prosperity and tolerance, can certainly be used as a mobilizer to facilitate the transition towards liberal democracy in the countries of Central Europe. For example Ján Čarnogurský, a Christian intellectual and former Slovak prime minister, applied Huntington's thesis of the 'clash of civilizations' to Slovakia in order to 'prove' the strategic necessity of integrating the country, which was Christian and thus traditionally Western, into the European Union, and other Western organizations such as NATO (Čarnogurský 1994: 12).[20] The obvious problem of this line of argument is that countries and people who happen to lie geographically and culturally beyond the borders of the West, however determined, are excluded.[21]

Two types of transition? The Czechs (Poles, Hungarians) and the rest

As the borders of some of the West's political institutions (the North Atlantic Treaty Organization and the European Union) are shifting eastwards, the nations of Central Europe are fiercely competing to show 'who is more Western, and therefore less Eastern, than whom' (Burgess 1997: 165). Belonging to the West should be a warrant not only for political stabilization but also for some tangible economic benefits that would flow from full economic integration into Western markets. Thus, it is not surprising that the political and cultural elites of the Czech Republic, considered a leader in the process of postcommunist transition, sought to distance themselves from other nations of the Visegrád Four group, especially the Slovaks. It is more of a surprise to see some academics adopting a similar stance when dealing with the changes in the geo-political configuration of Central Europe. Milada Vachudová and Tim Snyder, for example, proposed the differentiation between 'two types of political change in Eastern Europe' that was a timely modification of the thesis of 'two types of nationalism'. Only this time, as the borders of Western civilization were being redefined, the Poles, Hungarians and Czechs, who were no longer seen as epitomizing the East, were set against the Slovaks, Bulgarians and Romanians. The writers claimed that 'the most striking and important feature dividing them [the two groups] is the role of ethnic nationalism in domestic politics' (Vachudová and Snyder 1997: 2; cf. Carpenter 1997). In the same vein, Jack Snyder contrasted 'the sophisticated Czechs [who] were able to invent a working civil society almost overnight' with 'more rural and less politically sophisticated' populations of Serbia, Slovakia and Romania, who succumbed to the lure of 'counterrevolutionary nationalist appeals by former communist leaders' (Snyder 2001: 73). The underlying assumption of these comparative studies was that aggressive ethnic nationalism has been marginalized by the political developments in Poland, Hungary and the Czech Republic, while it has dominated politics in Slovakia, Bulgaria and Romania (or in Serbia, Slovakia and Romania in Jack Snyder's comparison).

The conception of 'two types of transition' is vulnerable to most of the criticisms that apply to the conception of 'two types of nationalism'. The study – as I shall show in more detail when dealing with particular case studies – is an example of how a misconception led to a misrepresentation of the actual developments in the region. The success of the democratic transition in the three countries of Central Europe shows, if nothing else, that ethnic nationalism need not be aggressive. Even ethnic nationalism, if culturally based, can be liberal.[22] It can well be argued that nationalism in the Czech Republic, Poland and Hungary has not been marginalized, but rather employed in a fashion conducive to the development of democracy and a free-market economy. Since the Czechs, for instance, pride themselves on being a 'democratic, well-educated, and highly cultured nation' (Holy

1996: 77), it was easy for their prime minister Václav Klaus to utilize their national feelings to elicit support for democracy and a free market economy, that was presented as a 'natural' way of life for any civilized nation (Holy 1996: 153). At the same time, many Czechs are yet to change radically their attitudes towards the Romany minority, in order to live up to their self-image of a 'democratic and highly cultured nation'.

In addition, it is misguided to evaluate the strength and relevance of nationalism in a country just by observing the rhetoric and deeds of the current governing elites. Notwithstanding the fact that government policy has a stronger influence on the development of a society that undergoes radical systemic change than in a long established democratic order, it is not the sole determinant. The character and political relevance of nationalism is rather a result of an ongoing contest between different conceptions of nationalism, in which the voice of the governing elite is but one of many. Vachudová and Snyder correctly observed that politicians were generally more successful in exploiting xenophobic nationalism in Slovakia than in the Czech Republic, Poland and Hungary, but that in itself does not warrant the thesis that there is 'an essential difference between the political evolutions' (Vachudová and Snyder 1997: 32) of the countries in question. Otherwise any change of the government and its political priorities would necessitate a new theory.

The Slovak elections of September 1998 and September 2002, for example, propelled into power two different broad coalition governments, which have both been certainly more open towards the legitimate demands of national minorities than the Mečiar administration ever was. In fact it was characteristic of the 1998–2002 government that the minister for minorities and human rights was an ethnic Hungarian, Pál Csáky, from the Party of Hungarian Coalition (SMK). This is not to say that Slovakia under prime minister Mikuláš Dzurinda would solve all the problems stemming from the coexistence of different national cultures; but the general claim that Slovak people are unlike anyone else in Central Europe and are susceptible to an 'essentially different type of nationalism' must be rejected.

Similar criticism applies to an analysis that employs the concept of political culture when looking for substantial differences between the countries. Michael Carpenter, for instance, identified 'two types of political cultures' in Central and Eastern Europe: civic and traditional, dividing the region into 'a nationalist-populist South and a social democratic North' (Carpenter 1997: 205). According to this scheme, civic political culture is characteristic of the Czech Republic, Hungary, Poland and Slovenia, while traditional political culture is typical of Albania, Bosnia, Bulgaria, Croatia, Macedonia, Romania, Yugoslavia and Slovakia. Carpenter states that the legacies of long lasting political subjugation and backward socio-economic conditions in the traditional political cultures led to political systems hallmarked by ethnic nationalism and authoritarian populism. Apart from the fanciful geographical division that posits Slovakia in the South and Slovenia

in the North, the argument cannot be sustained without the culturally deterministic assumptions that amount to a backward reading of history. Even
though Carpenter claims that he does not wish 'to imply deterministically
that all the countries with traditional political cultures will adopt nationalist-populist political systems' (1997: 205), the study ultimately argues
precisely that, at least for Slovakia. 'The triumph of nationalist populism' in
Slovakia is explained by a recourse to the history of the nation. Ten
centuries of Slovak serfdom in the repressive Hungarian monarchy should
at least partly account for the failure of postcommunist democracy.

Conclusion

These comparative studies exemplify how old classifications of nationalism
(civic and ethnic, equated with Western and Eastern) distort the perception
of recent political developments in the region. Thus it is evident that any
study of postcommunist developments will not be furthered by simplistic
concepts along the lines of 'two types of nationalism'. The actual outcome
of the dynamic political processes in today's Central Europe is not pre-determined by its 'Eastern' past, however defined. The attempt to find new
borders between 'the West and the rest' based on different types of nationalisms should be abandoned in favour of cautious and detailed analysis of
various nationalistic discourses within each nation. In that way any similarities in all the countries in focus can be highlighted without neglecting
national peculiarities.

One of the most important factors influencing the success of the postcommunist transition will be the result of the contest between different
forms of nationalism within the particular countries of Central Europe. The
crucial question is whether liberal nationalism can win the upper hand over
a nationalism that derives its strength from xenophobia and chauvinism.
Certainly, some recent developments could suggest that it is the latter that is
gaining momentum, and posing a danger to the development of liberal
democracy in all countries of Central Europe. The expressions of anti-
Semitism in Poland (associated for instance with Pater Rydzyk and Radio
Maryja), violent racist attacks on Romanies in the Czech Republic and
Slovakia, and expressions of chauvinism in Hungary, might at first sight
appear to have proven the conception of two types of nationalism correct.
Does this mean that the fears of Hobsbawm, Plamenatz, Schöpflin and
others who warned against the legacy of an illiberal type of nationalism in
Central and Eastern Europe are justified? Has, then, liberal nationalism in
Central Europe any chance of succeeding at all?

Despite the problems that have occurred within the societies of the Czech
Republic, Slovakia, Hungary and Poland, and even allowing for their
ambivalent historical legacies, the worst predictions of the doomsayers in
regard to the ominous influence of extreme nationalism have *not* been
fulfilled.[23] Rather, the signs are increasingly positive. The June 1998 Czech

elections, held in the midst of serious economic difficulties and problems with political corruption (i.e. an environment that traditionally leads electorates to move towards extreme populist parties) resulted in the exclusion from parliament of the extreme-right Republican Party of Miroslav Sládek, renowned for its xenophobic rhetoric against the Romany minority.[24] In Poland, too, the recognition of people 'as a differentiated, plural society composed of a multitude of groups continues to increase' (Morawska 1995: 67), and the expressions of anti-Semitism are countered by influential voices calling for more tolerance (e.g. Michnik). Furthermore, the successive defeats of Mečiar's (misnamed) 'Movement for a Democratic Slovakia' in Slovakia in 1998 and 2002 showed that even a country that is usually seen as the epitome of the backward 'East' could make real progress in weakening the forces of extreme and illiberal nationalism. The different coalitions of democratic forces led by prime minister Mikuláš Dzurinda (from 1998–2002 and from 2002 to date) have demonstrated a clear commitment to the protection of national minorities, and reversed the policies of Mečiar's previous administrations that were inspired by extreme nationalism (e.g. the amendments of the restrictive language law). Clearly, an unbiased approach to the study of nationalism(s) in Central Europe reveals that all the countries have a very good chance of sustaining their liberal democracies with the help of liberal nationalism.

2 Reflections on minority rights in Central Europe

One of the most serious challenges facing the postcommunist societies of Central Europe is to find a way in which different ethnic groups can live together peacefully in a stable, liberal democratic order. For that to happen, the needs and aspirations of minority cultures must be reconciled with the interests of the majority. How or whether that can be achieved, has puzzled political theorists from John Stuart Mill in the nineteenth century to the likes of Charles Taylor in our present day. How can political liberalism with its focus on individual freedom accommodate the political demands of groups and conceptualize a multicultural society free of culturally based oppression and domination? What sort of functions, if any, is a liberal state supposed to fulfil regarding national minorities? Should the state embrace and actively support ethnic diversity by acknowledging the special rights of the national minorities, or should it be indifferent, or even resistant to any special demands?

These questions are as urgent as they are difficult to answer. Even liberal nationalists cannot offer simple solutions for reconciling the needs and aspirations of minority cultures with the interests of the majority, although they would usually be sympathetic towards the legitimate demands of ethnic minorities. A respect for other nationalities is, after all, one of the defining characteristics of liberal nationalism. In this light, this chapter aims to explore how theories of multiculturalism that originated in the West can apply to the question of minority rights in Central Europe. After a brief consideration of some more traditional liberal approaches to the challenges of ethnic diversity, I will discuss the merits of two competing contemporary theories. Thus I will contrast Taylor's conception of the politics of recognition that calls for active state involvement in questions of cultural diversity, with Kukathas' politics of indifference that warns against extending the powers and influence of a patronizing state. I will then discuss different meanings of multiculturalism, and demonstrate that concepts derived from migrant societies such as Australia cannot be directly transferred to Europe. After consideration of some examples from the Czech Republic and Slovakia and the situation of, among others, the Romany minority, the strengths and weaknesses of both approaches will be re-examined.

Liberalism from J. S. Mill to John Rawls and the challenges of ethnic diversity

John Stuart Mill argued that democracy is virtually impossible in a state populated by different nationalities. From this point of view, the best state is the one that has no minorities; if it has some, as the next best option they should, if possible, be fully integrated into the dominant national culture. The integration of a national minority into the dominant culture can, according to Mill, be beneficial to its members if it allows them access to a civilization that is more developed. Thus, for a Breton or a Basque, it is better to be fully accepted as French, 'than to sulk on his own rocks...revolving in his own little mental orbit, without participation in the general movement of the world' (Mill 1991: 431). If Mill's premises were to be accepted, it would be a legitimate task of a liberal state – at least in some cases – to promote integration and in that way actively encourage the nation-building process, as this ultimately leads to a more stable democratic system.

Mill, with his concerns about the political implications of national identities, is an exception amongst liberal theorists, who traditionally viewed the questions of belonging as something private that is beyond the legitimate interest of the state. Liberals from John Locke to John Rawls derived the legitimacy of the state from a legal compact between free individual citizens that are thought of as bearers of some universal rights, rather than members of a particular national community (Czarnota 1998: 9). Thus, even if the state is inadvertently conceptualized as national, it is ideally seen as ethnically neutral towards its citizens. A parallel could be drawn with the approach of a liberal state towards religious diversity. Even if some religious beliefs are arguably more propitious to liberal democracy than others (the Protestant confessions, for example, with their stress on personal responsibility, can be seen as more favourable to the cause of liberal democracy than Islam, which stresses the importance of a religious community), ideally the neutrality of a liberal state towards them must not be violated.[1] But is such an approach applicable in dealing with the national identities of citizens?

Characteristically, one of the most influential contemporary philosophies of political liberalism, Rawls' *A Theory of Justice* (1971), does not explicitly deal with the questions of ethnicity and nationality. His ideal of justice as fairness, however, certainly demands that the political institutions of a liberal state be indifferent to citizens' particular national identities. The fictive participants in an 'original position', in which people deliberate on a just society, are behind a 'veil of ignorance', that is 'the parties are not allowed to know the social position of those they represent, or the particular comprehensive doctrine of the person each represents'. As Rawls further states, the same applies 'to information about people's race and ethnic group, sex and gender, and their various native endowments' (Rawls 1996: 25). In short, in order to attain a universal conception of justice, Rawls imagines a situation ('original position') in which participants can conceive a just society without being burdened by particularities of their personal position in society. As no one knows anything about his/her ethnicity and/or belonging to a national community, it cannot be in anyone's interest to treat any particular ethnic or national community favourably. Thus the state in an ideal, just society must be ethnically blind, i.e. perfectly neutral. But the question arises again – is this possible? Can the state maintain neutrality towards all the questions that affect national identities? How can the language of public administration, or the language of education, be determined in a neutral fashion? What is, for that matter, the language of deliberation in the original position?

The last question can be seen as inappropriate since the original position is, after all, 'both hypothetical and nonhistorical' (Rawls 1996: 24). At the same time, Rawls maintains that his conception must be 'a natural guide to intuition', and therefore 'it is important that the original position be interpreted so that one can at any time adopt its perspective' (Rawls 1971: 139). From this background it is legitimate to ask how far Rawls' thought experiment could approximate any 'real situation'. Indeed, it can be argued that

> there could be no such thing as rational choice behind the veil of ignorance. In order to secure the results that he desires, Rawls asks us to discount not only our race and sex, but also our religious values and our several 'conceptions of the good' – in short, all that makes truly rational choice conceivable.
>
> (Scruton 1996: 426)

For to make a rational choice presupposes that a subject has a frame of reference that is provided by societal culture, that includes not only different value systems, but also a particular language in which these systems are articulated. Herder, at any rate, would never have been able to adopt the 'original position's perspective'.[2]

This is not to say that Rawls underestimates the role of culture and language in the well-being of citizens. Indeed, when contemplating the option of emigration as a way of evading a government's authority, he highlights the fact that individuals are always born into a societal culture. According to Rawls, leaving one's country is normally 'a grave step', because

> it involves leaving the society and culture in which we have been raised, the society and culture whose language we use in speech and thought to express ourselves, our aims, goals, and values; the society and culture whose history, customs and conventions we depend on to find our place in the social world.
>
> (Rawls 1996: 222; cf. Kymlicka 1995a: 86–7)

In other words, people are usually embedded in their national cultures. 'The attachments formed to persons and places, to associations and communities, as well as cultural ties, are normally too strong to be given up, and this fact is not to be deplored' (Rawls 1996: 277). Rawls does not explicitly address the question of the appropriate treatment of minorities, but it is evident that integration, as proposed by Mill, is indefensible. If we cannot expect people voluntarily to abandon their national identity for the sake of emigration, it would be even less legitimate to demand the integration of people who have been born into a societal culture of a national minority.

Neither Rawls' *Theory of Justice* nor *Political Liberalism* deal with the practical consequences of these attachments. Furthermore, the original position is an abstraction also in regard to 'really existing' societies, in which majority and minority cultures and languages coexist, in that it assumes a 'closed society' that is self-contained and has no relation with other societies. 'Its members enter it only by birth and leave it only by death' (Rawls 1996: 12). According to Rawls, the question of justice as fairness is to be solved first at the level of a closed hypothetical society and only then transferred to a wider context of 'the just relations between the people' (Rawls 1996: 12). Thus it is tacitly assumed that the participants in the original position envisage a just society for *a people*, and at the same time (being behind the 'veil of ignorance') it is impossible for them to say anything about *this people*, their (national) culture, or in fact their language.

Rawls' failure to consider the practical consequences of questions of ethnicity and national identity for a liberal democratic order, goes deeper than being just an accidental consequence of his particular thought model. It is typical of all the liberal theories that tacitly presuppose the existence of national communities and national states without acknowledging their importance. As Kymlicka observed, liberal theorists 'have generally, if implicitly, accepted that cultures or nations are basic units of political theory' (Kymlicka 1995a: 93). The fiction of ethnocultural neutrality prevented political theorists in the past from any meaningful conceptualization of the relationship between the state and national culture(s). This has changed with the writings of liberal nationalists (Tamir 1993; Miller 1995) and communitarians[3] (i.e. Taylor 1992; Kis 1996; Kymlicka 1995a; 1998; 2001a). As Rainer Bauböck stated,

[I]f it is true that liberal democratic states cannot be culturally neutral because the working of their core institutions inevitably reproduces specific dominant cultures, then it follows that such national cultures cannot be allowed to undermine equal respect and concern for all citizens and the fair terms of cooperation.

(Bauböck 1998: 40)

Communitarian theories of multiculturalism are united in their criticism of a liberalism that underestimates the societal context that not only allows individuals to act as political beings, but also constitutes their identities. To that extent, theories of multiculturalism provide a good starting point for studying the political relevance of a multitude of national cultures within a society. Most communitarians believe that the state should actively endorse the politics of recognition and in that way do justice to the different identities of people inhabiting that state. The critics of communitarianism (Holmes 1993; Hardin 1995; Kukathas 1995; 1998; Ossipov 2001) warn, however, that active state support of diversity leads to more division and conflict within a society, and thus ill serves the main aim of a liberal state, which is to maintain peace between various groups and individuals following their own conceptions of the good.

The politics of recognition

Identities matter. If we agree with the premises on which the importance of liberal nationalism is based (i.e. not only on its relevance to a liberal democratic society, but also for the well-being of individuals), we cannot ignore the findings of communitarians who do not consider identities important only if they are national, or ethnic. Individual identities are partly constituted by the sense of belonging to different communities, be they racial, ethnic, cultural, or gender-based. To treat individuals fairly, hence, necessitates a fair treatment of all these communities, since 'my own identity crucially depends on my dialogical relations with others' (Taylor 1992: 34). Misrecognition is, according to Taylor, impermissible as it amounts to oppression. 'The projection of an inferior or demeaning image on another can actually distort and oppress, to the extent that the image is internalized' (Taylor 1992: 36). Patriarchal societies, for example, perpetuate the inequality of genders by imposing on women a sexist image of them that hinders their full emancipation long after more practical barriers have been removed. According to Young, marginalized groups cannot escape oppression from the dominant culture since their 'stereotyped and inferiorized images...must be internalized by group members at least to the extent that they are forced to react to the behaviour of others influenced by those images' (Young 1990: 60).

As Taylor stated, 'due recognition is not just a courtesy we owe people. It is a vital human need' (Taylor 1992: 26). On these grounds affirmative actions sponsored by the state are justified.

> Where the politics of universal dignity fought for forms of nondiscrimination that were quite 'blind' to the ways in which citizens differ, the politics of difference often redefines nondiscrimination as requiring that we make these distinctions the basis of differential treatment.
>
> (Taylor 1992: 39)

In other words, in certain circumstances the state has to discriminate in order to be genuinely non-discriminatory. Iris Young argues along the same lines:

> The politics of difference sometimes implies overriding a principle of equal treatment with the principle that group differences should be acknowledged in public policy and in the policies and procedures of economic institutions, in order to reduce actual or potential oppression.
>
> (Young 1990: 11)

The practical consequence of this, in the context of national communities, is that a liberal state does not have to be culturally neutral and can actively follow a policy that favours some culture and a particular 'definition of the good life' (Taylor 1992: 59). Taylor uses the example of the French-speaking Canadians in Quebec to demonstrate that it can be legitimate to expect from the state that it does more in order to preserve a particular culture than a strictly neutral conception of a state would allow for. Taylor argues that the state has to protect cultural diversity not only for the people currently living within their (French minority) culture, but also for the future generations. 'Policies aimed at survival actively seek to *create* members of the community, for instance in their assuring that future generations continue to identify as French-speakers' (Taylor 1992: 58). In that way, it is legitimate for the state in Quebec to demand from new migrants that they learn French rather than English, even if it violates their right to free choice. Another regulation outlawed commercial signage in any language other than French. Thus 'restrictions have been placed on Quebeckers by their government, in the name of their collective goal of survival' (Taylor 1992: 53).

As Michael Walzer highlighted, Taylor distinguishes between two different models of liberal society (see Walzer in Taylor 1992: 99–103). Against the popular model of a strictly neutral liberal state that treats everyone equally without promoting any particular conception of a good life (espoused by Rawls, Dworkin and others), Taylor contrasts a different model of a liberal society, which is organized 'around a definition of a good life' and which does follow 'strong collective goals' (Taylor 1992: 59). The second model of a society is liberal, Taylor maintains, as long as it secures some fundamental rights and liberties for those who do not share its common goals. Thus the English-speaking 'minority' in Quebec would not be able to claim a right for all commercial signage being written in English, as this is not a fundamental right.

> One has to distinguish the fundamental liberties, those that should never be infringed and therefore ought to be unassailably entrenched, on one hand, from privileges and immunities that are important, but that can be revoked or restricted for reasons of public policy – although one would need a strong reason to do this – on the other.
>
> (Taylor 1992: 59)

But how can the importance of 'privileges and immunities' be determined so fairly as to avoid their misuse? In the case of French-speaking Canadians, Taylor derives the urgency and legitimacy of their linguistic rights from the threat to the very survival of their culture. We need not worry too much about the feelings of English-speaking Canadians in Quebec, since theirs is the culture of the ruling majority and therefore certainly not threatened in its very existence. But this is not a convincing argument. Liberals can and should realize the importance of a culture (as all the liberal nationalists do) not for the sake of a particular culture as an abstract entity, but only as long as it benefits the individuals that are, after all, of primary concern for a truly liberal theory. Since there probably will always be *some individual* Quebeckers who are not interested in the survival of the French-speaking culture in Canada, the state's demands on them could be seen as an arbitrary imposition. Thus, when Taylor defends restrictions placed on Quebeckers 'in the name of *their* collective goal of survival' (my italics, Taylor 1992: 53), he actually departs from the liberal platform, since he allows the interests of individuals to be overtaken by the demands of the community as a whole.

Liberal democracy is based on the assumption that it is possible for everyone to accept the verdict of the majority as long as all the different views have a fair chance of winning majority support. This means that the democratic process must be open-ended, and should not be pre-determined by established allegiances. As some of the liberal classics feared, democracy can retard into 'the tyranny of the prevailing opinion and feeling' (Mill 1991: 9), in which dissenting views and ways of life have no chance to assert themselves. Even if Mill was not concerned with the protection of national minorities (in fact, as we have seen, he advocated integration), his argument in favour of the protection of dissenting individuals could be extended and applied to minority cultures. The remaining problem for a *liberal* theory of minority rights lies in cases of individual dissent from within the minority. Their dissenting views and ways of life must not be forfeited for the sake of the survival of the minority culture.

If Taylor's assumption about the intrinsic value of all cultures were correct, and if the survival of cultural diversity were the primary goal of the politics of identity, one could even speculate (as Hardin did) about the necessity of 're-creating' long-dead cultures. 'But many of those cultures were ill-suited to providing good lives to their members. Many of the cultures died from within, as individuals abandoned them for other opportunities' (Hardin 1995: 67). As János Kis rightly argued,

> interests attributed to the community are *derived*. We can say that a community has an interest in its preservation and the flourishing of its culture if it is also possible to say that the individuals making up the community have an interest in the preservation of their community and the flourishing of their culture.
>
> (Kis 1996: 227)

It is, however, not clear who is to determine what the interests of these individuals are. In the real world, minorities are represented by leaders who do not and cannot always fully reflect the interests of all the members.

Furthermore, Taylor's defence of the politics of recognition sounds appealing only when applied to a national minority. But the English-speaking Canadians could be equally concerned about losing their identity, as they are being culturally dominated by the United States. Can they therefore restrict the linguistic rights of the French minority, or of the new migrants to Quebec, on the grounds that they need to foster a unity badly needed *vis-à-vis* the challenge from the south? This is not just a theoretical construct. Consider the Slovak case. Were the moral claims of Slovaks to protection of their culture stronger when they inhabited larger states as a minority that had to defend itself against the potential or real dangers of assimilation, be it within the Habsburg Empire, or within Czechoslovakia, than they are now, when they constitute a majority? If yes, why?

To answer this question, it is instructive to recall the modern history of nationalism in Central Europe, which is notorious for turning majorities into minorities and vice-versa. This history also shows the limitations of the concept of ethnic neutrality when applied to modern states. The efforts of Maria Theresa (1740–80) and Joseph II (1780–90) to modernize and centralize the Habsburg Empire were accompanied by a series of failed attempts at linguistic assimilation. As much as language is seen as the distinguishing feature of a nation (Herder), these policies were destined to trigger a series of national 'revivals' – a development clearly not anticipated by the rulers. Hence the Germanizing policies of Joseph II gave rise to Hungarian nationalism (if only indirectly and with considerable delay),[4] which in turn gave rise to Slovak nationalism.

The rationale for the policies of linguistic (and hence cultural) assimilation was not always that of 'collective survival'. For example, concurring with Mill, who advocated the full assimilation of the Irish into the 'superior' British civilization, many Hungarian liberals considered Magyarization the most reliable means of empowering the masses, which included Slovak peasants. Count Károly Zay, the superintendent of the Hungarian Lutheran Church, argued in 1840 that

> The Magyar language is the staunchest defender of liberty and Protestantism in our country. The victory of the Magyars is at the same time the victory of Liberty and Reason. The Magyarization of the Slavs is the holiest duty of any true Hungarian patriot, of any fighter for Liberty and Reason, and of any loyal subject of the Habsburg dynasty.
>
> (cited in Jászi 1929: 309)

Towards the end of the nineteenth century, at the height of the forcible Magyarization of the Slovaks, Béla Grünwald declared that it 'would involve incredible narrow-mindedness that anyone could seriously wish to be a Slovak' (Seton-Watson 1965: 272). He also acknowledged the importance of education for the social advancement of the wider masses through assimilation. In his words, 'secondary school is like a big engine which takes in at one end hundreds of Slovak youth who come out at the other end as Magyars' (cited in Jászi 1929: 329). Whether justifications for the assimilation policies were based on the ideal of societal progress, or the perceived goal of the 'collective survival' of a nation, its moral validity must be questioned.

Similarly, the ideology of Czechoslovakism, which aimed at the creation of a united 'Czechoslovakian identity by way of incorporating the Slovaks into the Czech nation-group' (Bollerup and Christensen 1997: 121), was partly driven by the perceived threat to the Czech culture from the surrounding Germanic influence.[5] This had an ambivalent impact on the Slovak nation. Even though it is contested to what extent Masaryk's conception of Czechoslovakism implied cultural unity, there can be little doubt that the Slovaks were culturally and politically dominated in the first Czechoslovak Republic of 1918–38. Still, as the Slovaks were considered together with the Czechs a part of the *státotvorní* people (the official constituent nationality of the state) they certainly had more influence on the policies of the state than the other national minorities of the new republic, such as the Hungarians (Leff 1997: 24–9; for a more detailed account see also Chapters 4 and 5). Was it right, then, for the 'Czechoslovak nation', in the name of its struggle for survival, to ignore the demands for recognition of other minorities?

The 'struggle for survival'[6] was later used in Slovakia not only for the justification of the very existence of the independent Slovak state, but also to deny the Hungarians some basic minority rights, since they were, and still are, perceived by some Slovaks as endangering the very survival of the Slovak nation. In fact, some of the most adventurous justifications of more restrictive policies towards the Hungarian minority during the third tenure of office of Vladimír Mečiar in Slovakia (1994–1998) were derived from irrational fears about the unabated threat of Hungarian dominance. Roman Hofbauer, a member of parliament for the then governing party the Movement for a Democratic Slovakia and a senior journalist working for the *Slovenská republika* argued in the issue of 27 January 1998 that the Slovak nation is threatened by genocide (*sic.*) and must therefore be protected from both its enemies abroad and traitors from within (Kamenec 1998a: 5).[7]

The above examples do not imply that Taylor would support any restrictions of minority rights in the Habsburg Empire, or Czechoslovakia, let alone in present-day Slovakia. Taylor's argument was voiced, after all, in support of minority rights. Moreover, the suggestion in some cases to override the will of individuals in Quebec was meant to apply to new migrants, whose demands have a different degree of urgency and legitimacy. But the logic underpinning Taylor's reasoning remains problematic.[8] The suggestion that some collective goals can override the interests of an individual deserves scepticism. All the more reason to turn to the examination of a radically liberal alternative to communitarian projects, proposed by the Australian political philosopher Chandran Kukathas.

The politics of indifference

Opposing Taylor's second type of liberalism, Kukathas boldly states that the most viable response of the liberal state to growing demands for recognition is to ignore them. Confronted with the complex realities of multicultural societies, liberalism 'recommends doing nothing' (Kukathas 1998: 687). Kukathas claims that the philosophy of liberalism does not have a problem with multiculturalism, because 'liberalism is itself, fundamentally, a theory of multiculturalism'. Liberalism's answer to the religious and cultural diversity inherent in modern societies has been the realization that diversity should be accommodated and difference tolerated, but without an illusion that all the conflicting interests can ever be reconciled. As Kukathas states, 'division, conflict and competition would always be present in human society and the task of political institutions is to palliate a condition they cannot cure' (Kukathas 1998: 690). As the conflicting demands of different groups are unavoidable, it is better for political institutions to try, as much as possible, to be indifferent to them, rather than putting them in the very centre of the political agenda. Thus, 'a positive delight in the diversity of human cultures, languages, and forms of life' (Nussbaum 1996: 137) characteristic of virtually all the theorists of multiculturalism, can lead, ironically, to more conflict to the extent that the politics of recognition diminishes room for compromises. Something that becomes essential for personal identities cannot be easily compromised.

When the Protestants in Northern Ireland 'celebrate' their identity with marches commemorating a glorious event in their history, they inadvertently demean the identity of the Catholics, whose common reaction is to make the march impossible (even to the extent of using terrorist methods). This is not to say that some sort of politics of recognition is to be blamed for the persistent crisis in Northern Ireland; but it could be argued that a multiculturalism which cherishes differences could hardly prevent it. In contrast, Australia has managed potential religious conflict among the migrants from different parts of Ireland as well as from Britain by 'forgetting' about their divisive histories (Hirst 1994: 32–4). Arguably, it was this politics of indifference that made the peaceful living together of different communities in Australia possible. Similar problems could arise from the differing views of Slovak and Hungarian national histories, when personalities and events that marked an important step in the history of the Hungarian fight for freedom and independence, like Lajos Kossuth and the revolution of 1848/9, are for Slovaks associated with more oppression. As the revolution eventually led in 1867 to the reorganization of the Austrian empire as the Dual Monarchy of Austria-Hungary, Magyars acquired equal status with the German-Austrians. The demands of Slovaks, on the other hand, were largely ignored, and in fact the ensuing politics of Magyarization that aimed to turn Slovaks into Hungarians resulted in the suppression of the Slovak language (Johnson 1996: 156–8).

Historical memories, as important as they may be for the self-understanding of a national community, can also become a dangerous source of conflict. As Jerzy Jedlicki noted, 'the twentieth century history of Eastern Europe (taken here in its largest sense and borders) is a perfect laboratory to observe how genuine or apparent remembrances of the past may aggravate current conflicts' (Jedlicki 1999: 226). In some circumstances, Jedlicki argues, forgetting can be more important for good inter-ethnic relationships than 'inexhaustible collective memory'. In fact, the experiences of the United States show that 'an indifference to history can be a blessing' (Jedlicki 1999: 231). In the context of Polish society, Jedlicki contended that the intense feeling of hatred 'that the Poles harbored for the Germans in the wake of the Nazi occupation and war' could only start waning with a new generation (Jedlicki 1999: 226). Although Polish memories of Nazi atrocities could not be erased, Jedlicki observes that 'with the lapse of time...the trauma seemed to fade and no longer determined popular images of Poland's western neighbors' (Jedlicki 1999: 227). What is needed, hence, is a sober and critical approach to one's own national history:

> No, not oblivion, but a distance, resulting one may hope, in a certain devaluation of national sanctities (holy cities and battlefields, celebrated anniversaries, emblems, heroes' graves, nations' cradles) which would still be worth cultivating, but no longer worth the spilling of one's own blood and the blood of others – this seems to be a necessary condition for negotiating reasonable solutions of apparently insoluble crises.
>
> (Jedlicki 1999: 230)

Thus to stress and celebrate the importance of different histories in Central Europe can contribute paradoxically to more division than to mutual understanding. In that way, Kukathas' theory, which argues for a minimalist liberal state that ignores the political relevance of ethnic identities could be seen to be validated. The question remains whether Kukathas' proposition, which relies on the experience of a migrant country, offers a realistic option for Europe.

Two types of multiculturalism

The politics of indifference can only be equated with multiculturalism, however, when multiculturalism is just another word for tolerance of ethnic differences. Thus we should distinguish between *soft* multiculturalism which allows for and is even supportive of an overarching identity (defined by common language and some basic commitments to the ideals of a liberal state) that unites people of different ethnic backgrounds, and *hard* multiculturalism which implies that all the cultures and ethnic groups within a society are equal and should therefore be actively encouraged to fully realize their particular ethnic identities. Consequently, in the second version of multiculturalism there is no space for an overarching identity since this would inadvertently privilege one group (say Anglo-Celtic) over others. As Hirst convincingly argued, the success of multiculturalism in Australia can be attributed to the application of its soft version (Hirst 1994).[9] While the new migrants were not expected to give up their ethnic and cultural identities entirely, they did have to accept some basic Australian values and they had to learn English if they were to succeed in their new country. This experience cannot, however, be easily 'exported' to Europe, where the situation is radically different. As Kymlicka rightly pointed out, the moral claims for preservation of migrants' identities are different from claims of people living in the countries of their birth who constitute national minorities (Kymlicka 1995a; 1998).[10] The partial loss of one's culture is mostly a painful experience, but migrants are usually better prepared to accept this. Ideally, they made a voluntary trade-off and renounced the 'culturally comfortable' living within their familiar environment for better opportunities in a new country. This does not suggest that the state actively demands that the new migrants forget about their ethnic and cultural identities; the assumption is rather that they can be successfully accommodated within a very broad context of an Australian culture. Soft multiculturalism creates space for migrant cultures to negotiate the conditions of settling down. Instead of forced integration, a benign state makes the adaptation to the new environment easier by formally acknowledging the equality of all cultures.

In the context of Central Europe, however, soft multiculturalism that ultimately leads to assimilation (even if it takes generations) hardly offers an adequate solution for a peaceful co-existence of national minorities. Even though there are historic instances in Europe of states being relatively successful in incorporating some ethnic minorities into the dominant nation (like Basques and Bretons in France), in our times 'the attempts to suppress minority nationalism have been abandoned as unworkable and indeed counter-productive' (Kymlicka 1998: 281). In fact as long as assimilation policies were successful in the past, they were usually only made possible thanks to an unacceptable extent of coercion. Presently, there is a growing consensus that any practices leading to forceful integration or homogenization of the people are morally reprehensible. No liberals today would accept the reasoning of the likes of Count Zay and Grünwald (see above), who in the nineteenth century saw forceful assimilation of the Slovaks into the dominant Hungarian language group, as the best means of securing the enlightened causes of societal progress and liberty.

Unlike migrants, the members of national minorities have not actively chosen to live in a country that is dominated by a different culture, but were born into one. Therefore, they should not suffer permanent marginalization that would follow from state policies based on ignoring the differences. The large Hungarian minority in Slovakia, for example, cannot reasonably be expected to subordinate the importance of their ethnicity and culture to some higher good of the country as a whole. Even if political stability is easier to maintain with a population that shares a common culture, and the public administration is more effective when conducted exclusively in one official and dominant vernacular, the Slovak state cannot aim at full assimilation of a large minority that would lead to its cultural marginalization (or even cultural extinction).

Thus a harder version of multiculturalism is needed in the Central European context, one that does not only allow for a minority culture simply to exist, but actively provides for some of its basic needs. The state must, for example, fully accept its responsibility for education with languages of instruction mirroring the cultural diversity of the country. Moreover, depending on the size of the minority in question, the state should help to sustain the vibrant cultural life of the ethnic communities by providing assistance for newspapers, public broadcasting, theatre and the like. Inevitably, ethnic communities compete with other groups for limited resources that are available for redistribution, and ultimately not all claims can be fulfilled. This is yet another reason why it is crucial that ethnic communities secure adequate political representation which can articulate and persuasively follow its interests.

Surprisingly, besides the extreme-right Slovak National party, no one in the newly independent Slovakia actually questioned the obligation of the state to spend money on ethnic minorities; not even the former prime minister Mečiar, who was rightly criticized for his authoritarian style of government and some extreme nationalistic tendencies in his policies. What was contested was the extent and quality of state support for minority cultures. Yet, on the other hand, Mečiar's government (1994–8) found ways of perverting the purpose of affirmative policies, so that they primarily served the particular political interests of his party, ignoring the needs of the minority in question. In one telling instance, the government cultural fund 'Pro Slovakia' allocated a substantial subsidy for the creation of a Hungarian supplement to a Slovak extreme nationalist newspaper, *Slovenská republika*, that was closely affiliated to Mečiar's Movement for a Democratic Slovakia (Bútora and Skladony 1998: 40). The likelihood of any Slovak Hungarians ever reading this propaganda was negligible, but the government fulfilled two goals at once. First, it bettered the financial situation of its 'own' newspaper; and second, this being a 'truly democratic government', it was able to argue that it was taking its responsibility for supporting minorities seriously.

Thus far I have argued that a multiculturalism based on ignoring differences is not a plausible option in Central Europe. Kymlicka's conception of multicultural citizenship, which acknowledges and accommodates the ethnocultural diversity of the people, is more convincing than politics of indifference. But the critique voiced by Kukathas clearly shows the limits of active politics of recognition, and points at some serious practical problems that cannot be ignored. The implication of Taylor's and Young's assertion that denial or negligence of identity amounts to an act of oppression is that people who feel that their identities are not fully recognized have very strong moral claims to make. In that situation it would be unreasonable to expect them to make compromises in the daily business of politics, which in practice means that political processes can easily turn into a zero-sum game in which one side always has to lose.[11] Since oppression is morally reprehensible, it would not make sense to seek only a partial improvement of the situation. The existing oppression must be abolished altogether. This kind of language is unhelpful for policy-making in diverse societies that, more often than not, have to be based on compromises. Furthermore, the arguments underlying Taylor's 'politics of identity' (Taylor 1992) are based on the assumption that ethnic/cultural identity is more important than any other identity. Yet this view is mistaken psychologically, and unhelpful politically.

These criticisms of contemporary political theories of multiculturalism also point to the limits of Herderian romantic nationalism, which in its celebration of authenticity and cultural purity penalized those individuals who sought to transgress the boundaries of their own culture. For example, the people of Czech ethnic origin in the Austrian part of the Habsburg Empire, who chose to assimilate into the dominant language group (German), were condemned by Czech romantic nationalists as 'odrodilci' (renegades) – a notion with clear negative connotations.[12]

Hard cases: the protection of marginalized groups (e.g. Roma)

The other serious limitation of the politics of identity is the fact that the state can never fully secure undistorted recognition of various identities. This problem is particularly pronounced in dealing with marginalized ethnic groups, like Romanies, who are significantly more disadvantaged than other minorities. As Kymlicka pointed out, this ethnic group is unique, and its position in the societies of Central Europe is difficult to classify (Kymlicka 2001b: 73–6). Romanies do not fit into established categories. For instance, many people would argue that they do not really constitute an ethnic, let alone a national minority, because they have no common homeland, and are widely dispersed throughout the world. This has direct political consequences, since many states are only willing to grant certain rights to national minorities rather than ethnic groups.[13]

Yet the classification of ethnic (or any other) group is by itself very problematic. In the process of classifying a group, an observer (or a state) imposes an image on the people, and by doing this denies the group its authentic voices. For instance, a number of scholars argue that 'the Roma are not Europeans' (Barša 2001: 254). This may seem an innocuous claim that can easily be 'proven' by reference to the history of the Romanies, who are said to originate from India. Yet surely the European identity is not determined just by the historic origins of the group. (Following this logic, and depending on how far back one would go, there would be very few people in Europe left who can claim a 'truly' European origin.) To be European means many different things to many different people, but often Europe is equated with civilization. Hence to exclude Romanies from Europe, if only symbolically, can have undesired consequences, as it implies that they are barbaric. Not surprisingly then, many Romanies resist such claims. As Ian Hancock put it, 'we [the Romani people] are *quintessentially* European, being found in all of its countries like no other single European people' (Hancock 2002: 77–8). At any rate, if Romanies cannot even be seen as an integral part of a wider European culture and society, what hope is there that they will ever become an undisputed part of Czech society? Surely this is what their successful integration, advocated by Barša (see below), would require.

These are not just 'academic' disputes. The images that dominant cultures develop with respect to their minority groups influence their behaviour, and can hence further disadvantage the affected group. The Czech and Slovak languages, for example, are so deeply imbued with racism against Romanies, that much more than some formal political changes would be needed to secure their full equality. As in other European languages, the very term that the majority of the population uses to describe Roma (*Cikán, Cigáň*, in Czech and Slovak respectively) is derogatory, since it implies that Gypsies are people who lie, steal and are generally unreliable.[14] As a recent ethnographical study documented, anti-Roma sentiments are also manifested in a vast number of Slovak folk songs (Krekovičová 1999). These widely spread negative attitudes can be easily utilized by populist politicians. Miroslav Sládek in the Czech Republic and Ján Slota in Slovakia stand out as two leaders of extreme nationalist parties who sought to gain popularity by vilifying the Romanies.

While the liberal state should step in where it can to avoid excesses, such as open racial vilification by extremist politicians, not even a police state could fully eliminate a word and its implications in its daily use.[15] This change can only come about as a result of a slow process from within a civil society. Ultimately, the state can no more warrant that recognition of various identities be free of any distorting, or demeaning images, than it can secure the universal happiness of all citizens. The culture of tolerance has to develop and cannot be imposed on the people by the state, even though the state can help actively in promoting it. Havel's repeated interference on behalf of Romanies was a good example of this.

Apart from Havel, however, Czech state institutions[16] were not very successful in constraining the expressions of racist attitudes. When, for example, the leader of the extreme right Republican Party, Sládek, verbally provoked two Romany brothers, the Tancoš, who, in response, physically attacked him, the brothers were charged with racially motivated violence against an individual and a group of people, as they denounced Sládek as 'bílá svině' (white pig). Thus laws that were clearly created for the protection of minorities were in this instance interpreted in a way that assisted the defence of a politician who had for seven years programmatically incited racial hatred and violence against the Romany minority (Camrda 1998).[17] It required a radical step by the Czech President, who made use of his power by granting the brothers clemency, to restore a sense of justice. As the proper procedures of the rule of law were obstructed by his quick decision, however, the sense of legality suffered. Many observers criticized Václav Havel for over-stretching his competencies (e.g. Šustrová 1998). Yet, with his controversial decision, the Czech president was able to make a clear stance against racism that may have contributed to the failure of the Czech Republican Party to secure seats in parliament in the June 1998 election (for other examples of expressions of Czech chauvinism against Romanies see Chapter 4).

Feasibility versus desirability

The consequent politics of recognition in which the state would take full responsibility for due acknowledgement of often conflicting identities is, as we have seen, hardly a practical proposition when dealing with cultural diversity. But it could still be argued, at least from the point of view of an individual who can ignore the practical implications of such a policy, that such policies are, in any case, desirable. This depends ultimately, however, on individual preferences. Only for those people who value the acknowledgement of their identities more than other goods, which can be in conflict with this requirement, does the politics of recognition remain morally valid whatever its practical implications. For in some cases a choice has to be made between incommensurable options. One has to decide whether living within a closely knit 'culturally comfortable' community is more important than some other goals, like professional advancement or artistic independence, that can only be fulfilled within a broader society.

Any meaningful conception of minority rights will include some elements of affirmative action, which means that the state will inevitably interfere in the value system of a cultural minority. When the state, for example, takes responsibility for education it cannot but promote some sort of values. The idea that at least primary education is obligatory for all citizens is based on the rationale that only in that way can some basic equality of opportunity be maintained. This is supported *inter alia* by the European Convention on Human Rights (Article 2 of the First Protocol) that explicitly states that 'no person shall be denied the right to education' (Poulter 1987: 600). Moreover, liberal thinkers like J. S. Mill highlighted the importance of education for the stability of a liberal democratic order that – at least in the long run – relies on well informed and thus well educated citizens. Even an outspoken advocate of multiculturalism, Joseph Raz, stresses that 'a democratic political system depends on literacy, access to information, a certain understanding of political issues and of political processes' (Raz 1998: 202).

Yet many Romany groups, according to Ian Hancock (a senior Romany scholar and a representative at the United Nations and at UNICEF for the International Romani Union), consider too much formal learning 'as a threat to the Romani way of life' (Hancock 2000: 19; cf. Barany 2002: 132–3). They would hence reject compulsory schooling as the undesired imposition of a patronizing state. 'Our' instinct would tell us that it is surely in the interest of the Romany children to receive the best possible education, even allowing for some significant differences that would accommodate the specifics of their culture – at least some subjects, for example, should be taught in Romanes. The underlying assumption is, however, that 'our' life-style (typically based on education and wealth acquired through a successful career) is more valuable than the life-style of Romanies. If that is the case, the whole project of a multicultural liberal state is self-defeating as, in the process of assisting a minority culture, it undermines, if not destroys, the very culture it aims to protect. As Kukathas stated, 'there is no more reason to insist that gypsy [*sic.*] parents offer their children "rational choice" of life-style through public education than there is to require that other parents offer their children the opportunity to become gypsies' (Kukathas 1995: 248).

In both ways, the cases of discrimination seem to be unavoidable. Kukathas' politics of indifference can be seen as discriminatory because it precludes the individual members of Romany culture from an opportunity to fully participate in the dominant culture, by *practically* denying them access to an institutionalized education system. The politics of difference, on the other hand, which would provide Romany children with some form of institutional education, allows a patronizing state to promote values foreign to the actual culture even if the content and form of education takes Romany culture into account. Which conception, then, is more just? Both are open to the accusation of being racist. One could argue that the state makes itself either guilty of implementing a policy based on ideas of cultural supremacy (in the case of institutional education imposed on Romany children), or it does not live up to its pronounced adherence to individual rights that include the right to proper education. It will be rightly said that the state is able to accommodate differences by, for example, taking seriously the importance of the Romany language. Nevertheless, the question is not whether Romany children should be taught in Romany language, but whether they should go to school at all.

To complicate matters further, it is not even clear whether Romanes should be the preferred language of instruction. Ironically, the attempts of some non-governmental organizations and Roma rights activists in the Czech Republic to provide Romany children with high-quality education in their own language, have also been criticized as leading to exclusion. In fact, even Romanies themselves are not always in favour of a 'revival' of Romany culture. According to a recent opinion survey, some 80 per cent of Romany parents rejected the suggestion that their children attend schools with Romany as the main language of instruction (*Respekt*, 11 December 2000).

What sort of equality: Burkean equality of happiness, or the liberal equality of opportunity?

As we have seen, infringement of cultural autonomy is in some cases a result of the liberal welfare state pursuing social justice. The idea that the state has some responsibility for a downward distribution of wealth is presently hardly contested (with the notable exception of Nozick). In pre-modern times, when democracy was restricted to people with property, this problem could not have been significant. People were free to live within their communal culture, but were also 'free' to remain marginalized. Indeed, Edmund Burke defended the economic injustices of the *ancien régime* by espousing the idea of an 'equality of happiness'. All lives are inherently valuable regardless of material conditions. People should hence, according to Burke, be taught to seek

> the happiness that is to be found by virtue in all conditions; in which consists the *true moral equality of mankind*, and not in that monstrous fiction, which, by inspiring false ideas and vain expectations into men destined to travel in the obscure walk of laborious life, serves only to aggravate and imbitter that real inequality, which it never can remove; and which the order of civil life establishes as much for the benefit of those whom it must leave in an humble state, as those whom it is able to exalt to a condition more splendid, but not more happy.
>
> (my italics, Burke 1968: 124)

This is not to suggest that in order to meet the demands of cultural recognition, we should return to pre-modern times, or revive Burkean conservatism. Nor does it mean that the politics of recognition is *always* in conflict with welfare politics. But it is instructive to remember that pressure to homogenize the populations of larger states arose with the process of modernization (vividly described by Gellner [1983]). The attempt of the enlightened despot, Maria Theresa, to turn Romanies into 'new peasants' or 'new Hungarians' did not bring about their political emancipation, but rather a new form of systematic oppression. The failed policies of forced assimilation represented yet another aspect of modernization of the Habsburg empire. It is not surprising that the communist rulers, being even more ruthless modernizers than Maria Theresa, continued in her endeavour. Both oppressive regimes also accompanied their attempts at forced assimilation with policies, which aimed at preventing the cultural and biological reproduction of the Romanies.[18] We now know that these and similar policies are both morally indefensible and politically infeasible. The nationalist dream of a perfect cultural unity has never materialized. The question is how genuine cultural diversity can be accommodated in our 'post-socialist' times (to use the words of Nancy Fraser)[19] without endangering, but rather supporting the liberal democratic order.

The redistribution-recognition dilemma

Nancy Fraser has identified a dilemma of modern liberal welfare states that are concerned both with the politics of recognition as well as the politics of social justice. While the demands for recognition are commonly addressed by some form of affirmative action that leads to valorization of group-specific differences, the ultimate goal of social improvements is to minimize any group-specific differences (Fraser 1997). When, for example, Romanies are discriminated against on the labour market because of their ethnicity and/or 'race', social justice would require overcoming this unfavourable differentiation. As Fraser put it (writing about the discrimination against Afro-Americans),

> Eliminating 'race'-specific exploitation, marginalization, and depriva-tion requires abolishing the racial division of labour – both the racial division between exploitable and superfluous labour and the racial divi-sion within paid labour. The logic of remedy is like the logic with respect to class: it is to put race out of business as such.
>
> (Fraser 1997: 21–2)

Policies against racism are, according to Fraser, trapped in a dilemma. They must at once 'pursue political-economic remedies that would under-mine "racial" differentiation, while also pursuing cultural-valuational remedies that valorize the specifity of despised collectivities' (Fraser 1997: 23). Thus, in certain circumstances, struggles for recognition of diverse iden-tities are in opposition to struggles for a just distribution of material benefits. Affirmative action directed towards disadvantaged groups can actually lead to backlash misrecognition, as the groups that are in need of assistance are made visible and therefore more vulnerable to attacks from those people who are unwilling to accept their rights. In fact, the affirmative action itself can be perceived as yet another, albeit unwitting, act of oppres-sion. According to Iris Young, 'in its new usage, oppression designates the disadvantage and injustice some people suffer not because a tyrannical power coerces them, but because of the everyday practices of a well-inten-tioned liberal society' (Young 1990: 41).

Fraser believes, however, that the contradiction between the imperatives of social justice and the demands for recognition can and should be over-come. For that to happen, conventional affirmative multiculturalism and social policies that aim 'at correcting inequitable outcomes of social arrangements without disturbing the underlying framework that generates them' must be replaced with a more radical approach that is transformative, in that it aims at 'restructuring the underlying generative framework' (Fraser 1997: 23). Transformative remedies would redress disrespect of disadvantaged groups by 'destabilizing existing group identities and differentiations', and thus they 'would not only raise the self-esteem of members of currently disrespected groups; they would change *everyone's* sense of self' (Fraser 1997: 24). 'The long-term goal of deconstructive antiracism is a culture in which hierarchical racial dichotomies are replaced by networks of multiple intersecting differences that are demassified and shifting' (Fraser 1997: 31). In the economic realm, the remedies would also be directed towards a thorough restructuring of the underlying causes of unequal distribution, rather than simply relying on half-hearted remedies of the liberal welfare state. Here again, while the former remedies seek to undermine class differentiation, the latter more traditional remedies create 'strongly cathected, antagonistic group differentiations' (Fraser 1997: 25) and in that way perpetuate structural injustice.

Leaving aside the economic and political viability of the proposed socialist transformation (that by aiming at 'deep restructuring of the relations of production' (Fraser 1997: 27) very much resembles a communist revolution), Fraser's remedies are not very convincing even in the context of race and ethnicity. If the 'selves' were malleable to the extent that Fraser assumes, then the whole project of a multicultural society based on recognizing differences would not be needed, as it would be simpler to turn people into 'deconstructed' cosmopolitan citizens of the world, for whom the notion of a particular cultural identity would be obsolete anyway. Thus, Fraser, having rightly identified potential tension between the politics of recognition and the politics of the welfare state, obscures the problem by proposing a solution that is both inconsistent and unrealistic. This is not helpful, as it ignores the fact that the aims of social justice and the politics of difference are often caught in a conflict which cannot be reconciled.

The other problem with affirmative action is that its justification is often based on a misconceived understanding of ethnic identities. Identities are dynamic. The active politics of difference can, in fact, inhibit this dynamic. As Waldron observed:

> In general, there is something artificial about a commitment to *preserve* minority cultures. Cultures live and grow, change and sometimes wither away; they amalgamate with other cultures, or they adapt themselves to geographical or demographic necessity. To *preserve* a culture is often to take a favoured snapshot of it, and insist that this version must persist at all costs, in its defined purity, irrespective of the surrounding social, economic and political circumstances.
>
> (Waldron 1995: 109–10)

Any affirmative action must presuppose a certain conception of a minority culture. In order to determine what is to be affirmed, some elements of that culture have to be described, or even defined. This, according to Young, can lead to the perpetuation of basic injustices which are based on a reductionist view of members of the marginalized group, since seen 'as remarkable, deviant beings, the culturally imperialised are stamped with an essence' (Young 1990: 60). In order to overcome this dilemma, Young asserts that 'it is necessary to conceptualise groups in a much more relational and fluid fashion' (Young 1990: 47). It is difficult to imagine, however, how practical policies can be based on fluid and ever-changing identities. To decide on a suitable curriculum and language of instruction in minority schools, for example, it is of little help to state that everything is in flux. Moreover, if identities were as flexible as Young and Fraser at times assume, one of the basic rationales for the politics of difference would be seriously undermined.

It is important that ethnic/cultural minorities have a fair chance to assert their interest without being constantly overruled by the majority culture, especially in the areas that are culturally sensitive, e.g. minority schools, the media and the like. As Bauböck argued, ethnic minorities 'can claim collective rights which enable them to keep cultural boundaries relatively closed and traditions relatively stable, as long as this is what their members want' (Bauböck 1998: 46). But minority cultures are not monolithic and do not have a will and a purpose on their own; to that extent Young's argument against the essentialist approach to identities is valid. Rather, all their needs can only be derived from the individuals constituting this minority. For that reason it is crucial that they have authentic, democratic representation. What is inevitable, however, is that various representatives will have very different ideas about the best interests of their community. Moreover, minorities often have to confront the values and ideas which are imposed on them by the majority culture.

Stereotypes versus reality

The discussion about the value of institutional education in Romany culture offers a vivid example of the dilemma any conception of affirmative action has to face. The assumption noted above, that the Romanies dislike going to school, can be refuted as yet another instance of racism based on prejudices that have no relation to reality. In fact, the very same Ian Hancock who stated that many Romanies consider too much formal learning 'as a threat to the Romani way of life', complained on another occasion about many prejudices against Romanies which included the assumption that they don't like going to school. He listed among many 'bizarre things [that] have been written and presented as fact' about Romanies, 'claims that Gypsies originated on the moon; that they have an intrinsic horror of water and washing; or that they have no conception of obligation and danger or ownership', as well as claims 'that they have *no interest* in organization, *education*, or leadership' (my italics, Hancock 1997: 38). This prejudices can also be challenged by a number of educational achievements, whether at individual or community level. For example, when a Czech Romany community set up the first specialized Romany secondary school (the Rómska strední škola sociální), one of its founders stressed that the school is 'proof that Romanies want to educate themselves, and that they are capable of learning' (Bauerová 1998).[20]

It seems difficult to ascertain which description is more accurate. But it can be argued that both claims are incorrect as long as they – being crude generalizations – do not apply to *all* instances of Romany culture, and accurate as long as they describe *some* particular case in time. This should not be surprising to anyone who is concerned with cultural identities. As we have seen in the discussion on liberal nationalism, identities change with time, and at any particular point they are never monolithic. Different conceptions of what it means to be a Slovak, Czech or Romany compete for influence within a community. This is not only natural, but at least from a liberal point of view also very desirable. Yet, as disturbing as it may seem, there are 'some examples where stereotypes and reality are not far apart' (Lewy 1999: 81). As Guenter Lewy argued, certain traditional practices within Romany culture sanction behaviour which exacerbates the divide between the Romanies and mainstream society.

> Whether the result of exclusion, poverty or other factors, the fact is that certain characteristics of Gypsy life tend to reinforce or even create hostility amongst the population they encounter. These traits, customs and attitudes are reported not only by their enemies but also by well meaning observers, sympathetic anthropologists and, at times, by Gypsies themselves.
>
> (Lewy 1999: 80)

It is not surprising that after many centuries, in which Romanies were alternately victims of social isolation, forced assimilation, or persecution, these people themselves developed some prejudices, or even hostility towards all non-Romanies, who are called *gadje*. This exclusive term has a pejorative connotation and, according to the American anthropologist Anne Sutherland, allows the Romanies to approve of behaviour towards outsiders which would be unacceptable within their own community, including cheating and stealing. 'Stealing from other Rom is wrong...but it is not necessarily wrong when it is from *gaje*; although one should not be too greedy' (Sutherland quoted in Lewy 1999: 80). The danger stemming from such statements (regardless of whether they are genuine and disinterested observations of anthropologists, or unfounded expressions of plain prejudices) is that they fortify differences by tacitly assuming that certain traits are essential to the members of an ethnic community. If such findings translate into stereotypical notions that Gypsies cannot help themselves since lying and stealing lie in their 'nature', then there is little hope for improvement. To that extent, Young and Fraser were certainly right to remind us that minority culture should not be stamped with an essence which is immutable. This type of cultural determinism leads to racism.

The limits of tolerance

Yet it is certainly conceivable that *some* cultural practices that are considered a part of Romany tradition are incompatible with the demands of a liberal democratic state. In such cases the benign pressure of the liberal state can be legitimate, since it can lead to the adaptation of the affected culture. Hence there are significant limits to tolerance which cannot be ignored even in an ideal liberal setting. Joseph Raz listed four:

> First, all cultural communities should be denied the right to repress their members....Second, no community has a right to be intolerant of those who do not belong to it....Third, the opportunity to leave one's community must be a viable option for its members....Finally, liberal multiculturalism will require all groups to allow their members access to adequate opportunities for self-expression and for participation in the economic life of the country, and the cultivation of the attitudes and skills required for effective participation in the political culture of the state.
>
> (Raz 1998: 199)

The acceptance of Raz's prescriptions would lead to policies which are considerably more interventionist than Kukathas' politics of indifference, but they seem more pragmatic and fair. It is important, however, to realize that the limits of tolerance impose restrictions on minority cultures, and can be difficult to implement, especially when they are in conflict with the cultural practices of the community in question. This is why 'Romani communities themselves must make a greater effort to reduce their marginality – an effort that in some instances may involve a reappraisal of long-standing Romani traditions', as Zoltan Barany suggested in his recent comprehensive study of *The East European Gypsies* (Barany 2002: 19). However, it is vital that the kinds of restriction proposed by Raz are applied not only to minorities but also to the dominant culture (in particular, Raz's second imperative, which demands tolerance of the members of other ethnic groups, must be observed by all groups in a liberal society).

What is needed in order to improve the situation of Romanies in Central Europe is a transformation of both cultures. But there can be little doubt that mainstream society has to make the first step. Only in that way can the vicious circle be broken; the vicious circle which developed as both sides of the cultural divide were strongly influenced by their respective prejudices which led to mutual alienation. As Barša argued in a recent study of the

Political Theory of Multiculturalism, 'Czechs will basically have to cease regarding the Czech state as the possession of their ethnic group....If we do not provide them [other ethnic groups] space within Czech society, we will force them to create their own society outside it' (Barša 1999: 283; see also Barša 2001: 255). A critical survey of the post-1989 school curriculum in the Czech Republic revealed, for example, that none of the standard history textbooks cover the history of Romanies (Čaněk 1996: 77–8). This is not only to the detriment of all those Romany children who are expected to learn about Czech national heroes and nothing about their own history, but also to the detriment of the Czech children who have no opportunity to learn about Romany tradition and culture, and can only rely on prejudices and stereotypes.

The most serious impediment to satisfactorily accommodating the Romanies is the resentment to which they are subjected by the dominant cultures. Many Czechs and Slovaks, for example, believe that Romanies should be fully assimilated into their respective mainstream culture, while at the same time denying the Romanies the capacity of doing so (see also Chapter 4). This attitude is unacceptable, as it is based on the logic of racism. As Rainer Bauböck argued,

> Nobody should be seen as being incapable of assimilating into a national culture because of her ethnic or 'racial' origins, her gender or other innate features, or because of her present affiliation to a particular cultural, linguistic or religious group. Denying the capability of members of such groups to assimilate into a national culture 'naturalizes' cultural differences and defines them implicitly in racial terms.
>
> (Bauböck 1998: 41)

But is assimilation defensible, or even desirable, for a minority culture like Romanies? Paradoxically, the possibility of assimilation is not only denied to Romanies by mainstream prejudices, but often also by those well intentioned defenders of Roma rights who render the inviolability of ethnic identity their primary concern. They contend that the negative attitude of a large part of the Romany community towards some aspects of their own tradition (including language) is itself a result of long lasting oppression and racial prejudices that should be overcome. This attitude is seen as a strategic move of the members of victimized group to escape its 'inferior' status by full assimilation into mainstream society – a move that should not be necessary. Yet even assimilation must be considered a legitimate choice, provided it is not enforced, but rather corresponds with the genuine desires of the individuals concerned.[21]

A Slovak scholar specializing in Romany culture, Arne B. Mann, bemoans the instances of full voluntary assimilation. These people were, in her view, not able to 'overcome the handicap of their past, and awake in themselves a positive ethnic consciousness'.

I know a west Slovak Romany family, where the parents gave their children middle school and college education (as a chemist, agricultural engineer, aeroplane mechanic etc.), and did not teach them the Romany language. They all found non-Romany marriage partners. They justified this by saying that they had experienced enough poverty, and wanted their children to have a better life.

(Mann 1992: 262)

But it may well be that they were simply not that interested in 'ethnic consciousness', or at least they made a choice according to which career opportunities were more important than the 'culturally comfortable' way of life within their own culture. In an ideal world this choice should not be necessary. It should be possible to do both: remain true to one's own culture and acquire any career that one dreams of. And in some cases it is possible to have the best of the two worlds; the choices are not always either/or. A Slovak poet, Dezider Banga, who writes both in Slovak and in Romanes, did not need to abandon his rich cultural inheritance to become a part of the 'Slovak' literary establishment (Banga 1996). But there are occupations and life plans which demand that one transcends the limits of one's own culture in order to succeed.

Clearly, there are limits to what can be achieved to the full satisfaction of all conflicting demands. Furthermore, it is unrealistic to expect that the postcommunist countries can better resolve the problems of the coexistence of different ethnicities than can the well-established democracies in the West. As André Liebich reminds us,

No one should expect a 'solution' for the minority issue. What one can hope is that the East Central European countries will continue to try to learn through their own experience with the understanding encouragement of the outside world and in a favourable international climate. In light of the alternatives, past and present, muddling through may be good enough.

(Liebich 1996)

Conclusion

The presentation of these examples should not suggest that the state should fully withdraw from interference with minorities and ignore its responsibility for their well-being. Similarly, the fact that the existence of a welfare state makes its misuse possible is not an argument against welfare politics. But we are well advised by Kukathas and others that we should be realistic about and often suspicious of the state, and not expect any definite solutions to all the problems derived from the living together of different cultures. Ultimately, Kukathas is right to say that a liberal state can only ameliorate conflicts, not abolish them all together, but his argument in favour of a consequent politics of indifference is less persuasive.

To sum up, rather than proposing simple solutions, I have tried to identify some of the inherent contradictions involved in dealing with ethnic and cultural diversity. I argue against those who maintain that because of these contradictions a liberal state should withdraw from issues of ethnicity. Both affirmative action and minority rights are needed. But no rights are absolute, and even minority rights have to be weighed against other legitimate considerations, like the stability of a democratic order, or the individual equality of opportunities. The critics of the politics of recognition provide a useful corrective to some projects of communitarians who tend to raise expectations no state can ever fulfil. When demands for (say) social justice are incommensurable with demands for cultural recognition, a choice has to be made that excludes other options. Hence to strike the right balance between unity and diversity, and between individual and collective rights, requires careful consideration of intricate and often ultimately insolvable problems.

3 Nationalism in Poland

In no other country of Central Europe have different types of nationalism played such an important role in affecting the outcome of the postcommunist transition as in Poland. The Poles experienced nationalism as a liberating force that led to their emancipation from communist rule in 1989. But given the intermingling of extreme forms of nationalism and strong religious attachments, many observers feared that the emerging liberal democratic order would be seriously impeded by the very same nationalist sentiments that made emancipation possible. These fears did not materialize. Now, more than a decade later, Poland is widely considered one of the most stable countries in the region; its democratic credentials were underlined by the March 1999 accession to NATO (together with the Czech Republic and Hungary), and the December 2002 invitation to join the EU. Accordingly, scholars have argued that nationalism has become largely irrelevant in postcommunist Poland (i.e. Morawska 1995; Millard 1996; Vachudová and Snyder 1997: 34).

These accounts misconceived the nature of nationalism, and underestimated its potential impact – both positive and negative – on the political and economic transition of Polish society. The relative electoral success in September 2001 of extreme nationalist parties, such as the League of Polish Families, belied the overly positive assessments of those scholars who argued that nationalism was a thing of the past. Yet more, not less, nationalism was needed to make democracy work in Poland – but nationalism of a radically different sort. A number of Polish intellectuals have argued in recent years that the problems of postcommunist transition were, in fact, exacerbated by liberals abandoning the language of nationalism, which had proved such a powerful motivating force in the fight against communism (i.e. Cichocki 2000; 2002; Gowin 2001; Krasnodębski 2002).

Liberal nationalism could have advanced the goals of transition more than it did in two ways. First, a sense of national solidarity could have alleviated the negative impact of economic reforms that created an underclass of people excluded from the gains of transition. Second, a sense of belonging to the national community could have fostered political participation, and reduced the kind of cynicism that sees in all political processes just a corrupt game beneficial for those few who are fortunate enough to share in the spoils of political power.[1] As Cichocki has recently argued, the crucial task for contemporary Polish intellectuals is to endow nationalism with a new meaning; to redefine it in such a way that would address the current and future challenges of the Polish nation without losing the connection with the past (Cichocki 2002). This is not to say that there were no influential voices advocating the virtues of liberal nationalism in the early stages of political transition. As will be shown in this chapter, the likes of Marcin Król, Adam Michnik, Jerzy Szacki, Józef Tischner and Andrzej Walicki maintained their interest in 'the shape of the Polish soul' (Michnik 1993: 252) before and after 1989.

In this chapter, I will map out the different discourses of nationalism in Poland. Starting with the competing interpretations of the significance of pre-eighteenth-century history (Noble Democracy), and their impact on recent political developments, I move on to examine the different perceptions of the interwar period and the legacy of two competing political figures, Roman Dmowski and Józef Piłsudski. I will then deal with the impact of the Second World War on the self-understanding of the Polish nation, and the changing nature of the Polish-Jewish relationship. Further, I will assess the relevance of religious nationalism from communist times to the present. In connection with religious nationalism, the issue of church-state relations in liberal theory will be discussed, drawing on the example of the United States, and examining political practice in Poland. This leads to an assessment of the influence of the Catholic Church in the creation of the 1997 Polish constitution. Finally, the Polish version of liberal nationalism will be explored.

History

> Disputes over history are frequently equivalent to quarrels over our identity.
>
> (Michnik 1985: 325)

The history of Polish nationalism poses a twofold challenge to the theory of 'Eastern' nationalism (see Chapter 1). First, most historians of Poland question the assumption that nationalism is a relatively recent phenomenon. They 'tend to agree that the starting point in the long process of making the Polish nation was the medieval Polish nationality that had emerged at the turn of the thirteenth century' (Walicki 1997a: 232). This is another instance of the long-lasting conflict between primordialists (such as Smith) who argue that many nations can boast of a long history, and modernists (such as Anderson, Gellner, and Hobsbawm) who consider nations and nationalism to be a result of modernization.[2] Even if primordialists have good evidence to support their arguments in the Polish case, it seems that the present 'content' of Polish nationalism has been more influenced by the developments of the nineteenth and twentieth centuries – on which all the modernist interpretations of nationalism focus. But here it is not important to decide what the 'correct' interpretation of Polish history is. Rather, it suffices to observe different historic narratives as they influence the character of the 'imagined' Polish community. As the sociologist Roman Szporluk put it, 'it matters a lot *what* a nation imagines itself to be' (Walicki 1997a: 229).

Second, Walicki has successfully challenged the idea that Polish nationalism has always been ethnically and culturally based. Rather, even before the French Revolution, the Polish nation would have been best described by a conception of civic nationalism that transcended ethnic boundaries. The emergence of the Polish-Lithuanian Commonwealth, known as *Rzeczpospolita* (Republic), resulted in a shift from the ethno-linguistic national patriotism that had characterized the medieval Polish nationality to a form of 'multiethnic civic nationalism, based upon a vision of common political destiny and cemented by a fierce attachment to republican libertarian values' (Walicki 1997a: 233). The strongest bond of this nationalism was the so-called Noble Democracy, which gave its members considerable rights. Walicki consequently claims that 'Polish "nationalism", in Kohn's sense of the term, originated as a political nationalism, a nationalism of a definitely "Western" type. One might here risk the assertion that its origins were earlier than those of either French or German nationalism' (Walicki 1989: 7).

Noble Democracy: enlightened or feudal? Proto-liberal or proto-communist?

The claim that Polish nationalism was originally more civil than ethnic can be supported by the argument that Noble Democracy was indeed a precursor of contemporary liberal democratic political systems (a question that constitutes yet another controversy about the most accurate interpretation of Polish history). As Noble Democracy was limited to only one class, it was arguably far removed from the Enlightenment ideal-typical model of nationalism as a modern phenomenon that unites different classes. The defenders of the 'golden freedom' stress that the high number and social diversity of active citizens (i.e. the nobility, who enjoyed political liberty and civil rights) compares favourably with England and France (Davies 1981: II, 489; Walicki 1989: 6; 1997a: 232). Furthermore, even the typical Western nations seldom, in practice, lived up to their ideals. The American conception of a nation, to take an example, was originally exclusionary, or even racist since it did not include black slaves.[3] Critics of 'the myth of the golden freedom of old Poland' (Szacki 1995: 45) emphasize, on the other hand, that nine tenths of the Polish population was subjected to backward forms of feudal tenure and had no political rights or representation at all (Johnson

1996: 110). Similarly, the unique institution of the *liberum veto*, that enabled any single member of the Diet to prevent a political agreement, is hailed by Davies as the expression of traditional liberal values such as 'the right to resistance, the social contract, the liberty of the individual, the principle of government by consent, the value of self-reliance' (Davies 1981: II, 489–90), and criticized by Szacki as corresponding with a spirit of collectivism that stands in clear opposition to liberalism (Szacki 1995: 48). Depending on the viewpoint, then, communist rule in Poland either 'reinforced many of the most salient features of traditional culture' (Jowitt in Szacki 1995: 45), or was an alien graft, to which 'the Polish national tradition provided a particularly unreceptive soil' (Herer and Sadowski 1990: 47).

As contentious as the meaning of Noble Democracy was the advancement of liberal ideals marked by the Polish Constitution of 3 May 1791. Some historians argued that the term 'people' employed in the constitution was still very restrictive, since despite some vague promises towards the peasants and more real advancements regarding the burghers, it largely limited the real political power to the Polish nobles (Stone 1990: 67; Brzezinski 1998: 44). In that way, the constitution was still conceived around the premodern notion of privileges which were granted to certain social groups but withheld from others. This is in line with the critical observations of Wiktor Osiatynski, who stressed that the concept of individual rights, which is central to liberalism, had been missing from the Polish tradition of political thought (Osiatynski 1992: 15). Conversely, others praised the 1791 constitution as remarkably progressive for the time of its implementation. Andrzej Ajnenkiel argued, for example, that

> the constitution, as well as the practice of the Sejm that passed it, broadened the notion of 'political nation' to include not only nobility but also townspeople; what is more – an absolute novelty – it stated at places that the notions of 'nation' and 'citizens' concerned all inhabitants of the country.
>
> (Ajnenkiel 1993: 123)

Whether the 1791 Constitution was sufficiently liberal or not, it failed in one of its primary tasks, which was to prevent any further disintegration of Poland, due to the imperial aspirations of its neighbours. Only fourteen months after its adoption, the constitution became irrelevant as Prussia and Russia agreed to the second partition of Poland. Finally, the third partition in 1795 brought an end to Poland as an independent state (this time, as in the first partition in 1772, Austria was also involved). The constitution did not save the state, but it became a powerful 'symbol of Poland's national identity – an identity based on values of constitutionalism and limited, enlightened government' (Brzezinski 1998: 45).

The meaning of this symbol remains disputed. Is the constitution proof of the enlightened character of Noble Democracy, or yet another demonstration of its feudal, pre-modern character? Ultimately, for our purposes, it is not decisive which side of the argument will prove more convincing. Liberal democracy in Poland can be sustained because of its liberal traditions, or, paradoxically, in spite of its lack of these traditions. As the past shapes competing historical narratives, it influences present developments, but does not fully determine their outcome. The issues of Noble Democracy and the Polish Constitution of 3 May 1791 provide the Polish people, at any rate, with a good vantage point from which to elaborate the desirable features of liberalism. The historical experiences can be instructive for current aspirations – whether it be negatively as warnings which indicate how to avoid past mistakes, or positively as prototypical models which can and should be emulated.

Further developments in Polish history were seen against the background of these (contested) liberal traditions. After the third partition of Poland in 1795, for example, liberals and other proponents of independence strengthened their confidence in the righteousness of their cause by seeing it as originating in the glorious history of their nation. A pamphleteer of the November Uprising of 1830 wrote:

> The fatherland of political freedom is our land, Poland...in liberal principles and institutions we are ahead of all the nations of Europe....We must revive these institutions and extend them to all citizens, we do not have to imitate anything.
>
> (cited in Szacki 1995: 47)

Polish romantics firmly believed that their nation was a chosen nation, destined to succeed in its fight for freedom and political independence. The most prominent Polish poet, Adam Mickiewicz, popularized the evocative metaphor of Poland as a saviour of humanity, as the 'Christ of Nations', that would, one day, liberate the world from injustice (Mickiewicz 1944: 371–81; Porter 1996: 1474).[4] Polish romantic nationalism displayed elements of universalism that bear resemblance to the rhetoric of French revolutionaries, or nationalist fighters for Italian unification such as Mazzini. The watchword of the 1830 uprising was characteristically: 'For your freedom and ours' (Gomułka 1990: 6). Similarly, in the 1980s as the independent trade union Solidarność led the biggest protest against a communist regime, Poles were fully aware of the fact that their fight was relevant to other nations of Central and Eastern Europe locked in the communist bloc. Today, the Polish people are proud that it was they who initiated the end of communist power.[5]

Even though the loss of political independence at the end of the eighteenth century gave rise to a romantic conception of nationalism that is usually associated with a shared culture, language, religion and ethnicity, to be Polish still meant 'something more than just to speak Polish, and..."Poland" extended beyond the boundaries of the Polish tongue and the walls of the Polish Catholic Church' (Porter 1996: 1474). The defining feature of a nation thus conceived was not ethnicity, but the historic mission that this nation was supposed to fulfil. As Brian Porter argued, the Polish nationalists 'of the early nineteenth century *enacted* the nation rather than *embodying* it' (Porter 2000: 16). They idealized the old, multiethnic and multi-religious Commonwealth. Mickiewicz characteristically began his *Master Thaddeus*, a patriotic poem about Polishness, with the words 'Lithuania! My Fatherland!' (Gross 1995: 296; Walicki 1997a: 242). Not even different languages could divide the nation, as the romantic historian Joachim Lelewel wanted his contemporaries to believe, writing in 1836: 'Already for centuries the Ruthenian, Polish and Lithuanian languages have been brothers; they constitute no national division among themselves' (Millard 1995: 109).

But as repeated attempts to regain the political independence of the nation failed (the last significant uprising in 1863 was bloodily suppressed by the Russians), the content of Polish nationalism shifted ever closer to ethnicity, culture and religion. Increasingly, to be a Pole meant 'Polish born, Polish speaking and Roman Catholic' (Johnson 1996: 110). As the prospects for political independence faded, the conception of a nation based on language and ethnicity that was independent from the existence of a national state and its political institutions gained prominence. Even then, however, ethnocentric nationalism was not the only option under considera- tion. An influential group of the Warsaw Positivists appropriated some ideas of English liberalism in order 'to create a *national* liberalism (though they did not use this expression) that would make sense in the atmosphere of defeat and despair after 1863' (Porter 2000: 48). This was a new generation of political thinkers, who were highly critical of their romantic predecessors. In their view, the romantics – being preoccupied with the lofty ideals that would advance both their nation and humanity – seemed to have lost sight of the current problems of their fellow co-nationals in the here and now. The Warsaw Positivists sought to substitute the 'grand ambitions' of the past with practical concerns for their people. Instead of heroic actions prop- agated by romantic nationalists like Mickiewicz, the Positivists proposed mundane everyday work, which would improve the lot of their people within the constraints of the existing political situation. While the romantics saw their nation as a spiritual entity with a God-given mission, the Positivists saw their nation as a society in which individuals should contribute to the common good by small productive work (Porter 2000: 48ff).

Crucially, both the romantics and the Positivists explicitly rejected the ethnocentric vision of the Polish nation, which would put Poles above everyone else.[6] Their ideas significantly enriched the discourse of liberal nationalism. The Warsaw Positivists sought to empower the individual members of the nation by encouraging them to do what was currently possible in order to improve themselves and their nation. Importantly, they warned of 'national sentiments based on "international hatred" or "national self-exaltation"' that could only be described as 'false patriotism' (Porter 1996: 1488; see also Porter 2000: 68). It was this false patriotism, however, that was to dominate the Polish political scene just a few decades later.

Competing visions: Dmowski versus Piłsudski

At the beginning of the twentieth century the international situation changed dramatically. The position of all the three partitioning powers had either been weakened (Russia and Prussia), or suffered a fatal blow with the end of the First World War (Austria-Hungary). Thus, at last – after more than a century – a realistic opportunity arose for the Poles to assert their national independence.[7] Their desire corresponded with the policy of the victorious Allies, which supported the establishment of new states in Central Europe based on the doctrine of national self-determination (Cirtautas 1995: 24–46). However, the newly born Polish state (of 11 November 1918) faced many challenges. It had to unite three distinctively separate territories; it had to build whole new institutions necessary for a functioning state; and it had to secure its borders and their international recognition. Most important, for this study, was the impact the new political reality had on the understanding of the Polish national identity. The conception of a nation that came to dominate national politics was based on ethnicity and language, and clashed with the reality of Poland as a multinational state, in which the Polish majority amounted to only two thirds of the population. Regrettably, 'the multicultural Polish state of the early twentieth century was no longer accompanied by a multicultural vision of the Polish nation' (Porter 2000: 16). In fact, the interwar Polish national state became associated with extreme nationalism characterized by xenophobia and anti-Semitism. The 1919 programme of the Popular National Union (Związek Ludowo-Narodowy), which was the most successful party in the national election in that year, abounded in anti-Semitic and chauvinistic statements. The programme stated that the goal of the republic must be 'the greatest possible nation-state homogeneity' and lamented that the 'Polish organism' had been polluted by 'many foreign and hostile elements'. It stated further, that

> The control of nearly all commerce and industry by Jews, who have no connection with the nation, has obstructed the proper development of a Polish middle class, impeded the unity and mutual understanding of the educational strata of the nation and the peasant strata, and excessively inflamed all social classes.
>
> (cited in Sugar 1995: 251)

These ideas reflected the influence of Dmowski's vision of the Polish nation that was popular by the turn of the century. Dmowski, the leader of National Democracy (or the *Endecja* as it was usually called), despised the

Noble Democracy and 'placed the "national interest", as he saw it, above all else' (Sugar 1995: 267). He strove for a Poland that was to be ethnically as 'pure' as possible. His main competitor, Piłsudski, by contrast, drew a different lesson from the same tradition and envisaged a large, geographically more eastern, heterogeneous, federally organized and ethnically tolerant state.[8] It is not without irony that it is this second vision that is decisively closer to our modern image of liberal democracy, since at the beginning of the twentieth century it appeared to be vice-versa. Dmowski's *Thoughts of a Modern Pole* were, after all, modern and popular precisely because they proposed a state whose borders corresponded with an ethnically homogenous nation. Dmowski declared that 'the nation is the product of the state's existence' (Sugar 1995: 267). Despite the wide appeal of Dmowski's extreme nationalistic ideology,[9] Piłsudski had politically more success. A popular fighter for Polish self-determination, he enjoyed the strong support of the people when he declared Poland's independence in 1918, and served as the first president of the country until 1922. But Poland, even under Piłsudski (especially after the military coup in 1926 that established his dictatorship) had never quite lived up to his own ideals of a nationally tolerant state. As Korbonski observed, 'the official policy toward minorities was hostile from the start...[and] was characterised by widespread use of violence intended to enforce Polonization of reluctant Ukrainians and Belorussians' (Korbonski in Held 1992: 233). Piłsudski may have been stronger politically, but it was Dmowski's vision of the nation that determined the actual political developments.

However, the first attempt to establish a modern, liberal democratic Polish state failed not only because of the problems with integral nationalism. With the emergence of a powerful Nazi German state, and the consolidation of communist power in Russia, Poland had very little chance of survival. Once again it was to be partitioned by its traditional enemies in the West and the East, and ultimately fully occupied by the Germans. Polish resistance against Nazi Germany continued the long tradition of underground campaigns against foreign oppression, only this time the Poles suffered more than ever before. The war also reinforced the tendency to define the Polish nation in exclusivist terms.

One of the consequences of the Second World War was the fact that Poland became, for the first time in its history, virtually ethnically homogeneous (bringing it considerably closer to Dmowski's rather than Piłsudski's vision of the Polish nation). Although the process of ethnic homogenization started with the extermination of the Jewish population by the Nazis, it was only completed after the war by a series of population 'transfers', which followed the enforced revisions of the Polish borders.[10] Due to the concessions of the Western allies to the Soviet Union, Poland incurred significant territorial losses in the east, and was compensated by territorial gains in the west at the expense of defeated Germany. In effect, Poland was moved some 300 kilometres to the west (Ther 2001). The incorporation of the ethnically mixed territory of Upper Silesia posed a serious challenge for the postwar Polish authorities, who were determined to create an ethnically pure republic. The policies of enforced 'de-Germanization' and 're-Polonization' in Upper Silesia were presented as fulfilling historic justice by 'recovering' the ancient Polish territories that had suffered centuries of German domination. 'This myth was popularised by the National Democrats in Poland at the beginning of the twentieth century, and in 1945 it served as the ideological basis for Poland's successful claim to the eastern territories of Germany' (Linek 2001: 121). Similarly, the numerous ethnic Ukrainians in eastern Poland were 'exchanged' for the ethnic Poles whose homeland was incorporated into the Soviet Union. This massive population transfer could not have been enacted without the use of violence, which culminated in the infamous 'Akcja Wisła' (28 April–31 July 1947) – a military operation that finally broke the resistance of the Ukrainian underground fighters who sought the creation of an independent Ukrainian state and resisted the expulsion (Jasiak 2001).

As in the Czech case (see Chapter 4), the dispossession and expulsion of the German population, though understandable against the backdrop of the immeasurable suffering of the Polish population under German occupation, proved to have devastating consequences, not only for the victims of these policies but for the Polish nation as well. The principle of collective guilt, according to which the German nation as such was to be punished (rather than the individual perpetrators), paved the way for the communist takeover of the country.[11] Xenophobic nationalism directed against the Germans and Ukrainians served as an important source of legitimacy for the communist rulers and helped to consolidate their hold on power. 'A contradictory image of the new regime appeared – it was seen as a government forcibly imposed by a foreign power [the Soviet Union], but one that was nonetheless taking care of Poland's national aspirations' (Kersten 2001: 80). This perception was strengthened by Poland's strategic reliance on the Soviet Union, which was seen as the only foreign power that was willing to defend the Oder-Neisse border against the possible threat of German revisionism.

Communist ideology based on the ideal of proletarian internationalism may have been opposed to nationalism, but its practice was not. As Zaremba convincingly demonstrated, at different stages of the communist system of power the political authorities employed official nationalism to elicit public support (Zaremba 2001). It is a telling irony of Polish history that the last significant step towards ethnic homogenization of the country took place in March 1968, when the communist leadership instigated an anti-Semitic campaign which effectively resulted in the expulsion of some 15,000 members of the small remaining Jewish community in Poland (Vetter 1998; Biskupski 2000: 144).

In contrast, after the collapse of communism, the new political authorities sought to come to terms with the difficult aspects of Polish history, and extended conciliatory symbolic gestures towards the victims of expulsions.

With respect to the Ukrainians, the first freely elected 'Senate of the Third Republic of Poland passed a resolution on August 1990 that categorically condemned the *Akcja Wisła*' (Jasiak 2001: 190).[12] In a similar vein, the Polish foreign minister Władysław Bartoszewski, in an address to the German parliament in April 1995, expressed his regrets about the cruelty of the expulsion. The Poles apologized 'for the bitter fate they had inflicted on the Germans after the war; and the Germans, in their turn, begged the Poles' forgiveness for the horrible events of the occupation' (Naimark 2001: 137–8). These political gestures have already had positive effects on Polish-German and Polish-Ukrainian relations. Opinion surveys show significant improvements in the attitudes of the Poles towards these neighbouring nations.[13]

The collapse of communism also made it possible to openly discuss the political implications of different aspects of Polish political tradition. However, the conflicting views of the Polish nation espoused by the likes of Dmowski and Piłsudski remain highly controversial. Both national heroes – despite their failings – were a source of inspiration in the fight against communism, which was conceived of as a fight for national independence in many respects similar to the liberation struggle of the beginning of the century. Even many outspoken critics of Dmowski's integral nationalism sought to highlight the political pragmatism and programmatic flexibility of Dmowski's movement (Porter 2000: 11).

Adam Michnik evoked in his *Letters from Prison* in the 1980s the revolutionary heritage of both leading Polish nationalists. He condemned Dmowski as 'the co-culprit of Polish narrowness' while acknowledging that 'he was the co-founder of Polish pro-independence thought' (Michnik 1985: 306), and celebrated Piłsudski, who was, in Michnik's view, not a nationalist since he 'did not think it either proper or healthy to organize a national consciousness around the hatred of other nations' (Michnik 1985: 213). More recently, Andrzej Walicki warned of the danger of integral nationalism in contemporary Poland, which goes back to Dmowski's interwar conception of an ethnically 'pure' nation. 'Dmowski declared ruthless war on everyone whom he labelled as "half-Polish"' (Walicki 1997c: 36). *Pół-Polacy* (half-Poles) are defined by Dmowski as those people who 'lost their attachment to the aspirations of the nation'. They must therefore be compelled by 'physical and moral tyranny' to accept the moral values of the 'healthy spirit of majority' (Walicki 1997b: 46). Walicki used Dmowski's ideology to demonstrate that integral nationalism is hostile and aggressive not only towards other nations, but also towards those of its own people who do not endorse the values of their leaders.

Despite these critical voices, the Polish political elites seem to be currently unwilling to take an openly critical stance towards Dmowski's troubling legacy. In order to commemorate the sixtieth anniversary of Dmowski's death, on 8 January 1999 the Polish Sejm adopted a resolution which celebrated the extreme nationalist leader as 'an outstanding Pole who had rendered great service to his country' (Walicki 2000: 14). This could be seen as marking the rise of extreme nationalism in Poland, or simply explained away through a mixture of ignorance and political opportunism on the part of the members of parliament. However, as Walicki pointed out, a more balanced explanation for the official endorsement of Dmowski's legacy would have to take into consideration the complexity of his political ideology, which 'can serve many different, sometimes contradictory and mutually incompatible purposes' (Walicki 2000: 41). Consequently, 'it was perfectly possible to see positive relevance in some aspects of Dmowski's political thought without endorsing his anti-liberalism and his dangerous nationalist obsessions' (Walicki 2000: 42).[14] Yet Walicki does not seek to downplay the illiberal aspects of Dmowski's legacy; on the contrary he is highly critical of it, and dismayed by the lack of political sensitivity among contemporary Polish elites. A more critical attitude towards Dmowski is also needed for the improvement of the relationship between the Poles and the Jews.

Poles and Jews

Polish-Jewish relations were also profoundly affected by the experience of the Second World War. The Nazis used the occupied Polish territory for the genocide of the Jewish people of Europe. Given the history of anti-Semitism in Poland, some writers have argued that the Polish people made themselves guilty as accomplices in this crime. Most Polish intellectuals (including Michnik) have until recently dismissed these accusations, arguing that the Poles were themselves victims during the Second World War, and cannot, therefore, be held responsible for the fate of their Jewish compatriots. But there were critical voices challenging this view by acknowledging the historic responsibility of the Polish nation. Błoński, for example, contemplated that: 'Had we, in the past, conducted ourselves more wisely, nobly, more as Christians, the genocide would probably have been "less thinkable", made more difficult to carry out, and certainly would have met with greater resistance' (Błoński 1988: 353–4).

   This thesis started a fierce exchange of polemics carried out in the leading Polish Catholic weekly *Tygodnik Powszechny* that once again redefined the meaning of 'Polishness'. More recently, the debate has gained new impetus with the publication of a study by a New York-based historian of Polish origin, Jan T. Gross, which documented the destruction of the Jewish community in the provincial Polish town of Jedwabne. The book, entitled *Neighbors*, gives a detailed account of a massacre of some 1,600 Jewish inhabitants of Jedwabne, which took place on 10 July 1941. Particularly disturbing for Polish readers was the fact that in this case, there could be little doubt that Polish responsibility for the genocide was not limited to a lack of active resistance – in Jedwabne, according to Gross, Poles themselves killed their Jewish neighbours without any direct involvement of the German occupiers (Gross 2001).

Not surprisingly, Gross' study met with fierce opposition from those Polish historians who were unwilling to abandon the prevalent perception, according to which the Poles were themselves victims responding to various pressures (see for example the debate in *Rzeczpospolita*, 3 March 2001, especially the response of Tomasz Strzembosz). Jacek Żakowski argued that even if Gross' account was proved to be historically accurate, it is mistaken to assign collective responsibility to the Polish nation for crimes which were committed by individuals (Żakowski 2000). In a similar vein, Wojciech Roszkowski rejected the notion of collective responsibility and the idea that it is possible to differentiate between 'guilty' and 'innocent' nations. In his view the 'Polish-Jewish rivalry for first place in the hierarchy of suffering [was] regrettable' (Roszkowski 2002: 465). In response to these viewpoints, liberal nationalists could argue that when people see themselves as part of a national community, they also have to accept shared responsibility for the history of that particular nation. As Jan Nowak-Jeziorański put it:

> As we share in national pride derived from our victories, praiseworthy deeds and the great Polish contribution to universal human values through our national heroes, we also have to accept a sense of national guilt for those deeds that were despicable....If we expect others to come to terms with the responsibility for crimes which were committed against Poland and the Polish nation, we also have to be willing to come to terms with our own responsibility for evil which we inflicted on others.
>
> (Nowak-Jeziorański 2001; see also Kuroń and Lipski 2001)

The fierce arguments triggered by the publication of *Neighbours* were not restricted to the responses of intellectuals; it also became a major political issue. A number of populist politicians categorically rejected any suggestion of Polish guilt. The rise of the League of Polish Families (Liga Polskich Rodzin), which gained a surprising 7.9 per cent in the September 2001 elections, has been attributed partly to its well publicized uncompromising attitude towards the tragedy of Jedwabne (Stankiewicz 2002: 275–6). The party has strong links with the religious broadcaster Radio Maryja, which is known for its open anti-Semitism.[15] Another political group likely to have benefited from the Jedwabne controversy was Self-Defence of the Republic of Poland (Samoobrona Rzeczypospolitej Polskiej) led by the notorious Andrzej Lepper. His party received 10.2 per cent of the vote in the September 2001 elections. However, while extreme nationalist politicians sought to gain public support by objecting to the alleged 'world-wide campaign against Poland' (Kosc 2001), the Polish president echoed the sentiment of those intellectuals who called for the public acknowledgement of the historic responsibility of the Poles. Commemorating the sixtieth anniversary of the pogrom in Jedwabne, President Aleksander Kwaśniewski offered an apology:

Because of this crime we should beg the shadows of the dead and their families for forgiveness. Therefore, today, as a citizen, and as President of the Republic of Poland, I ask for forgiveness...in my own name, and in the name of Poles whose conscience is moved by that crime. In the name of those who believe that it is impossible to be proud of the greatness of Polish history without at the same time feeling pain and shame because of the wrongs Poles have committed against other people.

(Kwaśniewski cited in Tymowski 2002: 298)

Kwaśniewski's gesture was seen as an important contribution towards reconciliation between Poles and Jews. But this apology performed on behalf of the Polish nation is not without its own problems, even for those liberal nationalists who agree that 'it is impossible to be proud of the greatness of Polish history without at the same time feeling pain and shame because of the wrongs Poles have committed against other people'. By assigning responsibility to a national community, even if only symbolically, the question of guilt is arguably muddled. The argument that we (the Poles) are all somehow guilty (by virtue of belonging to our national community) can also serve to obfuscate the guilt of individual perpetrators directly involved in these actions.[16] At any rate, the process of coming to terms with the history of anti-Semitism in Poland cannot be deemed completed by the commemoration of the tragedy in Jedwabne. More will be needed to overcome the anti-Semitic sentiments which are still present in Polish society, despite the fact that hardly any Jews live in Poland today.[17]

An important part in this process must be taken by the leaders of the Polish Catholic Church, especially as popular anti-Semitic prejudices were in the past often reinforced by the church. And even today, although the Catholic Church has long ago, in the Second Vatican Council, condemned anti-Semitism in any form (Pawlikowski 1996), there are still some instances when Polish Catholicism supports anti-Semitism (e.g. Radio Maryja). But before returning to the more disturbing aspects of religiously inspired nationalism in Poland, it is useful to discuss the role of the Catholic Church in challenging the communist system of power.

Religious nationalism in Poland

When General Jaruzelski proclaimed martial law in December 1981 in order to suppress the political might of Solidarność, the people once again tried to reclaim their national tradition (returning to the romantic, messianic ideas of a Polish nation destined for freedom and independence). Women in Poland started wearing jewellery that had been popular after the defeat of the 1863 uprising against Russia: the Polish eagle mounted on a black cross (Johnson 1996: 130). This powerful religious symbol highlighted the influence of the Catholic Church, which had been seen as the only reliable institution supporting the cause of the Polish nation for almost 200 years (since 1795).[18] Roman Catholicism distinguished a nation occupied by German Protestants, then Russians who were Orthodox, and later controlled by communists who were atheists. During communism, probably more than ever before, the Polish Catholic Church functioned as the main vehicle of Polish national identity and defender of national survival. Polish Catholic leaders and intellectuals had on many occasions actively supported the opposition movements.[19] The communist state 'had in the Church an institutional rival that was much harder to suppress than were isolated dissident intellectuals' (Osa 1997: 351). National opinion surveys conducted in the mid-1960s, mid-1970s and mid-1980s had consistently shown the church 'ranking first as the best representative of the interest of the Polish nation' (Morawska 1995: 51). With the election in 1978 of a Polish pope, John Paul II, and his subsequent visit to his homeland in the following year, a renewed sense of spiritual community among the Polish people received further stimulation.

Cardinal Wojtyła had actively opposed the communist regime in Poland well before he became pope. He organized, for example, 'flying universities' which were illegal centres for intellectual life, countering the official propaganda of the state. His fight against communism was a fight for the nation. Wojtyła's New Year's Eve sermon of 1976 declared:

> We had to repeat again and again that the state exists for the nation, and not the other way around. After so many struggles, so many wars on various fronts, after so much suffering, this nation deserves to be free and independent.
>
> (Bernstein and Politi 1996: 126)

This must have been read as a direct attack on the communist Polish state that was perceived as something alien, serving foreign forces (the Soviet Union) rather than reflecting the genuine needs of the nation. Wojtyła continued his fight even more vigorously from the highest position in the Catholic Church. His visit to Poland in 1979 'had the most electrifying effect on popular sentiments of national pride and a sense of social unity since the installation of the communist regime....The overwhelming feeling among the millions who listened was national exhilaration and collective defiance (Morawska 1995: 57). The pope's visit was, however, more than just a demonstration of religious nationalism. John Paul II repeatedly expressed his concerns for human rights and spoke about the rights of citizens (Bernstein and Politi 1996: 128). This is not to suggest that the pope was preaching liberalism;[20] nevertheless, his contribution towards the ending of communist rule in Poland and in the whole of Europe should not be underestimated.

The Solidarność movement could and did build on these sentiments, and gained a level of support unparalleled by the communists. From the very beginning of the independent trade union movement, the importance of the church was symbolized by the ever-present crucifix at the meetings of Solidarność. Not only did all the gatherings have some religious connotations, but most religious ceremonies increasingly assumed the role of political demonstrations. For example, the regular monthly 'masses for the homeland' in Żoliborz, conducted during the period of martial law by the charismatic priest Jerzy Popiełuszko, were hugely popular because of their openly political content. Popiełuszko called on the people to pray for 'those deprived of freedom: sentenced, arrested and interned', for 'those sacked from their jobs', for 'Solidarity activists facing trial', and 'for ourselves, that we may create solidarity of hearts which no-one and no thing will be able to subdue' (cited in Ruane 2002: 49). Popiełuszko's sermons stirred patriotic feelings of ever-larger congregation, and his masses became rallying points for Solidarność supporters who saw their fight against communism as a fight for national freedom (*ibid.*). As Maryjane Osa observed, a paradigm of confrontation was created that turned any Christian celebration into a form of symbolic politics: 'the solidaristic nation (with a national historic and religious tradition of which the Black Madonna was its primary symbol and the Church its defender) versus the atheistic, artificial (traditionless) communist state' (Osa 1997: 352). The Catholic religion became the unifying force of Polish resistance to the communist regime.

In contrast, the numerous attempts by the communist leadership to gain political legitimacy by resorting to official nationalism proved futile (Ajnenkiel 1993: 131). Jaruzelski's government, while suppressing the opposition movement led by Solidarność, ostensibly sought wide-ranging national understanding. The state authorities ventured to rally public support around the 'Patriotic Movement for National Rebirth' (PRON) created in 1982, which consisted of all the officially recognized political and societal organizations (Bingen 1998: 55). Neither the proclamation of martial law in December 1981, nor the alternative nation-building project of the 'Patriotic Movement' was, however, successful in challenging the influence of Solidarność. Thus, despite some serious setbacks for the opposition which followed the implementation of martial law (e.g. arrests of dissidents and the 'disappearance' of Jerzy Popiełuszko in 1984, kidnapped by the security police), the communist system of power was unable to withstand the persistent pressure generated by Solidarność and the Polish Catholic Church. By February 1989 Solidarność had started formal negotiations with the government, marking the beginning of the end of communist rule.

After the end of communism in Poland, many analysts were concerned about the danger the existing conflation of nationalism with religion would pose to the establishment of liberal democracy. Typical was the assessment of Jerzy Szacki, who concluded his study of *Liberalism after Communism* with the rather pessimistic prediction that political liberalism was doomed in Poland, since it could not successfully compete with the long tradition of Catholicism. It is because of this tradition that many politicians and people in Poland oppose liberalism. More important than the ideals of individual freedom (that are essential for liberalism) is, according to Szacki, 'attachment to the idea of the common good as the foundation of political society and the belief that the nation-state above all should express the moral unity of the nation' (Szacki 1995: 204).

There were many instances of religious nationalism allied with xenophobia that seemed to have validated these concerns. As already mentioned, the religious broadcasting station Radio Maryja, led by the highly controversial priest Father Tadeusz Rydzyk, proved to be immensely popular despite (or because of?) its voicing of anti-Semitism. Similarly, even if not driven by religion, the populist leader of Samoobrona, Andrzej Lepper, is renowned as much for his contempt for proper democratic procedures as for his hostile attitudes towards the EU, international capital, and Jews. In his public statements, all the problems that beset Polish farmers, or unemployed workers, are usually attributed to foreign forces which are perceived 'as being un-Polish, as being forced upon people from outside and threatening the nation's existence' (Majman 1999). Characteristically, the May 1999 congress of Samoobrona opened with 'a dramatic rendition of a song containing the plea "May the Jewish oppression fall apart to dust and ashes"' (Majman 1999).

Another reason for concern was the popularity of the outspoken anti-Semite priest Henryk Jankowski, who had for years been connected with Solidarity circles and was even Wałęsa's long-standing confessor (Zygulski 1997). In the 1995 presidential election, anti-Semitism became a part of the anti-communist campaign that should have enhanced electoral support for Wałęsa, who competed against the former communist youth leader Aleksander Kwaśniewski. Wałęsa's supporters, including Jankowski, repeatedly denounced Kwaśniewski's alleged Jewish origin (Kuroń and Żakowski 1997: 9). Father Jankowski attempted to mobilize the Polish electorate by warning of foreign agents in the government: 'Poles bestir yourself. We can no longer tolerate governments made up of people who have not declared whether they come from Moscow or from Israel' (Tismaneanu 1998: 104). What is of even more concern is that Wałęsa failed in the election campaign to distance himself from the anti-Semitic rhetoric of his supporters.[21]

Kwaśniewski – despite his communist past – displayed more civic dignity than the (former) leader of Solidarność when declaring: 'In Poland, if someone is better educated and speaks other languages, they say you are a Jew. If that's the definition of a Jew, okay, I'll be a Jew' (Tismaneanu 1998: 104). Asked to confirm or deny the allegations concerning his Jewish origin, he replied: 'If I accept such a forum, I accept the whole discussion. The question is crazy. I'm a Pole, and I would like to be proud of being a Pole. But after such a question, that such a question is even raised, I am not proud' (Tismaneanu 1998: 104). Thus Kwaśniewski skilfully used the occasion to present himself as a modern, cosmopolitan European, who is proud of being a Pole only when it equates with tolerance of other religions and ethnic groups. In that way, Kwaśniewski took up a stance in favour of liberal nationalism. This paid off. Kwaśniewski won the presidential election, which according to Tismaneanu 'showed that anti-Semitism, religious fundamentalism, and fierce anti-Communism did not work well as electoral ploys' (Tismaneanu 1998: 105). In fact, Mirella Eberts observed a pattern in political processes in Poland. The stronger the involvement of the Polish Catholic Church in the election process, the less people supported the parties and candidates that were endorsed by the church hierarchy. The triumph of Kwaśniewski indicated 'people's opposition to the Church's active engagement in Polish politics. In 1996, according to a poll conducted by CBOS, an overwhelming 85.8 per cent of respondents declared that they were against the Church's direct participation in political life' (Eberts 1998: 832).[22]

Another potential rival to Wałęsa in the 1995 presidential election was a former adviser of Solidarność, Jacek Kuroń. Like Kwaśniewski, Kuroń has also been repeatedly attacked for his alleged Jewish origin, which has not prevented him from becoming one of Poland's most popular politicians.[23] He opposed the xenophobic nationalism of his compatriots, finding it disturbing 'especially since the Poles, as a nation were formed in a republic of many cultures and nations' (Kuroń and Żakowski 1997: 19). Ironically, if the Poles really wanted to exclude from their ranks people of different ethnic and/or religious backgrounds, they would have to do without some of their greatest national heroes.

> If we tried to look in Poland for entirely ethnically pure people, I doubt that we would find many that are one hundred per cent Polish. Almost the entire Polish culture would have to be discarded. Mickiewicz would today be considered Belorussian, what is more his mother was probably Jewish. Słowacki – half French. Chopin – half French. Kosciuszko – Lithuanian. Piłsudski – Belorussian, Lithuanian....We would even have problems with Copernicus, since he wrote in Latin.
>
> (Kuroń and Żakowski 1997: 19)

As a member of parliament for the Freedom Union, Jacek Kuroń was for many years leader of the parliamentary committee for the protection of national minorities, which means that his ideas have considerable political influence (Sadowski 2001). He is also a founding member of a movement called Świadomi tolerancji ('conscious of tolerance'), which organizes, among others, demonstrations against expressions of intolerance (Zdort and Janowski 1997). These examples demonstrate that the expressions of illiberal nationalism in Poland have been challenged by people endorsing a radically different conception of the Polish nation.

A Catholic tradition need not be seen as an insurmountable obstacle to liberalism. Even religiously inspired nationalism can be liberal. Mazzini, one of the first proponents of liberal nationalism, was after all a passionate religious nationalist (which is not to deny that he was quite hostile to the institutions of the Catholic Church). As a leading Polish dissident, Jan Lipski, argued, 'chauvinism, national megalomania, xenophobia, that is a hatred of everything that is foreign, and national egotism are incompatible with the Christian commands of love to your neighbour' (Lipski 1995: 11). Adam Michnik also sought common ground on which to lead an active dialogue with the church. He quoted from a pastoral letter of the Polish episcopate from 1972 that was indeed reminiscent of Mazzini:

> Through love for our own country, we move toward love for the entire human family....True love for one's country entails profound respect for the values of other nations...[But] it eschews hatred, for hatred is a destructive force that leads to a diseased and degenerated version of patriotism.
>
> (Michnik 1993: 149)

Michnik could not but agree with these noble ideals, but voiced criticism regarding the stance of the Polish Catholic Church represented by Cardinal Wyszyński, who lamented 'the widespread tendency to "dirty" our own [Polish] history'. While allowing for a healthy pride in national achievements, Michnik stressed that 'it is only the good traditions that we ought to respect' (Michnik 1993: 151). This view of history can be seen as a possible foundation stone of a liberal conception of nationalism, which I will explore below.

At any rate, the Polish Catholic Church as a whole should not be equated with Father Jankowski's views, nor the broadcasts of Radio Maryja. The pope, who certainly enjoys more respect and popularity than Jankowski or Rydzyk, is known for his stance against anti-Semitism.[24] Jankowski, on the other hand, had been repeatedly criticized for his statements by the official hierarchy of the church, and finally, in November 1997, he was suspended from his pastoral duties (Zygulski 1997). Regrettably, the Catholic authorities were less outspoken in their criticism of Pater Rydzyk, and the inflammatory programmes of Radio Maryja. Nevertheless, it is worth noting that the official Polish Catholic Church had been actively involved in the process of reconciliation between Catholics and Jews. Another gesture of goodwill, for example, was the establishment of a 'Day of Judaism' that aims at promoting respect and cooperation between people of different religious confessions (Henry 1998).

Clearly, Polish Catholicism is not a monolithic movement representing just one stream of thought, and hence should not be described solely on the basis of extreme examples. Adam Michnik summed up well the downside of such a reductionist approach:

> According to a well-known stereotype, Polish Catholicism is rustic and primitive, anti-intellectual and shallow, ethnocentric and intolerant. It would be a frivolous lie to claim that such Catholics do not exist in Poland. It would be equally false, however, to argue that they dominate the Polish Church.
>
> (quoted in Eberts 1998: 817)

Korbonski identified three different strands within Polish Catholic elites: 'the fundamentalists, the pragmatists and the liberals' (Korbonski 2000: 142). While the fundamentalists were keen to retain the dominant position of Church in Polish society by relying on authoritarian methods, the pragmatists (such as Tadeusz Pieronek) and the liberals (such as the late Józef Tischner) realized that in order to succeed, the Church had to adapt to the new political conditions which emerged after the collapse of communism.

Still, the xenophobic and anti-democratic elements within the Polish Catholic Church and their influence on political developments should not be underestimated. In fact, the more liberal forces within the church appear to have been on the defensive in the last few years. In line with this, Michnik became less optimistic about the role of the Church and warned that 'the "integrationist" trend, openly anti-liberal and succumbing to the language of religious war, has gained the upper hand in the Church' (Michnik 1998a: 68).[25] Given that during the postcommunist transition of Poland an institutional framework was being created that would determine the further political developments of the country, observers were rightly concerned about the character of the influence of the Catholic Church. The adoption of a new constitution in 1997, for example, was bound to have a lasting effect on Polish democracy. To what extent did religious nationalism find its way into the new constitution? Can the Catholic Church in Poland coexist with, or even be supportive of, a liberal democratic order? These questions merit thorough examination. But before returning to particular Polish developments, it is instructive first to examine the possible relations between the church and a liberal democratic state on a more theoretical level.

Church and state in liberal theory

The separation of church and state can be considered a litmus test of liberal democracy. There seems to be universal agreement amongst liberal theorists that the powers of the state and the church must be strictly separated. The most influential current formulation is arguably the conception of John Rawls, who argues in favour of a neutral state which does not espouse any comprehensive doctrine of a good life, and thus allows individuals to follow freely their differing conceptions of the good (Rawls 1971; 1996). This ideal is at times difficult to achieve. As we saw in Chapter 2, a strict religious neutrality on the state's part can in fact undermine some religious beliefs, in that this neutrality indirectly challenges the basic proposition of any orthodox belief system, which claims that it (and only it) has all the correct answers. An educational system, for example, that teaches about different religious doctrines could by default inculcate students with scepticism against any religion, or even lead to atheism. This would not seem to be a problem in a world that is becoming increasingly secular. In fact, one of the basic premises of the French Enlightenment was that religion, by being used to justify the divine right of kings, stood in the way of a more just and liberal democratic order. In contrast, John Locke saw the religiosity of citizens as a precondition for liberal democracy to be established and sustained. Thus he proposed a tolerance of all belief systems *except for* Catholicism and atheism (if the latter can be labelled a belief system). Similarly, that most astute observer of American society, Alexis de Tocqueville, saw organized religion – even including Catholicism – as the best breeding ground for the development of civic virtues, and the ultimate source of morality (Tocqueville 1994: 300f).

Nevertheless, all liberals were certainly wary of the political influence of religious sects and doctrines. James Madison, for example, thought that even the separation of church and state is insufficient for securing the individual freedom of citizens, and in *The Federalist Papers* no. 51 he advocates a 'multiplicity of sects', which would diminish their influence on the community as a whole, and prevent any particular religious doctrine from dominating political life (Madison *et al.* 1987: 321). The American political system and its constitution became primary examples of the separation of church and state. As de Tocqueville observed in *Democracy in America*, the prevailing spirit of the clergy was characterized by their retiring 'of their own accord from the exercise of power', and making it 'the pride of their profession to abstain from politics' (Tocqueville 1994: 309). Curiously, the clergy's conscious renunciation of their political power, accompanied by a focus on spiritual matters, only enhanced the moral authority of religious leaders. In fact, it would be self-defeating for any church to attempt to exercise some political control over the state. 'The church cannot share the temporal power of the state without being the object of a portion of that animosity which the latter excites' (Tocqueville 1994: 310).

Tocqueville, unlike most French *philosophes* of the eighteenth-century Enlightenment, considered the separation of church and state as the best means to secure the moral authority of religion, rather than a way of undermining the prevalence of religious feeling in society. Hence the formal separation was not supposed to marginalize the impact of religion on the wider societal life, but rather make it possible within clearly set rules. As Elshtain put it, 'Tocqueville insisted that the ideas of Christianity and liberty are so completely intermingled that if you tried to sever religion from democracy in America you would wind up destroying democracy' (Elshtain 1999: 8).

> Despotism may govern without faith, but liberty cannot....How is it possible that society should escape destruction if the moral tie is not strengthened in proportion as the political tie is relaxed? And what can be done with a people who are their own masters if they are not submissive to the Deity?
>
> (Tocqueville 1994: 307)

Surely, today we can imagine liberty without religious – or any other – faith. In fact, the prevailing models of liberalism in our times are based on the presumption that any belief in the 'eternal validity' of moral claims is potentially dangerous. Liberals like Karl Popper, Isaiah Berlin and Richard Rorty, from their different vantage points, have made it clear that traditional moral philosophy based on absolute ideas can be dangerous in the political realm. That is also the reason why John Rawls opposes the state espousing or privileging a particular version of any comprehensive doctrine of a good life. Tocqueville's conception of liberalism reminds us, however, that religious beliefs can also be seen as propitious for maintaining democracy. Leszek Kołakowski convincingly defends this tradition of liberalism, arguing that while 'strong beliefs easily breed fanaticism; scepticism or no beliefs, easily breed mental and moral paralysis' (Kołakowski in Niżnik and Sanders 1996: 76). In this light, conservative criticism of some recent tendencies in modern (or postmodern) liberalism, could appear less illiberal.[26] It is possible that nineteenth-century theories of liberalism are in some respects more instructive for present-day Poland than those contemporary theories of liberalism that are based on the assumption that there is no need for a comprehensive justification of liberal values.

In fact, many Polish intellectuals (e.g. Kołakowski, Krasnodębski, Król, Szahaj, Walicki) caution against some of the fashionable postmodern theories of liberalism (e.g. Rorty), questioning their relevance to the current Polish condition. It may well be that theories which are appropriate for the well established democracies of the West are of little use to the emerging democracies of Central and Eastern Europe, as they address a different set of questions. While the primary preoccupation of contemporary Western liberalism is how to maintain and/or improve the existing political order, political theorists concerned with postcommunist developments must focus on strategies that aim to create such an order in the first place. For that reason Rorty can afford to dismiss the political relevance of more fundamental moral values, while Król and Walicki are right to warn against such radical scepticism.

Marcin Król, in his study *Liberalizm strachu czy liberalizm odwagi* (*Liberalism of Fear or Liberalism of Courage*) describes the situation that arose from this misunderstanding as 'Polish tragicomedy'. The type of 'antipolitical liberal philosophy', which seeks to avoid ethical controversies within the political realm, is 'possible as an idle public discourse in established democracies'. But while this attitude can be harmful even for older democracies, it is certainly very dangerous, according to Król, for those countries which are still building their democratic systems. In the political discourses of those countries it is simply not possible to 'avoid making fundamental decisions and in general make choices between different systems of values' (Król 1999: 86; cf. Gawin 1997: 57). The intellectual and political elites in the postcommunist countries must have been disappointed, in Król's view, if they were subjected to the illusions of this type of 'antipolitical liberal discourse'. Hence Król advocates a 'liberalism of courage', which does not shy away from conflicts, by openly endorsing a clearly defined conception of the good.[27]

Similarly, Walicki challenged Rorty's suggestion 'that a democratic society should avoid foundationalism because it is not pragmatically useful and proper for such a society to put such notions as truth, transcendental truth, or reason in the center of its culture' (Walicki in Niżnik and Sanders 1996: 94), by explaining that the situation in postcommunist societies is fundamentally different from that in the West. In Poland,

> People are afraid that without objective universal standards it is much easier to become manipulated, duped, and enslaved. A contextual, situational, antitranscendental conception of truth is, in such conditions, suspect, because it is seen as strangely similar to the dialectical sophistries of Marxism....Many philosophers in Poland argue that we need Christian values, absolute values, or some form of foundations.
> (Walicki in Niżnik and Sanders 1996: 95)

In an open exchange at the Institute of Philosophy and Sociology of the Polish Academy of Sciences in Warsaw in May 1995, Rorty ultimately conceded that his 'romanticized version of the American Dream may not be what Poland really needs to hear about at the moment' (Rorty in Niżnik and Sanders 1996: 124). He granted that 'there is not much use for [his] brand of futuristic romanticism' until the standard institutions of constitutional democracy are firmly established (*ibid.*). If we take Tocqueville's classic interpretation of *Democracy in America* to have been more instructive than Rorty's account, the Polish situation appears not to be fundamentally different from the early American experience. Still, the successful symbiosis of religion and liberal democracy in the United States is probably predicated on the existing multitude of religious beliefs. But what if an overwhelming majority of people subscribes to one religious system, such as Roman Catholicism? Can a strict separation of church and state be secured in Poland, where the Catholic Church appears to be one of the most powerful institutions, enjoying the wide support of the population? Is this an insurmountable obstacle for establishing and sustaining a truly liberal democratic order?

The relationship of church and state in Poland: the constitutional debate

The political power of the Catholic Church in Poland, or the limits thereof, was tested during the long lasting and highly controversial debate that preceded the adoption of a new constitution in April 1997. The necessity for a new constitution in Poland arose immediately after the fall of communism, since the new political system based on a free market economy and parliamentary democracy needed to be formally instituted. The constitution of a country should determine the functioning of basic structures of its political system for the long term. Consequently, it is in the very nature of the document that any future amendments are difficult to implement, and the stakes for the parties involved are very high. As Piotr Winczorek accurately observed, 'the concentration of emotions and interests, of religious and ideological arguments, of economic and axiological considerations that accompany the drafting and the adoption of a constitution is quite extreme' (Winczorek 1998: 1). Hence the result can never live up to any abstract ideals of 'legislative rationality formulated by the theory of law' (Winczorek 1998: 1), or to some Rawlsian model of a perfectly neutral state.[28] Moreover, the actual implementation of the constitutional order is dependent on many external factors (social, economic, cultural), and even the best written constitution can never be a sufficient warrant of political stability and liberal democracy. No written document makes sense without interpretation, and interpretations can always be influenced by powerful groups and interests. This is not to question the importance of a written constitution: my argument is rather that the social context in which the constitution operates deserves as much attention as the written document itself.

One of the major concerns accompanying the creation and implementation of the new constitution in Poland was the extent to which the Catholic Church would succeed in imposing its views and values on the emerging political system. Whether the new constitution sufficiently provides for the separation of Church and state is an issue which can be examined by assessing the various aspects of possible state interference with the moral values of its citizens, such as the question of religious education, or the highly controversial issue of the legality of abortion. These issues divided Polish society even before the adoption of the 1997 constitution, and they partly explain why the process of its creation took so long.

Religious education

Religious instruction in public schools was introduced very quickly following the collapse of communist power, when Mazowieckie's government bowed to the pressure of the Polish episcopate in August 1990. This happened without any proper public debate on the issue. Only after the new regulation was implemented did a heated controversy take place in the Sejm, as well as in the media. Moreover, the new ruling was challenged twice before the Constitutional Tribunal by two ombudsmen (by Ewa Łętowska in 1990, and by Tadeusz Zieliński in 1992), who argued that the ruling violated the principle of church-state separation. The Constitutional Tribunal dismissed the charges on the grounds that religious education was optional, the programmes were determined by the church itself, and 'since the education programmes designed by the state were not filled with religious content, the neutral and secular character of the state was being preserved' (Eberts 1998: 823). The strategy used in defence of voluntary religious instruction in public schools by the minister of education, Andrzej Stelmachowski, was markedly different. He declared in 1992 that 'there is no such thing as separation of the state from religion, because no human being is one hundred per cent a-religious' (Eberts 1998: 823). Another victory for the Catholic Church was the Statute on Education, passed by the Polish parliament in September 1991, 'which states that the Christian values are to be respected in education' (Eberts 1998: 823). Given that the majority of people in Poland are in favour of religious education in public schools (67 per cent in 1995, Eberts 1998: 824), it is reasonable to expect that it will remain an integral part of the school system.

Abortion

The legal status of abortion caused even more controversy. In communist Poland, women had enjoyed considerable freedom to terminate unwanted pregnancies. Even though the Catholic Church has consistently opposed this freedom in the past, it was only after the collapse of communism that it succeeded in initiating a radical change of legislation. The anti-abortion law passed by the Sejm in January 1993 made abortions illegal except for some exceptional circumstances (such as unwanted pregnancy as a result of rape or incest; or when the woman's life is threatened). Notwithstanding the fact that even this ruling was considered too liberal by the church hierarchy, it 'was in effect extremely restrictive, since a decisive majority of Polish women who underwent the procedure previously did so for reasons other than those accepted under the law' (Eberts 1998: 827). This could be seen as another partial victory for the church, which was able to impose its values on Polish society, of which a majority opposed its uncompromising stance towards abortion.[29] But as the political parties opposing the new legislation were elevated to power after the September 1993 elections, amendments to the anti-abortion law were adopted which substantially liberalized the ruling. The struggle over abortion experienced yet another turn when a group of senators took the law to the Constitutional Tribunal, which in May 1997 concluded that some of the amendments were in fact unconstitutional. 'The Tribunal justified its decision on the basis that in a democratic state, human life, being the fundamental value, was implicitly protected from its conception by law' (Eberts 1998: 829). In December 1997, the newly elected parliament, with a more conservative majority, accepted the tribunal's decision.

Constitution

Issues of abortion and religious education were also crucial for the Polish Catholic Church in its determination to influence the content of the constitution. Moreover, the Church demanded that the constitution stress the importance of Polish national identity (*Rzeczpospolita*, 5 May 1997). As Bishop Pieronek stated in 1996, the church expected the document 'to respect national traditions and Christian values' (Eberts 1998: 834). Understandably, liberal critics feared that if the wording of the constitution fully reflected these demands, Poland could be turned into a denominational state, in which the separation of church and state was not secured. Furthermore, Leszek Kołakowski argued that to insist on a formal inclusion of Christian values in the emerging legal order would ill serve even the real interests of the Catholic Church, as it would turn Christianity into an ideology. 'Christian values becoming part of the constitution would not evangelize the worldly institutions, but rather the other way round, they would make Christianity heathen' (Kołakowski 1996: 209). Kołakowski concedes that 'it is both natural and necessary that the Preamble of the Polish constitution emphasise the importance of the religious tradition and of the Church in the history of the Polish nation' (Kołakowski 1996: 209), without, however, referring to Christian values.

Still, any reference to a narrowly defined national identity closely linked to Catholicism could lead to exclusionary policies that would affect all citizens who did not comply with the definition of the Polish nation. The adopted constitution, being a result of many compromises between the liberal streams in Polish society and more conservative elements concerned with traditional values, does not accommodate all the demands of the church. While religious education is made possible by the constitutional guarantee for parents to decide on the character of their children's upbringing (also allowing parents *not* to bring up their children according to any religious doctrine), on the issue of abortion, despite the demands of the church, 'the constitution does not ensure the protection of human life from conception until birth' (Eberts 1998: 834).

On the issue of national identity, the wording of the preamble is inclusive, and marks a clear departure from Dmowski's integralist vision of the Polish nation, which equated Polishness with Catholicism.

We, the Polish Nation – all citizens of the Republic,

Both those who believe in God as the source of truth, justice, good and beauty,

As well as those not sharing such faith but respecting those universal values as arising from other sources...

Hereby establish this Constitution.

Admittedly, the constitution does not provide a precise definition of the nation, even when referring to it as the source of supreme power (Article 4). 'The confusing Preamble attempts to include everything that relates to Poles in a way that excludes none from the term "nation"' (Osiatynski 1997). But as Kowalski and Stanclik have rightly argued, this can be seen as an advantage since it partly satisfies the desires of the more conservative parts of Polish society (e.g. the Catholic Church), which demanded reference to the nation, while allowing 'constitutional scholars to conclude that the concept means "political community" and thus all the citizens' (Kowalski and Stanclik 1998). Thus, for example, Mirella Eberts' overall assessment of the constitution was positive. 'The new Polish constitution, as a document of political compromise, incorporates many of the Church's demands, but does not turn Poland into a denominational state'. This is, according to Eberts, 'good news for the supporters of liberal democracy in Poland' (Eberts 1998: 835). Similarly, Piotr Winczorek commented in *Rzeczpospolita* that the text of the constitution 'corresponds with the European standards of democratic constitutionalism, and at the same time gives expression to the Polish national traditions of political legality' (Winczorek 1997a).

Even if the resulting text of the constitution fell short of the expectations of the Catholic Church in Poland, and pleased the more liberal observers (e.g. Winczorek), it is evident that church-state separation is far from being as firmly embedded in both the Polish political system and the practice of policy-making, as it is in the United States. The reasons for this are too complex and numerous to be elaborated here. But it is interesting to note that even the United States cannot always follow the ideal model of a religiously neutral state. While the actual ideal of church-state separation is hardly ever questioned, the American public has considerable difficulty in agreeing on the right extent of the separation. Thus some scholars argue that it is not possible, or even desirable, to enforce a very strict separation between church and state (e.g. Greenawalt 1995). Jean Elshtain has observed that attempts at instituting a consequent division between religious and public spheres can paradoxically lead to 'the betrayal of liberalism', in that the liberal ideal of the tolerance of differing views and lifestyles is being undermined by the attitude of 'liberal monism', which aims at minimizing (or eliminating) any public expression of religious belief. Liberal monism reduces a multiplicity of lifestyles and views to the only acceptable public attitude, one based on universal rationality. According to Elshtain, the liberal monist position, which can be associated with some ideas of John Rawls, holds that 'when religious persons enter the public sphere they are obliged to do so in a secular civic idiom short of any explicit reference to religious commitments and beliefs' (Elshtain 1999: 9). This is unrealistic and undesirable, since it presumes that it is possible for people 'to seal themselves into compartments' and be believers one moment, and purely rational citizens the next (Elshtain 1999: 6; cf. Rawls 1996: 140).

In defence of John Rawls, it is important to note that only a distorted version of his conception of *Political Liberalism* can be associated with Elshtain's exposition of a liberal monist position. Rawls demands the exclusion of comprehensive doctrines only in those public discussions which are concerned with 'constitutional essentials and matters of basic justice' (Rawls 1996: 1). Furthermore, Rawls states explicitly that other controversial issues inevitably remain and these can be the subject of a political process in which parties involved can legitimately resort to their particular comprehensive doctrines. In fact, one of his examples for the second type of political deliberation is to determine 'how more exactly to draw the boundaries of basic liberties when they conflict (where to set "*the wall between church and state*")' (my italics, Rawls 1996: 152).

At any rate, the notion of a religiously neutral state and a strict church-state separation can be useful as a normative ideal for designing a functioning and stable liberal democratic order. Even Elshtain, for all her criticisms of extreme positions of 'liberal monists', certainly does not advance the case for a denominational state. Rather she simply warns against the excesses of policies which are pursued in America in the name of religious neutrality; an excess that is hardly a danger in Poland. But it is important to bear in mind that the ideal of a neutral state is only that – an ideal. In the real world, different types of democracy have developed throughout the West, ranging from Catholic Spain or Ireland to the religiously neutral model of the United States. As Eberts has noted, Poland is likely to follow the Spanish model of 'a friendly or at least nonantagonistic separation of church and state, [which] recognises the special position of Catholicism in Spanish society' (Eberts 1998: 836). In that way, aspects of Polish national tradition can be accommodated, which in turn should contribute to political stability in Poland based on the rule of law. As Piotr Winczorek has argued, only a constitution that is popular with the nation and its elites can succeed (Winczorek 1997b).[30]

An additional reason for hope that religion will not endanger Polish democracy can be derived from those influential voices within the Polish Catholic Church which argue that church-state separation is not only in the best interests of democracy, but also serves to strengthen the moral authority of Catholicism. The most outspoken critic of the politicization of Christianity in Poland, Józef Tischner, warned that the 'faith that becomes the instrument of politics loses its essentially religious dimension' (cited in Michnik 1998a: 69). He argued, very much in line with Tocqueville and Kołakowski, that to allow for the political influence of Church hierarchies results in a betrayal of the true purpose of religion, which must remain untouched by earthly interests of secular power.

> The politicization of Christianity means allowing violence in the work of evangelizing. It means the primacy of political interests over shepherd [pastoral] concerns and, consequently, moving toward a religious state, whether in the form of a 'holy empire' or, nowadays, toward some 'hallowed democracy'.
>
> (Tischner cited in Michnik 1998a: 69; cf. Król 1999: 144)

Moreover, liberal democracy should be strengthened, and integral nationalism undermined by the continuing process of political and economic integration into the West European institutions. Poland became a fully fledged member of NATO in March 1999, and in December 2002 was invited to join the European Union. Surely there are some critical Euro-sceptics in

Poland (as in any other country of Europe) who fear the loss of national identity, including a number of Polish priests. But a majority of citizens had been in favour of the 'return to Europe'. Also, the official church hierarchy was largely in favour of EU accession because, in the words of Cardinal Józef Glemp, 'bringing people and nations closer together was a part of the Catholic Church's social teaching' (Kaczorowska 2003).

As demonstrated, the Catholic Church has played an important role in Poland's political transition. But increasingly, Polish people are becoming more and more secularized, and even practising Catholics have made it clear that they do not wish the church to intervene in political processes and/or have too great an influence on the institutions of the state. There are many indicators showing the weakening of the preponderance of the Catholic Church within Polish society since the end of communism, even if at the same time the church succeeded in implementing some political changes (i.e. regarding religious education). Support for the church between 1989 and 1990 declined by almost half, 'from over 90 per cent to slightly over 50 per cent' (Morawska 1995: 65). This can be explained primarily by the fact that the Polish Catholic Church was in a unique situation during the communist era, as it represented the only well organized institution which had the resources and the moral authority needed to challenge the despised political system, or at least to offer an alternative public space. For this reason, the Catholic Church would have been supported even by people who were possibly uninterested in religion, but saw in the church an important political ally in their fight against communism. Consequently, the collapse of communist power resulted in a decline in influence of the Polish Catholic Church. As Szacki poignantly put it:

> The thesis that 90 per cent of Poles are Catholics is nonsense. A very high percentage of people who were brought up as Catholics are not Catholics in their views or their behaviour. In any case, in Polish society there are (and over the past two centuries always have been) sizable groups of people who are real or potential clients of secular or religious ideologies far removed from Catholic orthodoxy.
>
> (Szacki 1995: 189)

Thus any political analysis which simply assumes that all Poles are Catholic,[31] or anti-Semitic, or conservative, or anti-communist, in a way perpetuates the mistake of integral nationalists (such as Dmowski), who render the nation a monolithic community. A conception of liberal nationalism, on the other hand, is based on the presumption that a nation is far too complex and diverse a phenomenon to be characterized in such a reductionist fashion.

Liberal nationalism

Liberal nationalism, as a very real societal force, can positively influence the process of postcommunist transition in Poland. Although it is not possible any more to revive the old concept of a multiethnic nation of the Commonwealth (which was probably never as perfect as many romantic writers would have us believe), 'the older tradition of libertarian nationalism has [not] been extinguished in Poland. It has survived, mostly among the intelligentsia, and plays an important part in Polish political life' (Walicki 1997a: 253). As early as in the mid-1980s Walicki called for a new kind of Polish patriotism (or liberal nationalism, to use the terminology employed in this book) which would build on Polish traditions by critically engaging with its three different aspects: 'a patriotism free from the archaic features of the democratic legacy of Old Poland, critical of romantic illusions, but no less critical of Dmowski's version of political realism' (Walicki 1990: 38). Similarly, Adam Michnik, who has consistently opposed chauvinism and xenophobic nationalism, can be quoted in defence of liberal nationalism:

> *We need national solidarity.* As its basis we must have respect for differ-
> ences, diversity, and pluralism. As a condition for it we must have
> concern for the positive development of our nation, for its collective
> ethos and its spiritual dimension. The threat that hangs over it consists
> in hatred for other nations, contempt for other cultures, and a megalo-
> maniac belief in one's own perfection.
>
> (Michnik 1985: 327)

In a similar vein, Marcin Król warned that

> whoever represents a dualistic vision of the world which is dominated
> either by liberalism, or nationalism is not only wrong about political
> realities, but causes irreparable damage, because the chances of imple-
> menting the liberal democratic project are decreased in direct
> proportion to the height of the wall which was created between liber-
> alism and nationalism.
>
> (Król 1999: 38)

Król's 'liberalism of courage', on the other hand, endorses liberal nationalist sentiments and sees in national tradition an important source of moral values. Król recalls the spiritual heritage of Polish romantics for whom 'Polishness was always a part of a broader, and an undoubtedly universal vision' (Król 1999: 174). While liberalism is universal in form, it must have a specific content which would reflect the particular historic experience of a nation (Król 1999: 121). In fact, the collective memory of the nation, and a sense of historic continuity, are, according to Król, vital for the establishment and consolidation of a liberal democratic order (Król 1999: 158–76).

More recently, Król radically revised his views and voiced serious doubts about the sense of historic continuity of the Polish nation. Echoing Habermas' argument in the German context (see Chapter 1), Król argued that after the revelations about Jedwabne, 'it was no longer possible for the

Poles to think of themselves with any certainty'. He believed that the Poles could no longer assume that they 'belonged to a certain community that could be described as "Polishness" (*polskość*) or "fatherland" (*ojczyzna*). That "Polishness" and that "fatherland" had died (*zakończyły swój żywot*)' (Król cited in Krasnodębski 2002: 90). Yet, without a sense of belonging to a national community, which links past, present and future generations, it is not clear why any Pole today should even contemplate the moral implications of the tragedy in Jedwabne, let alone accept some kind of responsibility for the event. It is precisely through the process of coming to terms with historic events, like Jedwabne, that one becomes painfully aware of the fact that one is not entirely free to choose one's own nation, and its historic legacies (Krasnodębski 2001). Furthermore, as much as a sense of pride in the best aspects of a nation's history demands that people do not ignore its darker aspects, one should also not limit a discussion of the historic experience of a nation to its failures. It is inconsistent to expect that 'we [the Poles] feel guilty for the antisemitism of our grandfathers, and [that] we [at the same time] must not revere the heroes of that generation and derive collective pride from their heroism' (Gowin 2001).

Król's change of heart could be seen as typical of that generation of dissident intellectuals who were committed patriots (or, in our terminology, liberal nationalists) before 1989, but grew increasingly wary of the potential dangers of nationalism after the collapse of communism. Krasnodębski has recently argued that after 1989, the mainstream Polish intelligentsia largely abandoned the kind of liberal nationalism that was characteristic of the Solidarność movement, which rendered the Polish nation an ethical community engaged in the fight for freedom. According to Krasnodębski, the progressive Polish intelligentsia failed its people by following the false allure of a utopian, 'post-nationalist' world of liberal democracy. Similarly, Jarosław Gowin bemoans the fact that in contemporary Poland 'patriotism is unfashionable, or even a matter of shame' (Gowin 2001). In a programmatic article critical of the decline of the patriotic spirit in postcommunist Poland, Marek Cichocki called on his fellow co-nationals to endow patriotism with a new meaning that would do justice to current and future challenges which the Polish nation has to face (Cichocki 2002). Cichocki, in particular, criticized the tendency amongst certain Polish liberals to advocate a narrow and rather dogmatic version of liberalism, which does not allow for accommodating the virtues of patriotism:

> It is important to decisively reject suggestions that patriotism is entirely in conflict with the idea of liberalism. This would lead to the absurd conclusion that a liberal could not be a patriot. It is true, however, that for a certain form of dogmatic liberalism, with which we have to deal at times in contemporary Poland, the idea of patriotism is quite troublesome, since it imposes obligations on individuals which go beyond the horizon of individual interests. Patriotism derives the justification for such obligations from the rationale of community ... from the conception of a

nation. For this reason it is impossible to separate entirely the idea of patriotism from such virtues as generosity, sacrifice, or solidarity [*od ofiarności, wyrzeczenia czy solidarności*]. The willingness for sacrifice remains at the heart of each patriotism, which impels one to reverse the hierarchy of individual values, putting the good of other fellow citizens above one's own needs or desires.

(Cichocki 2002)

At any rate, liberals would be ill advised to abandon the language of nationalism, since this would only give more opportunities to those populist politicians and opinion leaders who seek to gain popular support by relying on a more xenophobic version of nationalism. As Gowin argued, 'if we leave the monopoly for national values to the skinheads, "Myśl Polska" and [the extreme nationalist] member of parliament Tomczak, the results could be deplorable' (Gowin 2001).

In contrast, any form of liberal nationalism must be inclusive by its very definition. No one should be excluded from a nation either on the grounds of religious beliefs[32] (or lack of), or adherence to certain political values. No one, and no single group should be allowed to monopolize the meaning of Polishness by political means – not Catholics, nor for that matter anti-communists. This does not inhibit individuals and groups from arguing about the desired content of Polish nationalism. All claims about a nation are to an extent normative, describing what is to be achieved; and hence they can have a mobilizing character. According to Walicki, however, they should never be used for the political exclusion of groups that do not fit the desired image of a nation. It is one thing to reinforce the criticism of the former communists in Poland and their responsibility for past injustices by claiming that to support communism is not really a 'Polish' (meaning good) thing to do. But it is another thing to attempt the consequent exclusion of former communists from the political processes in postcommunist Poland on the grounds that it was un-Polish behaviour to support communism and the power of the Soviet Union in Poland.[33]

While the connection of anti-communism with the true meaning of Polishness was a useful and arguably legitimate strategy in the fight against the communist system of power before 1989, it has no place in a pluralist liberal democracy. Against this, one could argue that it is not uncommon even in well established Western democracies to exclude political groups whose programme is directed against the very existence of democracy (for example, the Nazi parties are forbidden by the constitution in Germany, as they are, for that matter, forbidden by the Polish constitution), but the party of the former communists in Poland has clearly accepted 'the democratic rules of the game'. Moreover, communist rule in Poland in the 1970s and 1980s, described unforgettably as 'totalitarianism with the teeth knocked out' (Adam Michnik cited in Garton Ash 1989: 240), cannot be compared with Nazi Germany.

Criticism could be raised that the Polish conception of liberal nationalism is beset by inconsistencies. Is it possible to celebrate the liberating aspect of the tradition of Polish anti-communism, and at the same time condone the inclusion of (former) communists in the national and political community? These people were, after all, responsible for the political oppression of the (freedom loving) Polish nation. Yet, one of the positive outcomes of the roundtable negotiations of 1989, which led to the collapse of communism, is the fact that the victors were able to show generosity towards their former enemies. Exemplary, though very controversial, was the conciliatory gesture of one of the most prominent leaders of the anti-communist opposition, Adam Michnik, towards the architect of martial law, General Jaruzelski.

Admittedly, these inconsistencies could have been avoided if the language of (liberal) nationalism had been disentangled from normative values which can be better conceptualized in a culturally neutral language free of particular references to a specific national community. Thus instead of saying that 'to support communism is not really a Polish (meaning good) thing to do', it should be simply maintained that these actions were wrong regardless of whether they were Polish or not. In response to this challenge, the proponents of liberal nationalism could argue that moral imperatives have a considerably stronger impact on the real lives of citizens if they are conceptualized within the existing societal culture. This strategy can find support in the study of *Ethics and Language* by Charles Stevenson, who argued that persuasive language could be legitimately used for the implementation of moral aspirations. Stevenson coined the term 'persuasive definition', which is a description used in order not to convey the true meaning of a word, but rather to suggest what it *should* mean. Such a definition is used 'consciously or unconsciously, in an effort to secure...a redirection of people's attitudes' (Stevenson 1944: 210). The various contested definitions of 'true' Polishness are hence very often the expressions of widely different ideals elaborating on what the nation should become, rather than simply describing what it is. As Józef Tischner argued, the Polish nation should be seen as an aspiration, an ethical task worthy of the commitment of the Polish people. 'Patriotism', in Tischner's view, 'is not just a sentiment. It is a type of responsibility. Responsibility for this country, its history and its future' (Tischner 1998: 26).

Consequently, it is not surprising that there are many different conceptions of what it means to be a Pole that compete for influence and are often inconsistent. But *some* inconsistency could be advantageous, or indeed desirable. Any exhaustive and definite conception of a nation would by necessity be illiberal, as it would inevitably lead to clearly defined exclusions. If a nation is to be liberal, on the other hand, its boundaries must be rather fluid and open to constant reinterpretation. As Leslie Holmes argued, all national communities have to draw boundaries and are thus by necessity exclusionary at least to an extent. What is important to observe is the character of these boundaries. Holmes advanced an instructive metaphor to illustrate the point: 'the boundaries between groups can be painted lines on the ground – which are easy enough to cross and are not *per se* threatening – or high barbed wire fences' (Holmes 1999: 140). Clearly, the latter image stands for a nation that is very exclusionary, while the former conception is fairly inclusive as it illustrates a case in which it is not very difficult to become a fully recognized member of the community. I would suggest, in addition, that for liberal nationalists the line should be conceived of as even more flexible (say, drawn in chalk), allowing constant re-definitions and re-interpretations of belonging. What follows is an exposition of yet another dispute about belonging, in respect to the former communists.

Lustration, de-communization

One of the main challenges to Polish society after the end of communist power was the question of how to deal with those citizens who were in the past actively involved in sustaining the regime, whether as active members and/or leaders of the Polish Communist Party, or as officials or collaborators of the secret police. In general, there were two basic approaches to the problem. On the one hand, politicians like Tadeusz Mazowiecki (the first non-communist premier of Poland) were in favour of a more conciliatory stance and argued that in order to smooth the path towards democracy and to prevent a possible anti-communist backlash, it was prudent to draw a 'thick line' behind the injustices of the past and move on towards the future (Bertschi 1994). At the other end of the spectrum were people like Olszewski (prime minister in 1991–2), arguing that the ultimate success of democratic reforms was predicated on a more radical approach towards the people responsible for the communist regime. While the former did not resist the involvement of the former communist elites in the newly emerging political institutions, arguing that their exclusion would actually destabilize the political and economic system, the latter were determined to exclude 'those most directly involved [in the evils of the past] from any senior posts in the future' (Goble 1998).

This practical political discussion had its equivalent at a more philosophical level. On the one side were those who were more supportive of the 'thick line' approach, relying on theories of procedural democracy which prescribe strict neutrality towards the moral values of the particular participants in the political processes. On the other side of the ideological divide were those who saw a danger in ideas which allowed for the theoretical justification of former perpetrators remaining in power on the basis that morality and politics must be kept separated.

Zdzisław Krasnodębski argued that Polish society should be wary of adopting theories which make a thick-line approach palatable.

> At times it would appear, that just as we had in the past followed the values of noble democracy ad absurdum (i.e. during the first republic), we are now probably doing the same thing with procedural democracy.

Being afraid of moral fundamentalism, we refrained from even referring to the basic moral values without which the very democratic order can lose its moral legitimacy and credibility.

(Krasnodębski 1997: 17)

Andrzej Walicki opposes Krasnodębski, relying on Rawls' conception of political liberalism that calls for a state which does not espouse any comprehensive doctrine of a good life, and in that way allows individuals to follow freely their differing conceptions of the good. This is, according to Walicki, far removed from moral relativism, since Rawls is deeply convinced of the universal validity of liberal values (Walicki 1997c: 25).

The Polish right sees in liberalism the danger of moral relativism that would pave the way to totalitarianism; the liberals, on the other hand, consider the source of totalitarianism precisely in the tendency to support one, or another political authority that espouses 'absolute values', or 'absolute truth'.

(Walicki 1997c: 36)

Walicki stresses that Rawlsian political liberalism could help the Poles to minimize the influence of integral nationalism, because 'it would not be possible (meaning morally acceptable) to demean the majority of the people by excluding them from the community of "real Poles" ' (Walicki 1997c: 27). What is evident from the arguments on both sides is the fact that the practical process of 'de-communization' cannot be separated from the broader issue of the understanding of Polish national identity. While Krasnodębski's conception has more appeal to those anti-communists who feel that a just society must be based on some form of reckoning for past injustices, Walicki's ideas open the way for a much more inclusive notion of a nation, and are therefore significantly closer to the conceptions of liberal nationalists.

The first rather misguided attempt at de-communization started with Olszewski becoming prime minister after the October 1991 elections. His government, a coalition of the Centre Alliance and the Christian National Union, was determined to 'break with the communist past and with the "forgive and forget" policy of the two previous governments' (Bertschi 1994: 444). When the interior minister Antoni Maciarewicz sought to apply the idea, however, the methods used proved inadequate. In order to proceed with the lustration of elected officials, Maciarewicz compiled a list of sixty-four alleged collaborators with the secret police. Next to the names of some genuine informants, the list included people who were innocent, which opened Olszewski's government to accusations that it had used the lustration process as a pretext for its own political agenda. Consequently, the government was dismissed by the parliament in June 1992, and it took another five years before the Polish parliament agreed on a new strategy for dealing with the past.

The controversy about the right approach towards the communist past has not abated. One of the undesired side-effects of the failure of Olszewski's administration was ironically the boost that it gave to critics of any attempts at de-communization. Based on the fact that accusations were often made on the basis of unreliable information, even the real former collaborators were able to 'portray themselves as innocent victims of a witch hunt' (Bertschi 1994: 446). Some of the former victims were also rather critical about some approaches of the right-wing anti-communist parts of the Polish political spectrum to the nation's past. Jacek Kuroń, for example, who spent nine years in prison under communist rule, observed that it was 'paradoxical that so many anti-communists appeared on the Polish political scene at the time when communism ceased to be any real threat to the country, and when there was no communist political force to speak of' (Kuroń and Żakowski 1997: 138). Kuroń warned against any indiscriminate condemnation of the former communists which would ignore their vastly different motives and the various extents of their personal responsibilities, suggesting that such an attitude 'has something racist about it' (Kuroń and Żakowski 1997: 139).

Amnestia – tak; amnezja – nie

Adam Michnik, very much in line with Jacek Kuroń, also rejected collective punishment of the former communists. At the same time, he called on all those who had actively taken part in the past dictatorship honestly and openly to discuss their individual responsibility for the past. According to Michnik, only after having fulfilled this basic duty can the former perpetrators seek a genuine reconciliation which cannot be based on forgetting. Adam Michnik introduced the formula: 'amnesty – yes (except for the criminals); amnesia – no' (Michnik 1995: 6). In a programmatic article written together with the member of parliament for the once-communist Party of the Democratic Left (SLD) Włodzimierz Cimoszewicz, Michnik advocated an open dialogue in Poland between those who belonged to different political camps, and were 'historically on different sides of the barricades' (Michnik and Cimoszewicz 1995: 6). To come to terms with the national past was vital for the successful development of the nation at present and in the future:

> We are aware that Polish history is a collection of events and facts that no one can change. This is our common heritage. Our awareness of this heritage can be a source of strength – if we succeed in honestly evaluating it; or a source of destructive conflict – if we bequeath the emotions and obsessions that we experienced to our children.
>
> (Michnik and Cimoszewicz 1995: 6)

This joint statement by Michnik and Cimoszewicz did not gain much support; in particular, the anti-communist opposition had problems accepting their rather tolerant attitude towards the former communists (Michnik 1997: 18). Still, the resulting lustration law, which was adopted by the Polish parliament in April 1997 (though not implemented until the middle of 1998), appears to be a compromise between any projects venturing radical de-communization, and the thick-line approach of Tadeusz Mazowiecki, and in that way it is not too far removed from Michnik and Cimoszewicz's idea of accomplishing 'reconciliation through truthfulness'. The political compromise was achieved to a large extent thanks to the proposal of Kuroń's Freedom Union (UW), which consistently argued against extremes on both sides of the political spectrum. One of UW's resolutions 'specifies that those who committed crimes under communism should be tried as individuals and cautions – citing Pope John Paul II – against the "logic of revenge"' (Snyder 1998). The adopted lustration law comes very close to this ideal. The law requires 'all senior officials, parliamentary deputies and judges to declare whether they worked with communist-era security organs' (Goble 1998). The rule encourages and rewards honesty, since provided that guilt of past involvement is freely professed, the person affected is not forced out of public office. Those, however, who 'do not acknowledge such involvement and are subsequently found to have lied will face fines and a 10-year ban from such posts in the future' (Goble 1998). Importantly, the law does not target former members of the communist party and functionaries of the state bureaucracy.

It remains to be seen whether the forces of liberal nationalism, which are in favour of an inclusive attitude towards collaborators with the former communist system, can effectively exercise influence on the ongoing discourse for the right meaning of Polishness. But judging from the tolerant character of the adopted lustration law, the chances of that happening are promising. The protracted political disputes about the correct strategies for dealing with the communist past in Poland are indicative of the importance of an issue which transcends the temporary political interests of the parties involved. As Charles Bertschi commented, 'there was clearly much more at stake than mere collaboration – this was a struggle for the Polish national identity' (Bertschi 1994: 446).

Kukliński: national hero or traitor?

As the former communists and those who worked for the secret service were considered to be the villains responsible for the past injustices, Ryszard Kukliński, a former senior military official of the Polish army who defected to the American secret service, was consequently seen by many as a national hero. Having become a NATO general, he was celebrated by thousands of Poles in May 1998 when he visited his home country after seventeen years of exile in the United States. As the time of his visit coincided with the decision of the American Congress to admit the country into NATO, to many this was the last proof – if any was needed – that Kukliński, while working for the Americans, had indeed served the best national interests of Poland. But not everyone admired Kukliński as a new Polish patriot. Even though he was legally cleared of the original charges of treason (he was sentenced to death *in absentia* in 1984), and courted by the new political representation (including Aleksander Kwaśniewski), for many critics he remained a traitor who broke his oath. Perhaps surprisingly, one of the strongest opponents of Kukliński's 'patriotism' was Adam Michnik.

Michnik's criticism was twofold. On the one hand he challenged the moral integrity of the new hero, explaining that preceding Kukliński's involvement with the CIA, he had held very senior positions in the Polish army. It should not be forgotten, cautions Michnik, that Kukliński

> was in the army in March 1968 during the antisemitism campaign and the brutal suppression of the opposition student movement; that he was in the army during the invasion of Czechoslovakia; and that he did not publicly condemn those actions, leave the army, leave the party, and somehow join the opposition.
>
> (Michnik 1998b: 31)

Michnik recalls the ethos of the Polish opposition, which prided itself on using methods that were morally justifiable while security services, even if they operate within a democratic state, cannot avoid using dubious means. Most leading figures of the opposition were therefore convinced that 'even total opposition toward the authorities of the communist regime...cannot lead to collaboration with foreign intelligence services' (Michnik 1998b: 27).

Moreover, if Kukliński is to be celebrated for having prevented an open military confrontation – as his supporters claimed – a similar argument could be used to defend the proclamation of martial law by General Jaruzelski. The event could be interpreted alternately as a 'brutal attack on Polish freedom', or as 'an act which served to defend the limited sovereignty of the nation in crisis which was threatened by an intervention' (Michnik and Cimoszewicz 1995: 7). In both cases the moral responsibility of the actors involved is ambiguous and difficult to evaluate.

Popular attitudes

One of the main imperatives of liberal nationalism is to keep the political system open to all the people of a community regardless of their ethnic origin or ideological persuasion. Thus far, it is evident that the ideas of liberal nationalism are espoused by intellectuals like Kuroń, Michnik and Walicki.[34] However, more important for the stability of liberal democracy in a country is ultimately the support these and similar ideas enjoy among the wider population. Obviously, this is more difficult to measure and evaluate; but if a recent study of different discourses of democracy in Poland is any guide, then there are sound reasons for optimism. Two out of three different discourses which were identified in an elaborate process of examination of various sources (newspapers, electronic media, and more importantly discussion groups of various representative cohorts of the population) showed considerable support for the statement that 'political power should be *open to all kinds of people*, and a democratic state should *welcome people of all nationalities, religions, ideologies, and capabilities*' (my italics, Dryzek and Holmes 1998: 8; see also Dryzek and Holmes 2002: 225–39). Thus discourses labelled 'civic republicanism' and 'majoritarian democracy' can accommodate the basic feature of liberal nationalism, i.e. its inclusive character in terms of ethnicity and religion.

The results of Q-methodology research conducted by Dryzek and Holmes are also supported by a number of studies on Polish nationalism, which observed that a majority of Polish citizens have so far refrained from endorsing extreme nationalism.[35] Ewa Morawska discerned a 'popular change of mind' of the Polish population after the collapse of the communist regime:

> As Poland regained state sovereignty under a government recognized as legitimate by practically all Poles, a shift occurred in the primary civic-political concerns of the majority of the Polish population – a shift from the idea, and the accompanying emotions, of the *nation* to that of the *society*. Put differently, while the primary interest in the undifferentiated and deindividualized national community – Benedict Anderson's 'imagined community' – has considerably weakened, the recognition of Poland as a differentiated, plural society composed of a multitude of groups continues to increase.
>
> (Morawska 1995: 66–7)

Even more optimistic was Frances Millard, who observed 'The Failure of Nationalism in Post-Communist Poland 1989–95':

> Numerous right-wing parties attempted to base their appeal on modern nationalist themes, but they failed to mobilise the population whether in support of decommunisation, a clerically oriented state based on identification of the nation with the Catholic Church, or an economically interventionist, xenophobic populism.
>
> (Millard 1996: 219)

Conclusion

My study is in partial agreement with both assessments, since they can be read as showing that the forces of *extreme* nationalism have failed to dominate the political discourse of Polish society. The study of different kinds of nationalisms in contemporary Poland demonstrates, however, that the uncritical and one-dimensional use of the concept of nationalism as standing exclusively for the movement towards 'the undifferentiated and deindividualized national community' (Morawska 1995: 67) is not beneficial to the understanding of current developments in the country. I doubt that most Poles suddenly lost interest in their nation, in favour of an abstract society (are they now emotionally attached to *society*?). Rather, a vast majority of Poles were successful in imagining their community in less exclusionary terms than those propagated by some extreme-right political parties (e.g. the League of Polish Families). If liberal nationalism is a viable concept, then the civic-political concerns of the people do not – *per se* – disallow for feelings of national solidarity, but can indeed support them. Millard's generalization with regard to the 'failure of nationalism' also needs some clarification; importantly, it was the extreme and exclusionary version of nationalism that failed to gain the support of a majority of the people, but they were receptive to other, more inclusive concepts of the Polish nation.

Despite some predictions to the contrary, Poland has so far succeeded in transforming its political system from communism to a reasonably stable liberal democracy. As one of the main challenges for the transition foreseen by many analysts was nationalism (and too often the term was used without sufficient clarification) and its alliance with intolerant Catholicism, it is not surprising that just about all the studies published after 1995 argued that nationalism 'miraculously disappeared' (or became marginalized, lost relevance) from the Polish political scene. My exposition of different discourses of nationalism in Poland presents a more complex picture. The relative success of the extreme nationalist League of Polish Families and the populist Samoobrona movement in the September 2001 elections, should dampen the optimism of mid-1990s scholarly assessments of the decline of nationalism in Poland. Yet the argument advanced in this chapter is that more, not less nationalism was needed – though nationalism which allows for both a strong identification with a nation *and* an endorsement of universal values of liberalism. Undoubtedly, it is not always easy to find the right balance between the two – often conflicting – imperatives. The 'cosmo-Polak' Adam Michnik (Michnik 2002) is aware of this inherent tension when he demands from intellectuals: 'Remain loyal to your national roots, but do not give up your eternal unrootedness' (Michnik 1993: 272; cf. Berlin 1969: 172, Tamir 1995: 440). Contradictory as it is, Michnik's liberal nationalism can still serve as a source of inspiration for the new generation of intellectuals and politicians. Today, Polish liberals should reinvigorate the kind of liberal nationalism that was characteristic of the Solidarność movement, and adapt it in order to strengthen the viability and stability of democracy in Poland.

4 Nationalism in the Czech Republic

While the dominant discourse of Polish nationalism since the beginning of the nineteenth century had been directed towards the restoration of full political independence and statehood, Czech nationalism had more modest aspirations. When the Czechs achieved their statehood, it was more as a result of changing external circumstances rather than a persistent fight for full political independence. Leaders of the Czech National Revival in the nineteenth century like Palacký envisaged the political future of their nation within the framework of a reformed Austrian empire. Not surprisingly, and very much in line with this tradition, Tomáš G. Masaryk, before becoming the founder and the first president of the 1918 Czechoslovak Republic, worked as a member of parliament for Austria-Hungary. Finally, even the new Czech state founded on 1 January 1993 was a result of unresolved disputes between Czech and Slovak politicians as to the right shape of constitutional order of the new (postcommunist) federative republic. To claim that the new Czech state was imposed on Czechs by Slovaks (*Lidové noviny*, 12 September 1992, cf. Pithart 1998: 57, 188) is a crude overstatement, but there can be little doubt that the creation of the Czech Republic was something of an historical accident rather than the fulfilment of some age-old national project.

Given these historical circumstances it is not surprising that the Czechs pride themselves on being immune to nationalism. As the British anthropologist of Czech origin, Ladislav Holy, observed, Czechs 'manifest their nationalism through its vehement denial'. According to this widespread perception, 'nationalism is something that plagues others – Slovaks, Serbs, Croats and various nations of the former Soviet Union, but not the Czechs' (Holy 1996: 189). Characteristically, in 1968 Milan Kundera celebrated the traditional roots of Czech patriotism, which is based on a rational and critical attitude towards one's own nation and is free from fanaticism. These properties make the Czechs, according to Kundera, 'one of the least chauvinist nations in Europe' (Kundera in Havel 1990a: 188).

It should be noted, however, that nationalism in Czech usage has had until very recently distinctively negative connotations, and usually stands for exclusive and xenophobic nationalism, which is, as in the Polish case, distinguishable from desirable patriotism (see Chapters 1 and 3). Petr Pithart, for example, remonstrates against nationalism as a form of collective egoism, while defending the virtues of patriotism, which he defines as 'a positive relationship to one's own national community, which need not be affirmed by the existence of an imagined enemy who usually becomes real' (Pithart 1998: 38–9). Consequently, Pithart concedes the importance of a sense of national identity without which 'people cannot lead satisfactory lives' (1998: 64) and which is also an invaluable source of solidarity (1998: 38).

This conception of patriotism is vulnerable to objections raised by Walicki against the Polish understanding of patriotism (Walicki 1997b: 33–5; see also Chapter 1). First, patriotism is not necessarily immune to chauvinism. In fact, a chauvinist is by a common definition 'a bellicose *patriot*' (*New Shorter Oxford English Dictionary*). Second, patriotism refers to the home country or region, *patria*, while in Pithart's understanding it is explicitly about the relationship to a 'national community'. Still, Pithart's definition is very much in line with the common perception of the term in Czech (and in Polish, or Slovak), and it would be both presumptuous and futile to attempt to change this. In the context of this book, however, a positive attitude to one's own national community combined with respect for others' constitutes one of the defining characteristics of liberal nationalism.

Such a misleading use of terminology (which equates nationalism with chauvinism) is typical of many journalistic accounts and academic studies that have dealt with the postcommunist developments in Czech society. The Czech Republic had for a long time been considered the leader amongst all the postcommunist countries of Central and Eastern Europe in its achievements in the transition towards liberal democracy and a free market economy (e.g. Elster *et al.* 1998: 279). A seemingly necessary corollary of this view was the conviction that nationalism did not play a role in Czech political discourse, which was dominated by civic principles. Scholars even applied the concept of two types of nationalism in Europe, in order to argue that the Czechs now epitomize the Western, or civic type of nationalism and distinguish themselves therefore from other nations further to the East, whether these be Slovakia, Romania and Bulgaria (Vachudová and Snyder 1997); or Albania, Bosnia, Bulgaria, Croatia, Macedonia, Romania, Yugoslavia and Slovakia (Carpenter 1997); or even Slovakia, Poland and Hungary (Bednář 1998: 133). Thus the assessment of Jiří Kořalka was typical; he observed in 1991 that 'all the important attributes of "western" nationalism were finally becoming present in Czech society' (Kořalka 1994: 275). Similarly, Bollerup and Christensen concluded that in contrast to the post-1989 developments in other countries of Central and Eastern Europe, 'the Czech-dominated revival was *liberal* rather than *national* in its aim and scope' (original emphasis, Bollerup and Christensen 1997: 131).

As I argued in Chapter 1, such distinctions are not only unhelpful methodologically, but are also morally questionable, since, by distinguishing between so-called more advanced and backward nations, they offer a sophisticated version of chauvinism. Furthermore, to consider nationalism as being in necessary opposition to civic values offers an incomplete and even distorted picture. Nationalism can also be conducive to liberal democracy. Not only did Czech and Slovak nationalism play an important role in the collapse of the communist system of power, but without some conception of nationalism, the newly created Czech Republic would not make sense as an independent state. The important question thus is not whether the Czechs can do without a sense of belonging to a nation, but rather what it means to be a Czech in relation to the emerging political order. The wide consensus, reflected in the new constitution, that the state must be built on civic principles and the principle of a free market economy, did not exclude questions about the specific character of the Czech Republic, one which would accommodate its unique national traditions. As Václav Havel argued in an interview with Adam Michnik for the Polish newspaper *Gazeta Wyborcza*, these universal principles are not a sufficient reason for the foundation of an independent state.

> [Why] could we not become the seventeenth state of the Federal Republic of Germany, why have an independent state because of something which is a universal programme? I think it is necessary to seek other dimensions of Czech political traditions and Czech statehood. Something, to my mind, that has occurred repeatedly in Czech political life from time immemorial is a sense of a broader responsibility. Whenever Czech politics was egotistic it was not successful. When there was a realization that the stability and prosperity of the Czech lands is only possible against the background of broader European stability, it was successful. This sense of responsibility and the feeling that the Czech concern is a human concern [*věc česká je věc lidská*] can be found in St Wenceslas, Charles IV, George of Poděbrady, Comenius, Masaryk, Patočka. I think that this political line should become a part of the foundations of the new Czech state and even a warrant of its prospects.
> (Havel in *Lidové noviny*, 11 September 1992; see also Havel 1991: 111–15)

The aim of this chapter is to examine the roles of different types of nationalism in Czech political discourse, and their influence on recent political developments. I will explore some of the traditions which Havel recalls and assess their potential for strengthening the cause of liberal democracy in the Czech Republic. Attention will be paid especially to the types of thought that combine universalist liberal aspirations with particular Czech traditions. The notion *věc česká je věc lidská* (the Czech concern is a human concern), which Havel adapted from T. G. Masaryk,[1] can be read as a shorthand for liberal nationalism, which 'celebrates the particularity of culture together with the universality of human rights, the social and cultural embeddedness of individuals together with their personal autonomy' (Tamir 1993: 79). This is not to say that Czech history should be interpreted as a unidirectional movement towards liberal democracy. In fact, it will become clear that many aspects of Czech national history were used in the past in order to strengthen the legitimacy of un-democratic regimes and illiberal policies.

History

Writings about national histories often reveal as much about the concerns of the time in which they were written as about the past events they set out to investigate. Present aspirations, achievements or failures tend to influence particular interpretations of the past. When the future appears promising, as it did for instance to Palacký in the middle of nineteenth century, or to Masaryk at the beginning of the twentieth century, historical narratives explain reasons for the feasibility of ambitious political programmes, as their success appears to be supported by the logic of history. Thus Masaryk's contemporary, the writer Karel Čapek, spoke in the 1930s of Czechoslovak democracy as being as 'hereditary and inborn as the democracy of the American nation' (cited in Beneš 1964: 267). By contrast, in times in which hopes for a better future were abandoned or postponed, histories were more likely to show that present failures were to an extent inevitable, or at least logical when seen against the background of past experience (Patočka, Šimečka). This is not to say that there is only one way of interpreting the past at any one time. Different historical accounts coexist in national discourse, and can be used alternately as the source of inspiration for political action or as justification for inaction. Furthermore, even a history of failure can be used as a morality tale which shows what went wrong and how it could have been prevented. In 1989, at any rate, potent symbols of national history were effectively used in order to challenge the existing repressive political system, which was seen as an alien concept imposed on the freedom-loving Czechs by communist Russia.

The mass demonstrations of October/November 1989 showed that historical figures and events were important not only for a handful of intellectuals like Václav Havel, but that they were also meaningful symbols for a wide cross-section of the population. As Ernest Gellner reminds us, 'there can be few nations...which live on terms of quite such constant intimacy with their own history as do the Czechs' (Gellner 1993: 3). Ladislav Holy showed how the participants in spontaneous demonstrations made use of the 'symbolic map' of the city of Prague, which reflects the historical experience of the nation in its fight for freedom and independence (Holy 1996: 33–42). The repeated demonstrations marking the fiftieth anniversary of the closing of the Czech Universities by the Germans on 17 November 1939 followed a particular route. They started at the statue of St Wenceslas on the square of the same name, and moved on to the next rallying point, which was the statue of Jan Hus in the Old Town Square. In that way, even if often unconsciously, the demonstrators appropriated two major figureheads of Czech history.

While St Wenceslas, who ruled in Bohemia in the first half of the tenth century, is considered the founder of the first Czech state and the patron saint of Bohemia, Jan Hus is regarded as the spiritual father of the nation. Both are celebrated as national martyrs who died for their firm commitment to truth and, particularly in the case of Hus, freedom (Pynsent 1994: 196–201, Holy 1996: 33–42). The spiritual heritage of St Wenceslas has been reclaimed repeatedly whenever the Czech nation has felt threatened by foreign domination, or celebrated its independence. Fittingly, the writing on the pedestal of the statue states: 'Do not let us, or our descendants perish!' (Sayer 1998: 100). The statue of St Wenceslas witnessed not only demonstrations in 1989, but had provided the background for the celebrations of the creation of the new republic on 28 October 1918, and had served as a rallying point of resistance against the Soviet occupation in August 1968 (Pynsent 1994: 198).

The timing of the demonstrations in 1989 was as important and symbolically potent as the places in which they took place. The first telling gesture which captured the imagination of people far beyond the narrow circle of dissident groups was the detention of Václav Havel, following his attempt of 16 January 1989 to lay flowers at the statue of St Wenceslas in honour of Jan Palach, a student who set himself on fire at the same place twenty years earlier in protest against the suppression of the 'Prague Spring' by the military intervention of the Soviet Union and their Warsaw Pact allies. Havel's arrest sparked a wave of protests that culminated in the November demonstrations, which ultimately toppled the communist regime. These events were linked through personalities and historic events. The person remembered in association with Jan Palach on the Czech independence day on 28 October 1989 was yet another student, Jan Opletal, who suffered fatal injuries in a demonstration on 28 October 1939. While Jan Palach was seen as a martyr who sacrificed his life for freedom from communist Soviet oppression, Jan Opletal became a national hero for dying in protest against Nazi Germany. The Czechoslovak communists tried to suppress the memory of Palach,[2] and at the same time appropriate the anti-fascist tradition represented by Opletal. Thus 17 November was officially celebrated every year as the international day of students, commemorating repressive actions of Nazi rulers in November 1939, including 'the closing of Czech universities, the execution of nine students, and the internment of some twelve hundred students in concentration camps' (Holy 1996: 42).

It is worthwhile noting that Palach's heroic action indirectly evoked the legacy of Jan Hus, who was burned to death by Church authorities because he refused to renounce his beliefs (Pynsent 1994: 209–10; Holy 1996: 45). In contrast, the continuous attempts of the communist authorities to appropriate the heritage of Jan Hus by turning him into a proto-communist revolutionary were troublesome. First, the spiritual dimension of Hus' heritage was difficult to square with the official atheism of the communist regime[3] (Sayer 1998: 277–80). Second, the famous dictum associated with Jan Hus and the Hussite movement, 'truth prevails' (*Pravda vítězí*), which was adopted by Masaryk as the motto of the presidential standard, proved of limited value for communist propaganda. Though the Czechoslovak communist leadership retained the presidential motto after 1948, and sought to align it with its own idea of the one and only 'truth' (i.e. the truth of Marxist-Leninist ideology), the ever-growing discrepancy between the noble ideals of the communist ideology and the oppressive nature of the political system ultimately undermined its legitimacy. In 1989, the people on the street were able to reclaim the motto with their posters declaring that 'truth prevailed' (Macura 2001: 544).

In November 1989, the police forces unwittingly created a new martyr in their desperate attempts to dissolve a peaceful demonstration – an event that decidedly exposed the hypocrisy of the existing regime, which claimed to be ruling in the best interests of the people, while ruthlessly suppressing any expression of popular will. It was alleged that on 17 November 1989, the police 'martyred' an innocent student demonstrator, Martin Šmíd. The monument to St Wenceslas at the top of Wenceslas Square became in the following days a shrine of remembrance. The brutal actions of the police ultimately undermined the very political regime they were trying to protect. By violently suppressing a demonstration commemorating an act of Nazi oppression, the communist regime put itself into a position in which it became virtually indistinguishable from another totalitarian regime – that of the Nazis. In fact, the police who sought to violently disperse the peaceful masses were likened by demonstrators to the 'Gestapo' and their behaviour seen as un-Czech (Holy 1996: 48). The demonstrators chanted that they were not like *them* ('Nejsme jako oni!'); making clear the division between *us* (the demonstrators), representing the true interests of the nation, and *them* (the police), who could not be considered truly Czech. As Holy observed,

> The reason that the demonstrators opposed the communist system as Czechs rather than as citizens or democrats derived from their perception of the communist system as yet another form of foreign domination which served first of all foreign – specifically Soviet – rather than Czech interests and, moreover, was alien to what the Czechs perceived as their national tradition.
>
> (Holy 1996: 51)

This perception is somewhat distorted and one-sided. Many observers (including some Czech intellectuals such as Patočka, Milan Šimečka, Uhde, Kučera) showed that the Czech people could not be entirely freed from their responsibility for the existence of the communist system in Czechoslovakia (Šimečka 1990: 107–9; Uhde 1995: 215; Kučera 1998a: 72–81; Sayer 1998: 167). There can be little doubt, however, that regardless of the historical accuracy of the popular belief that communism was imposed on an otherwise highly cultured and democratic Czech nation, this interpretation of Czech history proved to be an effective source of political mobilization. In a similar vein, the mobilizing potential of Martin Šmíd was unaffected by the fact that he was never killed by the police. His alleged martyrdom was discovered to be false. But by the time this truth had been established, the fictive 'ersatz martyr of Prague had accomplished his mission' (Kukral 1997: 79).[4] The story of a young student who died while peacefully defending the freedom of the Czech nation fitted all too well into the 'logic' of a long history of resistance of heroic individuals (Hus, Opletal, Palach, Patočka) and the corresponding 'Czech self-definition through martyrs' (Pynsent 1994: 147–210). Undoubtedly, with all their symbolic actions, the demonstrators strengthened their call against political repression by allying themselves success-fully with their national tradition (whether imagined or real).

Symbolic gestures on their own, however, would not have been sufficient to dissemble the communist system of power in Czechoslovakia, a country that had one of the most repressive and well functioning regimes in the whole of Soviet-dominated Eastern Europe. The symbolic value of Palach's sacrifice, for example, was significantly stronger than Havel's non-violent action twenty years later. But the circumstances of both deeds were very different and so was their impact. While in January 1969, no one could doubt the determination of the Soviet Union and its allies to suppress any new attempt at liberalizing the existing communist system (let alone an open anti-communist revolution), in November 1989, the examples of Poland, Hungary and East Germany showed clearly that the Soviet Union was serious about changing its foreign policy, and that changes were possible. In fact, the November demonstrations were partly inspired by a mass exodus of East German citizens, who left their native country in search of a better life in West Germany, to this end travelling first through Hungary and later via the West German Embassy in Prague. The fall of the Berlin Wall on 9 November 1989 was for many Czechs the last impetus needed to spark them into action. They were mobilized by the idea that even the Germans, who were traditionally seen as the embodiment of obedience and respect for authority,[5] had dared to challenge their rulers.

The Czechs, particularly since Palacký, contrast their democratic creden-tials with the German tradition of authoritarianism. Interestingly, the notion of peace-loving Slavs versus vengeful and militaristic Germans was also endorsed by the German philosopher Johann Gottfried Herder and his *Ideen zur Philosophie der Geschichte der Menschheit* (Doležal 1998: 19). Palacký's ambivalent stand towards the German nation, which is emblem-atic of the complex relationship between Czechs and Germans, was thus partly inherited from Herder;[6] though it has significantly longer pedigree within the history of Bohemia.

'Czech-German struggle' from 'Dalimil' to the Battle of the White Mountain

In fact, the first literary expression of Czech nationalism, the so-called Dalimil's Chronicle from the fourteenth century, seems to be full of anti-German sentiments. Dalimil sought to mobilize his readers against the corrupting influence of foreign elements by celebrating the heroic deeds of those Czech rulers who were most ruthless in dealing with the perceived German threat. In Dalimil's view, 'since all Germans were ill-disposed towards the Czechs', the land had to be cleansed of them – a task best achieved by chopping off the noses of their German enemies (Pynsent 1999: 226). Though it is disputed to what extent Dalimil's Chronicle can really be seen as an early example of Czech xenophobic propaganda,[7] it is clear that this view of Czech history, which sees it as an age-long struggle between Slavic and Germanic elements, predates the mythopoetic views of the nineteenth-century Czech revivalists, such as Palacký.

Palacký and the birth of the modern Czech nation

Even if it is plausible to trace Czech national history back at least some ten centuries, the actual content of modern Czech nationalism was arguably more strongly influenced by developments at the beginning of the nineteenth century. Gellner's theory of nationalism which claims that nations – at least as we now know them – are a result of the radical process of modernization is possibly best suited to the Czech case, which is not surprising given Gellner's background (see also Chapter 1). Thus, while the Poles are able to discuss the proto-liberal qualities of 'their' pre-eighteenth-century kingdom, and Andrzej Walicki can mount a strong case against all theories of nationalism based on modernization by demonstrating their deficiencies in the Polish case (Walicki 1997a), a defence of the idea of a continuous and long lasting history of the Czech nation seems more difficult. Accordingly, there are many more voices from within Czech intellectual discourse in our century, which convincingly challenge the mythological character of many historical narratives (e.g. Pekař, Patočka, Pithart). This is not to say that developments predating the Czech National Revival in Bohemia do not matter. But it can be argued that they could only exercise their strong influence thanks to nationalist leaders, such as Palacký, who recognized the importance of history in forging a sense of national identity, and actively promoted the understanding of crucial historic events and ideas.

Palacký's monumental six-volume *History of the Czech Nation in Bohemia and Moravia* is as much a foundation stone of Czech national historiography as of the modern Czech nation itself. Palacký was fully aware of the impact his work could have on the development of national identity. In fact, his was a conscious effort to 'revive' or 'reawaken' the Czech nation that had 'slumbered' for centuries under German dominance, unaware of its historic role. Palacký was committed to serve his 'beloved nation by giving a faithful account of its past, in which it would recognize itself as in a mirror and regain consciousness of what it needs' (Palacký 1939: I, 5; Sayer 1998: 128). This would finally bring to an end the time of national *úpadek* (decadence/decline) and allow for the full fruition of the Czech national character determined by the 'old-Slavonic democratic spirit' (Holy 1996: 81). As already mentioned, Palacký's view of Czech history is predicated on the conflict between two major political forces reflecting two contradictory philosophies of life: the Slavic spirit based on the historic experience of primitive democracy was peaceful and egalitarian, and this competed relentlessly with the Germanic spirit characterized by aggressive authoritarianism and aristocratism (Palacký 1939: I, 19–20, 58–60). The strongest expression of this ancient opposition was the Hussite revolutionary movement of the fifteenth century, which was, according to Palacký, not only a fight against the spiritual dogmatism of Rome, but also a rebellion against German feudalism. Even though the long lasting struggle ultimately ended with the military defeat of the Czech nobility in the famous Battle of the White Mountain in 1620,[8] this has no bearing on the moral superiority of the Czech cause 'to free the human spirit from the restrictive authority of the Middle Ages' (Palacký 1939: VI, 52–3).

Ironically, the 'Father of the Nation' wrote the first two volumes and a part of the third volume of his work in German as *Geschichte von Böhmen*, and started to write *Dějiny národu českého v Čechách a v Moravě* in Czech only after the eventful year of 1848. Palacký was not unusual in using the German language for the Czech national cause. In fact, many ardent Czech nationalists were more fluent in German than in Czech. For instance, the most prolific journalist of the Czech National Revival, Karel Havlíček Borovský, had to make a conscious effort to master fully 'his sacred sonorous mother tongue' (Sayer 1998: 108). Symptomatic are some transmutations of Palacký's work in the two different languages. Whereas the German title refers to *Böhmen* (Bohemia), which is an ethnically neutral term for the description of the territory concerned, the Czech title is explicit about its focus on the Czech nation and Czech territory.[9] The more accurate translation of the Czech title should therefore be *History of the Czech Nation in 'Czechia' and Moravia*.[10] Characteristically, the ensuing Czech editions of Palacký's works were more detailed in their descriptions of the democratic credentials of the Czech nation than their German original.[11]

Palacký's Manichean reading of Czech history based on the idea of the eternal struggle between German and Czech elements proved to be a double-edged heritage for the later developments of Czech society. The obvious danger of the concept lies in its inherent potential for chauvinism. By valuing Czech traditions above German, the concept lent itself to the justification of nationalist excesses such as the post-Second World War expulsion of ethnic Germans from their homeland in Czechoslovakia. But to see virulent Czech nationalism as a legitimate heir to Palacký is a gross misrepresentation of his liberal attitude. In the famous statement from the 'Letter to the Frankfurt Parliament', Palacký made unambiguously clear his opposition to any particularistic nationalist claims: 'with all my ardent love of my nation, I always esteem more highly the good of mankind and of learning than the good of the nation' (Palacký in Bannan and Edelyeni 1970: 147). Likewise, the 'Manifesto of the first Slav Congress', of which

Palacký was the leader, is universalist by demanding 'liberty, equality, and fraternity for all who live in the state' (Fischer-Galati 1970: 157).

Moreover, Palacký's extensive arguments against conservative centralist tendencies in the Habsburg empire in favour of a federal arrangement, further underline his commitment to basic liberal values. His vision of a multinational federalist state in which all communities are treated equally and can therefore live peacefully together, appears modern even by the standards of late-twentieth-century political theory, and are comparable with some present-day conceptions of multicultural societies and 'the politics of recognition' (e.g. Taylor 1992). Remarkably, Palacký's point of departure was the respect for the individual rights of citizens. He firmly believed that the equality of nations was derived directly from a natural right. The equal treatment of national communities was, according to Palacký, necessitated by the liberal imperative of the equal treatment of individual citizens. As he stated in Havlíček's *Národní noviny* (*National Newspaper*) in 1849:

> The laws in a free constitutional state must apply equally to all citizens ... In other words, the constitution must be nothing else but the realization of the well-known and eternal principle of all legality and justice: *do not do to others what you dislike yourself.*
>
> (Palacký in Znoj and Sekera 1995: 42)

It is not accidental that the principle is reminiscent of Kant's categorical imperative. As the contemporary Czech political philosopher Miloslav Bednář argues, Palacký's conception of freedom was strongly influenced by the Kantian notion of freedom as the moral autonomy of individuals (Bednář 1998: 110; see also Scruton 1990b: 51). This is the basis on which Palacký opposes any granting of privileges as unlawful and unjust. Hence he objected to the situation in Austria, in which the German-speaking elite benefited from the dominance of the German language in administration and public life. Thus it was of little use that the Austrian authorities formally acknowledged the equality of all nationalities if they did not, at the same time, practically allow for their political and cultural development freed from German domination. In fact, given the multiplicity of nationalities living in Austria, 'their full equality must not only be at the very basis of the constitution, but it must also be the moral basis of the whole empire' asserted Palacký (Palacký in Znoj and Sekera 1995: 43). The ultimate goal was to change the monarchy 'into a free association of peoples organized on the basis of modern democracy, constitutional parliamentarianism, and recognising the civil and political rights of the individual' (Beneš 1964: 271).

The most vocal propagandist of Austria becoming a 'central European union of free nations' was the Czech journalist Karel Havlíček, who stressed – even after the failure of the 1848 revolution – that the methods used in achieving this ambitious goal were to be peaceful and moderate. As he stated in 1849:

let us maintain continuous and unified opposition to the government, an opposition conducted strictly within the limits of the law, making up with spiritual force for the lack of our material resources. In all our striving let us always be sustained by genuine democracy, which has from the very beginning constituted the life and soul of our national endeavour.

(Havlíček quoted by Masaryk in Kovtun 1990: 72)

This strategy was later fully endorsed by Masaryk, who was convinced that humanist goals could only be achieved through humanist means.

Not with violence but with love, not with the sword but with the plough, not with blood but with work, not with death but with life – that is the answer of our Czech genius, the meaning of our history and the heritage of our great ancestors.

(Masaryk in Kovtun 1990: 80)

The same political tactic – although not phrased in such romantic language – was to be adopted by the dissident movements in communist times. The signatories of Charter 77 (e.g. Havel, Patočka), for example, only demanded from the state the adherence to its own (communist) system of law.[12] The conscious renunciation of any violence in political struggle was the salient feature of the anti-communist opposition (Havel 1991: 97) and resulted in the 'Velvet Revolution' of November 1989.

Despite the liberal ideas which permeated the political thoughts of Palacký and Havlíček, it would be anachronistic and exaggerated to claim they were impeccable liberals who would satisfy all our current expectations. For example, one of the serious limitations of Palacký's liberal nationalism is his reliance on the then popular notion of *odrodilec* (a linguistic renegade). The condemnation of individuals who opt out of their language community is in conflict with the liberal demand for respect for individual autonomy (see also Chapter 2). The concept of *odrodilec* allows for national values to override the interests of individuals whenever their interests are perceived to endanger the interests of the community (Palacký 1939: I, 20). But these and similar shortcomings can serve as a point of departure for the exploration of universal liberal values in the specific context of Czech history. Tomáš G. Masaryk argued in 1898 that Palacký did not always live up to his own moral imperatives. While approving of his endorsement of universal human values, Masaryk held against Palacký that he 'often emphasised national antagonism – especially between Slavs and Germans – to a greater extent than the need for cooperation and harmony between nations', and objected to his simplistic concept according to which 'the Slavs had a special propensity for democracy' (Masaryk in Kovtun 1990: 112–13). Even more critical of Palacký was the historian Josef Pekař. He rejected many popular myths about the meaning of Czech history (including those espoused by Masaryk) and instead made a conscious attempt to create a non-nationalistic historiography which 'saw Czech history not as the unique achievement of the Czech nation but as the unfolding of events in the wider context of European history to which Czechs were responsive' (Holy 1996: 124; see also Pynsent 1994: 182).

The most radical follower of Pekař's critical approach was probably Jan Patočka, who bemoaned the very fact that Palacký became such an influential figure in the forging of the Czech nation (Pynsent 1994: 185–6; Tucker 1996). Patočka strongly preferred the conception of yet another contemporary of Palacký, the Bohemian philosopher and mathematician Bernard Bolzano. A passionate teacher, Bolzano urged his students in Prague to transcend sectarian nationalist sentiments and 'love and embrace each other as children of a single shared homeland' (Bolzano in Sayer 1998: 60). His was a civic patriotism which countered the linguistic nationalism of the time (espoused by the likes of Jungmann, Šafařík and Palacký). Bolzano did not consider the language an important national attribute (let alone the defining feature of a nation), and conceptualized nation as a political community, which may have been constituted by different national tribes ('národní kmeny'), but was to be bound by shared moral obligations. The stress on the moral purpose of a national community meant that the nation was not seen as something given; rather it was the task ahead, the challenge that had to be met. In this view, the nation was just an instrument that was to be subordinated to the goal of furthering the universal human values (Patočka 1990: 51–3).

While Bolzano was as critical of German domination and the attempts at the Germanization of Bohemia as Palacký, he had no sentimental attachments to any particular language. In fact, he considered linguistic difference 'the greatest hurdle in the way of unanimity in our homeland'. As he argued,

> he who could bring it about that all the inhabitants of our homeland spoke only one language, would become the greatest benefactor of our nation; just as he who could introduce a single speech for the whole world would be the greatest benefactor of the human race.
>
> (Bolzano in Sayer 1998: 60)

Surely today it would be easy to dismiss Bolzano's vision as both unrealistic and undesirable (see the arguments of liberal nationalists elaborated in Chapters 1 and 2); but there can be no doubt that his radically modern ideas enriched the Bohemian discourse and proved to be useful as yet another source of inspiration for the ongoing debate about the meaning of Czech identity.

Moreover, to ask hypothetical questions about past events and developments helps to undermine the deterministic view of history in which there remains little space for individual responsibility. As Petr Pithart rightly pointed out, Patočka's musing about Bolzano was in some ways more directed towards the present and the future than the past. 'Patočka's seemingly anachronistic reference to Bolzano as a non-nationalistic alternative to the developments of Czech history ... was not only a formulation of an exciting and a challenging problem, but it was foremost an invitation to action'. To speculate about what could have happened if ... , serves as a reminder that 'in any given situation, there always exist alternatives, and therefore one can and must decide and act [in order to achieve these alternatives]' (Pithart 1998: 233). Patočka 'saw opportunities where others could not, or did not want to see them', which allowed him to become one of the crucial leaders of the Czech dissident movement, the goals of which at times considered as unrealistic as some of Bolzano's utopian visions (Pithart 1998: 234).

Despite Patočka's admiration, it was Palacký rather than Bolzano who was to exert a decisive influence on later Czech history and the content of Czech national identity. His thoughts on the historical necessity of cooperation between the nations of Central Europe as a defence against 'the universal monarchy' in Russia as well as against possible German dominance, seemed to have been fulfilled in the twentieth century. But it was unfortunate that the course of history made Palacký's preoccupation with conflict more relevant than his persistent calls for tolerance. The two world wars turned his thesis about the ongoing struggle between Germans and Slavs into a prophecy. The experience of foreign military domination not only had tragic consequences for the people directly affected by war, but also decisively weakened liberal tendencies in the development of Czech national identity. Even the humanist cosmopolitan Masaryk, who before the war criticized Palacký for focusing too much on national antagonisms, shifted with time more towards a conception that saw the newly created Czechoslovak state as a 'bulwark against German and Hungarian aggression' (Doležal 1998: 21). Anti-German sentiments were later skilfully utilized by the Czechoslovak communist state, the founding myth of which was the fight against German Nazism.[13] Peculiarly, it was possible to synthesize Engels's logic, which allows for the condemnation of a whole nation on the basis of its contribution (or lack of it) to the revolutionary progress of humanity, with Palacký's latently anti-German attitude.[14]

Masaryk and the Czechoslovak First Republic

Before the First World War, Masaryk was firmly convinced that political independence was not the most important goal of the Czech nation. 'Political independence will not save us', argued Masaryk, stressing instead 'an ever greater need for cooperation with other nations' (Masaryk in Kovtun 1990: 79). In 1918, in his programmatic speech to the National Assembly entitled 'Our People is Free and Independent', Masaryk appears to be markedly more reserved towards both Germans and Hungarians, despite his numerous assurances to the contrary (Masaryk in Kovtun 1990: 203). This was understandable given the historic context. The creation of the Czechoslovak First Republic was, after all, only made possible by the victory of the Western Alliance over Germany and Austria-Hungary. The First World War, in Masaryk's view, was a struggle between theocracy, represented by 'Prussianism, Austrianism and Genghis-Khanism' and modern 'non-militaristic democracies, defending the ideals of humanity' (Masaryk in Kovtun 1990: 192).

> We Czechs and Slovaks could not stand aside in this world-wide struggle....The building of our state and our resistance against German eastward expansion, our Reformation and its ideals, our suffering during the anti-reformation violence caused by the Habsburg rulers' misuse of religion for their base materialistic aims, as well as our national rebirth led by the idea of humanity and its consequence: democracy – the fate of our people is quite logically linked with the West and with modern Western democracy.
>
> (Masaryk in Kovtun 1990: 193)

This statement revives precisely those themes of Palacký which Masaryk had once rejected and even more ominously, it unambiguously excludes large portions of the population in the newly created state as the legitimate source of power as they were not *státotvorné národy*, that is the official constituent nationalities (Leff 1997: 24). Not included in 'we' and 'our people' were more than 3 million Germans, tellingly described as colonists, and some 700,000 Hungarians. The German 'minority', which actually outnumbered Slovaks in the first Czechoslovak Republic (3,123,000 versus 2,190,000 – see Craig 1984: 476), was forced to accept the new arrangement 'in the best interests of their economic progress' (Masaryk in Kovtun 1990: 199). In fact, the whole concept of a 'Czechoslovak' people was created in order to outweigh numerically and politically the influence of the German population (Pithart 1997: 547).[15] Whatever Masaryk's original intentions, 1918 brought into existence a unitary nation-state. As Erazim Kohák astutely observed, 'in one of history's ironies, the erstwhile supporter of a humanistic, federalized Austria and a critic of national chauvinism returned to his homeland at the war's end as a triumphant hero of Czech nationalism' (Kohák 1989: 10–11).

Still, measured against the many failures of democratic regimes in continental Europe in the 1920s and 1930s (e.g. Poland, Hungary, Italy, Germany), the Czechoslovak First Republic was a remarkable success in terms of political stability and economic prosperity. Even if the collective rights accorded to national minorities were rather minimal (Weidenhofferová 1996: 13), the observance of some basic rights of members of national minorities compared favourably with many of the country's contemporary neighbours (Hahn 1990: 99). Moreover, the Czechoslovak government, at times, included German ministers and it was not entirely inconceivable that a conception of an inclusive political Czechoslovak citizenship would at some stage replace the more restrictive notion (implied in the quotation above). But this was not to be.

The expansionist policies of Nazi Germany spelled an end to the democratic experiment of the First Republic. Hitler skilfully exploited the grievances of the German minority living in the Czechoslovak border territories (Sudetenland) and managed, in the name of national self-determination, to gain concessions from Britain and France. In September 1938, at the notorious conference in Munich, the Western powers accepted the secession of a large part of Czechoslovak territory in the hope of retaining 'peace in our time'. Tellingly, the Czechoslovak leadership was not even invited to the negotiations, and President Beneš was simply confronted with an ultimatum, which he unwillingly accepted. The policy of appeasement did not bring the results that the Western powers hoped for. By March 1939, the entire territory of the Czech lands was controlled by German troops and the former Czechoslovakia was divided into a Protectorate of Bohemia and Moravia, and the Slovak quasi-independent Nazi puppet state (while some parts of the borderland were incorporated into Poland and Hungary). Munich became a painful reminder of the limited power of the Czech nation to defend itself against more powerful neighbours, and the starting point of an ominous chain of historic events in which violence became the standard means of solving political and national conflicts. Thus, when the Czech-German writer Libuše Moníková attempted to locate a point in time when 'totalitarianism in Czechoslovakia originated', she pinpointed 1938 (cited in Eder 1999: 91).

The question remains, however, to what extent Czechoslovakia was just a victim of the inimical international context, or whether its failure was partly made possible from within. How liberal was the Czechoslovak First Republic? Was it an island of democracy and Western values in the middle of a Europe which was increasingly dominated by totalitarian regimes, as the defenders of Masaryk's heritage want us to believe? Or was it merely a precursor of Beneš's 'totalitarian democracy' of 1945–8 (Kučera 1998a), which in turn paved the way for the communist takeover of February 1948?

The 'meaning' of the Czechoslovak First Republic

Norman Davies noted that 'Czechoslovakia had a reputation for democracy that was stronger abroad than among the country's own German, Slovak, Hungarian, Polish and Ruthenian minorities' (Davies 1996: 979). But from the early years of the republic up to the present times, there have also been many vocal and influential Czech critics identifying the flaws of the Czechoslovak First Republic. Masaryk's contemporary Emanuel Rádl objected to the very founding idea of the newly created state. The idea that the Czechs, as one of the 'state creating' nations, conceded rights to other national minorities already implies an unequal relationship between nationalities, one which violates the basic principles of equality (Hahn 1990: 107). This ideology was, according to Rádl, the expression of a specific Central European nationalism which had a mystical character and the tendency to put national goals above the interests of individuals. Against the mythical concept of an organic connection between the nation (*lid*) and the state, Rádl proposed a conception of a contractual state (*smluvní stát*).

> In a contractual state, justice is more primary than state and law; the laws are thus not serving the state, or the people (*lid*), or the nation, rather their only purpose is to secure order which would allow the people to follow all those tasks which are not prohibited by law.
>
> (Rádl in Znoj and Sekera 1995: 346)

Rádl's stress on the priority of individual rights, rather than any higher goals of the state or the nation, bear a striking resemblance to some contemporary theories of liberalism. His *smluvní stát* could, in fact, be translated into more contemporary language as a 'procedural republic' (Sandel 1996: 4) which is predicated on the idea that the organization of societies must be based on clearly defined set of rules, which people of vastly different opinions and conceptions of the good can reasonably agree on; justice is hence produced through just procedures. As Rádl put it, 'reasonable people accept that it is not possible to live in a society, unless [they] endow it with a state and laws...which will correspond with their needs' (Rádl in Znoj and Sekera 1995: 346).[16]

Rádl paid close attention to the treatment of national minorities in the Czechoslovak First Republic. In particular, he criticized the lack of respect for the needs of the German and Hungarian citizens who were forced to accept unfavourable laws and conditions simply because their people lost the war. Rádl was convinced that individual human rights can only be fully realized if the state also accepts collective rights. He introduced a notion of collective human rights (*lidská práva kolektivní*), which are a logical extension of individual rights (rather than standing in opposition to them). Rádl's way of reasoning anticipates some of the arguments of present-day communitarians and their conceptions of a multicultural society, in which respect for the needs of a collective is considered a necessary corollary of the respect for basic individual rights.

Individual human rights, according to Rádl, are founded on the idea of the moral responsibility of individuals, and hence they take precedence over the interests of the state since the 'moral consciousness of individuals stands higher than any law of the state' (Rádl in Znoj and Sekera 1995: 348–9; cf. Havel 1999a: 6). Similarly, the interests of the state must be subordinated to the interests of its national minorities:

> Races, tribes and nationalities have a right to life, i.e. human societies and states must be organised in such a way that would avoid any restrictions of that right, apart from all those rules in a free society which also restrict any of its individual members. In this sense the right of nationalities is natural, original, basic and more primary than any other law of the state. *The state is the servant of nationalities and not their ruler.*
>
> (Rádl in Znoj and Sekera 1995: 351)

Rádl's critical voice directed against narrow-minded ethnocentric Czech particularism was not isolated. The content and the political expression of Czech nationalism were not only affected by intellectuals, or politicians, but they were also strongly influenced by new and exciting artistic developments. As Derek Sayer has impressively demonstrated, Czech avant-garde culture of the interwar period was outward looking and thrived on the fruitful exchange between Czech, German and Jewish elements within the multicultural society of the Czechoslovak First Republic. Modernist writers and artists challenged, or even ridiculed the state-sponsored 'official Czechness' that was strongly indebted to the tradition developed in the nineteenth century, and keenly endorsed *'a new style, a style of all liberated humanity, an international style*, which will liquidate provincial culture and art' (quoted from a 1922 poetic manifesto of the group 'Devětsil' in Sayer 1998: 213). Undoubtedly, some of the cosmopolitan aspirations of the avant-gardists appear today no less utopian than Bolzano's concepts from the middle of the nineteenth century (see above). But they are a clear illustration of the fact that the Czechs were not destined to turn towards ever more ethnocentrism, resulting in the 'ethnic purity' (Pithart 1993) of the present Czech Republic.

With the benefit of hindsight, it is easy to argue that Rádl's conception of a genuinely multicultural Czechoslovak state had as little chance of succeeding as the cosmopolitan projects of avant-garde culture. But Rádl's ideas have been instrumental as a point of reference for the exploration of liberal values within Czech society – whether it be in academic journals (e.g. Znoj 1997: 504–5), or in the popular press. Characteristically, shortly after the birth of the Czech Republic, the former prime minister Petr Pithart recalled Rádl's 1928 seminal work, *Válka Čechů s Němci (The War between Czechs and Germans)*, in order to strengthen the civic principle in the newly created state (Pithart 1993).

Despite Rádl's original insights, what is still hotly disputed amongst contemporary political analysts and historians is whether the failure of the Czechoslovak First Republic was brought about primarily by international developments, or rather by the inherent flaws of the existing model. While Jaroslav Opat, for example, has defended 'Czechoslovakism', the founding idea of the state, by arguing that it was 'conceptualised and realised by Masaryk as *a regional project of democratic Europeanism*' (Opat 1999: 14), Bohumil Doležal has dismissed it as a clever and 'dishonest Czech trick which simply substituted Czech with Czechoslovak' (Doležal 1998: 22). Correspondingly, Opat is convinced that the failure of the republic was ultimately caused by the Western policy of appeasement which made the German occupation possible, whereas Doležal argues that the Czechs must also blame themselves as 'they created a state which could not have been reformed' (Doležal 1998: 22). As Doležal put it, 'it is true that the Czechs attained freedom and democracy – but only for themselves, despite the fact that they included in their state also other peoples. But this fact had a negative impact on the quality of Czech democracy' (Doležal 1998: 23).

According to Jan Patočka and Petr Pithart, Czechs are also responsible for the actual downfall of the republic, since they failed to defend it against the invader, missing the historic chance 'to play an honourable role in the European crises' (Tucker 1996: 208). As Pithart put it, 'in the autumn of 1938 we failed to understand that it was not only Europe which could have helped us, but rather we should have helped Europe' (Pithart 1998: 138, 149). The Czechs should have been able to make sacrifices in order to defend their liberal democratic state, but unfortunately, they largely accepted Beneš's capitulation in 1938 and eventually adapted themselves to the new regime installed after the ensuing German occupation of the whole territory of Bohemia and Moravia in March 1939.[17] What followed was, according to Patočka, a long history of petty provincialism and collaboration with the powers that be – whether it was with Nazi Germany post-1938, or the Soviet Union post-1948, or again after the fall of Alexander Dubček in April 1969.

The significance of the Czechoslovak First Republic remains as much contested for the Czechs as does the meaning of the pre-partition 'noble republic' for the Poles. In both cases, these debates reach far beyond the limited circles of the academic community, as they are of concern for anyone who wants to understand, or redefine the very meaning of national identity. It is revealing that the title of Patočka's historical study is *Was sind die Tschechen?* (*What are the Czechs?*). Likewise, a recent collection of essays by Petr Pithart dealing mostly with Czech history is called *Po devětaosmdesátém: Kdo jsme?* (*After 1989: Who are we?*). Hence the disputes about the correct interpretation of past events cannot be settled once and for all, since all debates about the desired content of national identity must remain by their very nature open-ended.

At any rate, this is not the place to decide which account of the failure of the Czechoslovak First Republic is more accurate (even though any balanced analysis would have to conclude that the reasons for collapse were both internal *and* external). What proved to be crucial for the further path of history was that Palacký's original understanding of Czech history as a constant struggle between Slavic and Germanic elements was reinforced to the detriment of more liberal elements of Czech nationalism. In addition, this concept made it easy radically to change strategic alliances, as after the betrayal of the West it seemed only logical to turn towards the Stalinist Soviet Union. As Derek Sayer has commented,

It is one of the more tragic ironies of modern Czech history that because events of 1938–45 so brutally confirmed the old stereotypes of the *obrození* [National Revival] – Germans as the oppressors, the Czechs as an exposed Slav peninsula jutting into the indifferent seas of Western Europe, Russians as liberators – this nineteenth-century discourse could be revived and mobilized as a central component of postwar reconstruction and eventually used to legitimate a revolution whose methods and objectives would have horrified most *buditelé* [leaders of the National Revival] themselves.

(Sayer 1998: 223)

Thus concepts of Czech history and the self-understanding of the Czech nation, from Dalimil's Chronicle through the Hussites and from Palacký to Masaryk, proved to be a highly ambivalent heritage, which could have been used as much for the legitimation of revolutionary violence and chauvinistic excesses, as for the establishment of a tolerant liberal democracy. The equivocal character of this Czech tradition manifested itself during the eventful years of the aftermath of the Second World War. The postwar republic led by Masaryk's former colleague, President Edvard Beneš, adopted features of parliamentary democracy, but also imposed some damaging restrictions on certain political subjects, and denied basic human rights to its German and Hungarian citizens. Beneš's republic, following the approval of the victorious Allies at the Potsdam Conference (May 1945), sanctified the expulsion of the German minority and in that way accepted the use of violence as a legitimate means of political struggle. While it is open to debate whether Kučera's term 'totalitarian democracy' accurately describes the political character of the post-Second World War republic (Kučera 1998a), there can be little doubt that its shortcomings made the communist takeover considerably easier than it otherwise would have been.

Was Beneš's 1945–8 republic a totalitarian democracy?

During his exile in London, Beneš made the decision to once and for all 'solve' the problems of Czech-German coexistence by the violent expulsion of up to 3 million Germans living in Czechoslovakia, as rightful revenge for their support of Nazi occupation (Kučera 1998a: 75). As he stated upon his return to Prague, in May 1945:

> It will be necessary…to liquidate out [*vylikvidovat*] especially uncompromisingly the Germans in the Czech lands and the Hungarians in Slovakia, in whatever way this liquidation can further the interest of a united state of Czechs and Slovaks. Let our motto be: to definitively de-Germanize [*odgermanizovat*] our homeland, culturally, economically, politically.

(Sayer 1998: 241)

President Beneš found an enthusiastic supporter in Klement Gottwald, who was then deputy prime minister and the leader of the communist party. In Gottwald's interpretation, the expulsion of Germans was a logical result of undoing past injustices; an attempt at 'redressing the White Mountain' and 'correcting the mistakes of our Czech kings, the Přemyslids, who invited the German colonists here for us' (Sayer 1998: 241). The advocacy of chauvinist policies based on the idea of collective guilt would appear inconsistent with the ideology of the party which subscribed openly to the ideal of proletarian internationalism. Some fifteen years earlier, the very same Gottwald had claimed that his 'party held other social solidarities to be more binding than nationality' (Sayer 1998: 167). In his maiden speech to the Czechoslovak parliament in 1929, he openly admitted the close links of his party with the Russian communists against the charges of lack of patriotism. Attacking the liberal democratic parties, he said: 'we are the party of the Czechoslovak proletariat and our highest revolutionary headquarters really is Moscow. And we go to Moscow to learn, you know what? We go to Moscow to learn from the Russian Bolsheviks how to wring your necks' (Gottwald cited in Sayer 1998: 167).

The attitude of the Czechoslovak communists is hence not entirely inconsistent. First, they remained true to their basic strategy of using violence as a legitimate means of political struggle.[18] Second, the Czechoslovak communists still found inspiration in Moscow. Stalin fought not only against Nazism but also against the German people. Turning himself into a spokesman of neo-Slavism, he declared blatantly:

> I hate Germans. The First World War took place at the expense of the Slavs, and the Second World War…is being solved on their back.…This time we shall destroy the Germans so that they can never again attack the Slavs.
>
> (Stalin in Zeman and Klimek 1997: 236–7)

The abomination of Germans as a nation bearing responsibility for Nazi crimes against Jews and the fomenting of the Second World War was understandable, and surely not limited to Russian or Czech political leaders. But while the condemnation of a whole nation is on one level congruous with the revolutionary logic of communists, who are primarily concerned with collectivities (they only needed to substitute classes for nations),[19] the notion of collective guilt is incompatible with any concept of liberalism which is concerned foremost with individuals and their rights. It was therefore particularly tragic for the further development of Czechoslovakia that Edvard Beneš, who was the leader of liberal democratic forces, pushed forward the concept of collective punishment of a whole ethnic group.

It has to be stressed that the Western allies also endorsed the expulsion of the German population from the Czech lands (even though with significantly less enthusiasm than Stalin), but this does not free the Czech political leadership and its supporters from responsibility for these actions. The standard defence of these policies is, in fact, based on the consent of the Western Allies to this postwar settlement. Characteristic of this line of argument is the description of events in a recent historic study on Czechoslovakia by Pavel Machonin:

the victors decided that the *transfer* of the German population from the Czech borderland to *their motherland* would best serve the preservation of peace in Europe....The Czechoslovak president, the coalition government, with the participation of both socialist and civil democratic parties and the Czech and Slovak people, welcomed and carried out this decision immediately after the war.

(my italics, Krejčí and Machonin 1996: 150)

This account turns the logic of events on its head. While Beneš was in fact anxious to receive the approval of the Western Allies for his plans (Zeman and Klimek 1997: 226), in Machonin's interpretation the Czechoslovak political leaders simply followed the directives of 'the victors'.[20] The quote is revealing in two further respects. First, because it employs the euphemism 'transfer', a term which has been a subject of controversy in Czech and German historic debates as it implies – unlike the enforced expulsion – an orderly and peaceful resettlement of a group of people. Thus while apologists of the postwar 'solution of the German problem' usually talk about *odsun* (transfer), critics of the policy of revenge term it *vyhnání* (expulsion).[21] Second, the term 'motherland' applied to Germany deprives Czechoslovak Germans of their home country and in that way accepts the Nazi logic which defined belonging to a country by virtue of blood, reflected in its call *Heim ins Reich*.

The corollary of the view that the 'transfer' of the Czechoslovak Germans was simply the result of a decision by the major powers is the widespread perception that the establishment of the communist system of power was largely a result of agreements at the Yalta conference in which the West accepted Stalin's strategic interests in Central Europe. In contrast to this type of reasoning, Rudolf Kučera has convincingly argued that Beneš was not only personally responsible for the morally reprehensible actions against the German population of Czechoslovakia, but his policies also unwittingly paved the way for the communist takeover, as they undermined the conception of a state of law and respect for basic human rights. Moreover, despite the persistent popular belief that communism was only imported into Czechoslovakia as an alien ideology from the East, increasingly, Czechs are openly confronting the fact that this ideology had strong indigenous roots and enjoyed 'genuine support in the Czech working class and intelligentsia before 1948' (Williams 1997: 134).

The support for simplistic solutions offered by the ideology of communism was increased by the general radicalization of politics after the Second World War, and was also strengthened inadvertently by specific arrangements which privileged the Communist Party of Czechoslovakia. The Košice Government Programme of May 1945, endorsed jointly by communists (led by Gottwald) and liberal democratic forces (led by Beneš), created a political framework which allowed for illiberal practices and the ensuing communist takeover of February 1948. According to Kučera, the newly created system relied on the existence of 'totalitarian institutions' – such as local national committees (Národní výbory) and the state-wide National Front (Národní fronta) – which were dominated by the communist party and proved to be an effective instrument of its political power. Both institutions were crucial, for example, in the implementation of anti-German policies. From early on, however, the Czechoslovak communists were aware of the necessity to control and influence not only daily policies but also the very thoughts of their citizens. Hence they had totalitarian aspirations. Willing to determine the thoughts and ideas of a nation, the Czechoslovak communists 'used the National Front in order to control national consciousness and to impose the content and form of post-war national identity which would best serve their own interests' (Kučera 1998a: 79). This strategy was applied with enhanced vigilance after 1948.

Kučera's critical assessment of this eventful period in Czech history is increasingly becoming accepted in the mainstream. In fact, it is telling that when the Czech upper house decided, on the tenth anniversary of the fall of communism, to establish a memorial centre, the Památník doby nesvobody ('Memorial of the Age of Unfreedom'), the time covered by the centre was to be 1939–89. Despite isolated proposals that the time should not include 1945–8, a clear majority of senators decided in favour of its inclusion. As senator Daniel Kroupa (ODA – Civic Democratic Alliance) argued, 'the three years after the Second World War must be included in the age of unfreedom'. Even though the people celebrated May 1945 as a liberation from totalitarian Nazism, 'they at the same time freely decided to enter into a new slavery, which was communism' (*Mladá fronta dnes*, 14 November 1999). This interpretation of postwar developments poses a serious challenge to one of the most pervasive Czech myths – that of being repeatedly a mere victim of external circumstances. By acknowledging the mistakes of the democratic elites and the extent of popular support for totalitarian alternatives, people also accept domestic responsibility for communism.[22]

The communist regime derived a great deal of its legitimacy from presenting itself as a logical result 'of the great traditions of the Czech nation' (Sayer 1998: 311; see also Kemp 1999: 95). In that way, the revolutionaries were able to combine (somewhat paradoxically) a radical new beginning with a comforting sense of continuity. Zdeněk Nejedlý (1878–1962), a passionate nationalist thinker who had a successful academic career already in the First Republic, was the very embodiment of this sense of continuity. In 1945 he became minister for education and national enlightenment representing the Communist Party, and remained in influential political positions until his death in 1962 (see Sayer 1998: 303–313; Kemp 1999: 104–123). Nejedlý's major accomplishment, according to a standard 1972 Czech encyclopaedia, was that he 'always saw the ultimate fulfilment of all the progressive traditions of Czech and Slovak history in socialism and communism' (Academia 1972: 768). This view represents a succinct definition of the (then) new official historiography which helped to sustain the communist regime. To rephrase this, adding a touch of cynicism: 'the red chauvinism of the communist ideologist Zdeněk Nejedlý' (Doležal 1998: 18) became 'a central pillar of the totalitarian system' (Skilling 1989: 101).

The Czechoslovak dissidents, if they were successfully to challenge the existing order, had to reclaim a sense of national identity and prevent its monopolization by the communist regime. Thus it is not accidental that some of the most controversial debates within opposition circles concerned Czech history and its impact on the self-understanding of the nation. The first dissenting views of history came from within the established professional circles in the 1960s, as a result of partial liberalization of the regime (Skilling 1989: 103–5). However, after the suppression of the Prague Spring in 1968 and the 1970s policy of normalization, the spread of alternative views was only possible through samizdat publications. One of those, issued in 1977 under the pseudonym Danubius, sparked a lively debate about the significance of the expulsion of Germans. Danubius argued that the use of violence against the Germans could not be excused, and was not 'the behaviour of the nation of Hus and Masaryk and Štefánik. An ancient cultured and civilised nation must find within itself the strength to re-evaluate the deeds of its politicians and draw a lesson from them'. To come to terms with this historic legacy was necessary in order 'to help the nation to absolve itself of its guilt, concealed in collective silence and tacit approval' (Skilling 1989: 117).

After Danubius was found to be the prominent Slovak historian and Charter 77 signatory Ján Mlynárik, he was imprisoned without trial for a year and subsequently emigrated (Skilling 1989: 119). His treatment is testimony to the communist regime's determination to guard the one and only right view of history. Mlynárik was attacked not only by the communist regime, but was branded a 'Czechophobe' even by some of his fellow dissidents. These attacks were misguided. Liberal nationalists should not blindly revere their own nation. 'They can be critical of it; they can aspire to change it, develop it, or redefine it' (Tamir 1993: 89). Hence there is no contradiction between Mlynárik's critical stance and the claim in his defence stating that 'he wrote [the study] out of love for the Czech nation' (Skilling 1989: 259). It is worthwhile noting that Mlynárik was concerned with the Czechoslovak tradition, recalling not only Czech national heroes (Hus, Masaryk) but also the Slovak politician Štefánik (see also Chapter 5).

Mlynárik's thesis undermined one of the founding myths of the communist regime, and offers an instructive illustration of a critical approach to national history which is characteristic of liberal nationalism. Both communists and liberals used history partly as a didactic device to 'draw a lesson'. But while communists had to rely on myths and distorted views of history, liberal nationalists were able to engage in an open-ended debate which does not shy away from examining 'darker' aspects of history and which can challenge the dominant understanding of one's own nation.[23] In that sense liberal nationalists can and should do without a 'mythopoeic vision' (Williams 1997: 132) of their nation, and rather utilize debates about past achievements and failures in order to situate universal liberal values within the particular context of their national culture and history. Controversies about the right interpretation of the past can serve as a frame of reference for addressing more general issues. Kučera, for example, concluded his study on the 1945–8 'totalitarian democracy' by arguing that the adopted principle of collective guilt was 'incompatible with any concept of liberal democracy as it builds on the collectivistic ideal of a unified and closely-knit national community, while liberalism is based on individuality' (Kučera 1998a: 78). In other words, 'liberal democracy is not about the rule of a nation, or a united national community, but the rule of law' (Kučera 1998a: 78).

Against the background of these debates within dissident circles, it seems logical that very shortly after Václav Havel was elected president of Czechoslovakia (29 December 1989), he turned his attention to the Czech-German relationship. Three days after his election he visited the two German states (then still divided) and apologized for the postwar expulsion of Sudeten Germans. Havel was convinced that an honest examination of national history was a precondition for the success of the new liberal democratic project. In line with Mlynárik, he repudiated the principle of collective guilt and saw the crimes committed in its name destructive not only for the victims, but also for the perpetrators themselves. As Havel put it, speaking on behalf of his nation at the official visit of German president Richard von Weizsäcker to Prague in March 1990,

> [W]e hurt ourselves even more [than our victims]. We settled accounts with totalitarianism in a way that allowed the spirit of totalitarianism to penetrate our own activities and thus our own souls. Shortly afterward, it returned to us cruelly in the form of our inability to resist a new totalitarianism imported from elsewhere. And what is more, many of us actively helped that other totalitarianism into the world.
>
> (Havel 1997b: 23)

Havel's apology to the Germans was a conscious attempt to break with the logic of revenge, but it could also be seen as a practical expression of his rejection of the Marxist understanding of history, which sees all human developments as histories of violent revolutions and ruthless struggles for power (Havel 1991: 97). Moreover, Havel's symbolic gesture could have been defended also on pragmatic grounds, since a good relationship with neighbouring Germany was vital for political and economic reasons. But the decisively conciliatory stance *vis-à-vis* Germany proved one of the first controversial decisions of the newly elected president. It was met with widespread disapproval by the public, and was strongly criticized in particular by the Czechoslovak communists who, once again, tried to capitalize on the latent chauvinism of large sections of the Czech population (Obrman

1994).[24] It could also be argued the idea of a symbolic apology in the name of the Czech nation is inconsistent. While Havel's apology rejects the notion of the collective guilt of the Germans, it implies a sense of collective responsibility for 'the Czechs', who are seen as guilty for the expulsion.

Although Havel's moral determination to do what he believed to be the right thing cost him popularity, and thus was damaging for him politically (at least in the short term), what must be considered his achievement was the initiation of an open debate about the meaning of Czech history, which concerned the very foundations of the new liberal democratic system. As Havel reiterated in March 1993, referring to the recently created Czech state,

> We are building a new democratic state based on law; we are building a civil society. This state cannot be based on misguided notions, lies, or prejudices. I am concerned about the hygiene of our national consciousness. We thus have to be able to face our own past.
>
> (Havel cited in Obrman 1993: 45)

The willingness of the Czech political elites to 'face the past' was, however, rather limited. The first tentative attempt to deal with the postwar expulsion of Germans found its expression in the official Czech-German Declaration adopted in January 1997 by the prime ministers and endorsed by the parliaments of both countries. While the declaration stated that 'the Czech side regrets that the forced expulsion and forced resettlement of Sudeten Germans...inflicted great suffering and injustice on innocent people', it did not explicitly address the question of the moral legitimacy of these policies. The declaration was meant to mark a new beginning in Czech-German relations, as both sides also agreed that 'injustice inflicted in the past belongs in the past' (Kramer 2001: 23). However, those politicians on both sides who hoped that the declaration would settle the controversies about the expulsion once and for all were proven wrong.

In anticipation of the enlargement of the European Union, Hungarian, Austrian and German politicians (e.g. Viktor Orbán, Wolfgang Schüssel, Edmund Stoiber) called on the Czech Republic to repeal the Beneš decrees, which they saw as contravening European law and the underlying principles of the European Union. In response, the (then) Czech prime minister Miloš Zeman defended the decrees, arguing that the expulsion was a more 'benign' solution to the postwar problem of Czech-German coexistence, considering that treason (committed in Zeman's view by the Sudeten Germans) was ultimately worthy of a death sentence (Coudenhove-Kalergi and Rathkolb 2002: 13). Václav Klaus, then leader of the largest opposition party, the Civic Democratic Party (ODS), was equally uncompromising and demanded that the institutions of the European Union actually acknowledge the inviolability of the Beneš decrees. Even Václav Havel changed, to some extent, his earlier position by defending Beneš as a politician who had to face difficult moral dilemmas, not unlike his Western counterparts – the likes of Churchill and Roosevelt (Havel 2002: 36; cf. Mandler 2001: 110).

While the controversial issue did not impede the process of European enlargement, the external pressure reinforced the divisions within the Czech political sphere, and seemed to have strengthened the position of those politicians who advocated a more uncompromising stance towards the expulsion. This may partly account for the unexpected success of the Czech Communist Party in the June 2002 elections (18.5 per cent), which once again sought to mobilize its supporters not only by stressing economic grievances, but also with its anti-German rhetoric. Later, the narrow victory of Václav Klaus, who became the Czech president in February 2003, was to some extent due to the fact that he was seen as the best defender of Czech national sovereignty (Němeček 2003). Klaus received support from the communist members of the parliament and the upper house, who found him less objectionable than the alternative candidate, Jan Sokol, known for his 'pro-German' stance.

These recent developments have demonstrated the potency of ethnocentric nationalism within Czech society. This is not to say that 'the Czech nation is xenophobic' by nature, but it is plausible to suggest that some Czech historic myths are quite xenophobic (Třeštík 1998: 146). Hence it was possible to stir anti-German sentiments by using references to historic figures and events. As the Czech historian Dušan Třeštík argued, it is lamentable, for example, that Dalimil became 'the prototype of "the loyal Czech" rather than of little Czechness' (Třeštík 1998: 146; cf. Pynsent 2000: 352). What the Czechs need, according to Třeštík, is 'to re-invent the nation' in order to make it better (*ibid.*). Yet liberal nationalists need not rely on the creation of new myths, but rather they can critically engage with the prevalent conception of national history. Furthermore, some aspects of Czech national history can also be employed in support of liberal values.

Debates about liberalism: is there a Czech way?

Havel has consistently argued that political concepts and systems must be firmly grounded in moral principles that are unconditionally valid. Accordingly, he has sought to reconstruct the foundation of liberal democracy by employing concepts like 'transcendence' and 'the order of Being' that point to an older tradition of (metaphysical) philosophizing. The intimate link between morality and political actions had been exemplified by Havel's own personal experience as a dissident who was able to resist the pressure to conform to a morally reprehensible political system. Later, when he became president, it seemed possible for him to turn his ambitious aspirations towards changing the style and nature of politics, from a cynical power game to an occupation with a higher moral purpose; the Czechs were to enjoy another philosopher-king head of state.

Havel's ideal of responsible politics is congruent with his notion of 'living in truth', which he considers to be not only his personal maxim, but a more universal lesson which the Czech nation, with its unique historical experience, can share with the wider world.

> It is certainly not accidental that precisely here, in this part of the world in which identities – whether they be personal, cultural, or national – were repeatedly threatened and had to be defended, that a strong and lasting tradition of an idea of truth as a significant moral value has developed, for which one has to be prepared to pay. This tradition goes back, after all, to Cyril and Methodius through Hus, Masaryk, Štefánik and Patočka.
>
> (Havel 1991: 113)

This approach to politics is certainly integral to the Czech political tradition (going back in various degrees to Palacký, Masaryk, Rádl, Patočka) but it has also been under considerable attack by influential liberal thinkers in the West. Paradoxically, the political philosophy of dissidents who responded to the challenges of a communist totalitarian regime can be criticized by the theoretical tools developed as earlier responses to Nazi and Stalinist totalitarianism (e.g. Popper, Berlin). Since the publication of Karl Popper's *The Open Society and Its Enemies* (Popper 1945), for example, the notion of the 'philosopher king' has had distinctively negative connotations, since it could imply an enlightened dictator who can free his subjects from the 'burden' of freedom by making the right choices for them. Later, Isaiah Berlin explicitly warned against the employment of metaphysical concepts as the ultimate justification for liberal societies, as they could interfere with individual conceptions of the good. More recently still, Richard Rorty has attempted to redefine the terms of discussion, claiming that liberal societies would profit from abandoning useless, or even dangerous 'language games' concerned with 'devotion to truth', or 'fulfillment of the deepest needs of the spirit'. He envisaged a culture of liberalism 'in which no trace of divinity remained, either in the form of divinized world or a divinized self' (Rorty 1989: 45; cf. Rorty 1991).

In line with these arguments, specialists concerned with the processes of democratic transition and consolidation consider the political tradition which developed as a response to the totalitarian communist state a possible liability for a 'standard' democratic system. Juan Linz and Alfred Stepan, for example, explicitly warn against the 'anti-political' tendencies implicit in the notion of living in truth. While 'ethical civil society represents truth', a mature consolidated democracy must be built around a political society which represents interests (Linz and Stepan 1996: 272). What is needed, therefore, are not so much high-principled, heroic politicians like Havel, but pragmatists who can represent 'normal interest-based political parties' (Linz and Stepan 1996: 273).

Czech intellectuals, like their Polish counterparts (see Chapter 3), have questioned the wisdom of the dominant versions of political liberalism in the West (e.g. Rawls, Rorty) and its applicability to the problems of post-communist transition, or even its usefulness to the well established democracies of the West. The Czech philosopher Miloslav Bednář, for example, has lamented the 'contemporary crisis of democracy' which stems, in his view, largely from the incapability of many current political philosophies 'to overcome relativistic indifference in moral and spiritual affairs' (Bednář 1998: 89; cf. Pithart 1998: 219). An alternative can be offered by the Czech tradition of political philosophy which 'systematically repudiates a conception of politics which pushes religion and spiritual values exclusively into the private sphere' (Bednář 1998: 107). In congruence with the maxim that the Czech concern is a human concern (*věc česká je věc lidská* – see above), Bednář is convinced that the lessons to be learned from the Czech experience with totalitarianism can be useful for the wider world.

> To take this lesson seriously [at the centre of which is the priority of spiritual and moral dimensions in dealing with political issues] means to rethink thoroughly the dominant concepts of liberalism, human rights and democracy....The democratic world has to find its way back to its original mission, which has been clearly formulated by the Czech tradition of political philosophy.
>
> (Bednář 1998: 125)

Bednář's preoccupation with the spiritual and/or philosophical dimensions of politics may come as a surprise given that the vast majority of Czechs, in contrast to the Polish people, appear to be indifferent, or even hostile to religion. As Doležal wryly remarked, 'the most popular Czech denomination seems to be nihilism' (Doležal 1999). Nevertheless, any study of the history of Czech political ideas would reveal a continuing interest in the philosophical (or in Rorty's terminology 'metaphysical') groundings of liberal democracy. The most plausible explanation for the endurance of this tendency could be (as in the Polish case – see Chapter 3) that the problems facing contemporary Czech society are closer to the concerns of Western classics (e.g. Locke, Kant, Mill, De Tocqueville), who were primarily interested in establishing a liberal democratic order, than to some contemporary liberal theorists who take the existence of a relatively stable liberal democracy for granted. As Roger Scruton argued, Czech thinking is strongly indebted to Kant and his moral philosophy which offers a comprehensive defence of basic liberal values, building on his doctrine that all autonomous human subjects must be treated as 'equal citizens of a "kingdom of ends"' (Scruton 1990b: 50).

Even Jan Patočka, who was influenced by the (anti-metaphysical) philosophies of Heidegger and Husserl, concedes 'the unconditional validity of [moral] principles' which ultimately define what 'being human means' (cited in Kohák 1989: 340–1). As he wrote in one of the crucial texts of Charter 77:

No society, no matter how well-equipped it may be technologically, can function without a moral foundation, without convictions that do not depend on convenience, circumstances, or expected advantage....The idea of human rights is nothing other than the conviction that even states, even society as a whole, are subject to the sovereignty of moral sentiment: that they recognize something unconditional that is higher than they are, something that is binding even on them, sacred, inviolable.

(Patočka in Kohák 1989: 341)

Patočka has exercised a tremendous influence not only on professional Czech philosophers (e.g. Pešková 1997; Bednář 1998), but also on Václav Havel, who revered his former private teacher and fellow dissident (Havel 1990a: 152–5; 1990b: 134–6; cf. Findlay 1999). Consequently, when Havel defended NATO's intervention in Kosovo, he adopted Patočka's line of reasoning by arguing that intervention was morally justified, even if it violated the idea of state sovereignty, since the inviolability of states is less important than the protection of individual human beings. The war in Kosovo marked, according to Havel, a decline in the importance of the nation-state and a move towards 'a global civil society'. In his view, 'human rights, human freedoms, and human dignity have their deepest roots somewhere outside the perceptible world'. This leads Havel to the assertion that 'while the state is a human creation, human beings are a creation of God' (Havel 1999a: 6).

One does not need to accept the charges of 'religious fundamentalism' laid against Havel by the influential Slovene philosopher Slavoj Žižek to realize that there are some inherent dangers in his conception of politics based on a higher morality (Žižek 1999: 4). When political decisions are motivated purely by moral considerations, however noble these may be, the principles of representative democracy may suffer, since countering arguments of competing interest groups may not get a fair chance for consideration. This problem was exemplified by a few decisions Havel made without proper consultations with the parties affected. Shortly after becoming the first (and last) postcommunist president of Czechoslovakia, Havel concluded that a country committed to the idea of international peace should stop exporting weapons. The self-imposed restrictions could only have been implemented swiftly by overriding the interests of workers employed in factories producing these weapons. The attempts to convert the large military plants to non-military production were not very successful and ultimately led to redundancies. This in turn partly exacerbated Czech-Slovak relations, as Slovakia was more deeply affected by the policy than the Czech lands. This example demonstrates a basic dilemma of intellectuals in politics who may be inclined to disregard the practical consequences of their actions in order to avoid compromising (their) truth.

In fact, it can be argued that an overly anti-political stance towards political processes could undermine the process of democratic transition. Havel, for example, repeatedly expressed scepticism towards aspects of standard institutional arrangements of liberal democracy, such as the working of political parties. In January 1990, he allegedly suggested radical solutions for a united Europe to the German prime minister Helmut Kohl: 'Why don't we work together to dissolve all political parties? Why don't we set up just one big party: the Party of Europe?' (Keane 1999: 464). Whether this was only an expression of initial enthusiasm growing out of the Velvet Revolution which seemed to defy all conventional wisdom about politics, or whether he was misquoted, the statement was consistent with Havel's political philosophy, which was permeated, especially during the times of his anti-communist resistance, with scepticism towards conventional political institutions (cf. Linz and Stepan 1996: 331–2). Later in his presidency, Havel and his advisers were criticized for being too far removed from the daily concerns of citizens (Kučera 1998b: 7).

Another problem with a conception of politics that is based on ethical values rather than relying primarily on institutional arrangements, is the need for morally impeccable leaders. Yet even Havel, who fully deserves admiration for his courage and determination in 'living in truth', did not (and probably could not) always live up to his own moral aspirations. In fact, increasingly, he was attacked for not accepting responsibility for his own mistakes, while freely criticizing many other political actors in Czech society. According to journalists Petr Fiala and František Mikš, for example, Havel lost his moral credibility by pretending that he could not have been held responsible for the Czech situation because he was 'too busy solving global and planetary problems' (Fiala and Mikš 1998: 73).[25]

Still, the problem of the appropriate source of morality in the political realm is urgent, and not only in the postcommunist world. Even the best institutional arrangements cannot sustain liberal democracy if they are not supported by public culture. Hence, despite the potential weaknesses of Czech liberal thinking (be it traditional or contemporary), the insights gained from its preoccupation with ethical aspects of politics could also inform contemporary Western theories of liberalism. As Michael Sandel argued in his influential study of *Democracy's Discontent* in America, 'the public philosophy by which we live cannot secure the liberty it promises, because it cannot inspire the sense of community and civic engagement that liberty requires' (Sandel 1996: 6). Havel's inspirational ideas, which are in some respects close to more traditional Western liberal thought, can thus be relevant to contemporary societies far beyond the Czech context. This may partly account for his popularity abroad and the emerging interest in Patočka's political philosophy (e.g. Lom 1999; Findlay 1999; Tucker 2000; Patočka 2002).

Václav versus Václav

While Havel was admired internationally, his domestic popularity had continuously declined, reflecting an overall sense of disillusionment which characterized Czech society in the late 1990s. The most outspoken domestic critic of Havel was probably Václav Klaus, the architect of Czech economic reform, and until November 1997 also a remarkably successful prime minister. In March 2003, Klaus celebrated a comeback as the Czech president. Klaus was highly critical of Havel's preoccupation with global civil society, and dismissed Havel's predictions about the decline of the nation-state as yet another transmutation of an unrealistic and potentially dangerous dream of a third way, which goes back to the Prague Spring of 1968, and is characterized by a futile search for a compromise between capitalism and socialism. Bemoaning the lack of commitment to the principles of the free market, Klaus went so far as to accuse Havel of being 'a half-socialist' (Keane 1999: 439).[26] Rather than looking for some specifically Czech way of approaching the problems of transition, Klaus consistently advocated the adoption of 'standard' democratic institutions and procedures. He was probably the first prominent politician who foresaw, immediately after 1989, the importance of a well organized political party with a clearly defined programme. Even Klaus, and his party the ODS, however, did not ignore the importance of accommodating universal liberal values within the context of a particular culture. As he put it,

> When I stress normal, standard and, therefore generally applicable solutions to political, social, and economic problems of the postcommunist countries, and not only them, I do not deny or underestimate all the diversity of culture, historical heritage, recent experience, natural endowment, climate, and so on; but our tasks and our challenges have undoubtedly more general than specific features.
>
> (Klaus 1997: 35)

In accordance with this view, new Czech liberals surrounding Klaus have, from very early on, attempted to enlist historical tradition 'to present a vision of the Czech nation as Europeans naturally inclined to democracy, hard work, commerce and self-reliance' (Williams 1997: 134). Klaus himself, despite being usually seen as a dry technocrat, made numerous references to Czech national history, recalling the heritage of St Wenceslas, St John Nepomucene, or T. G. Masaryk. Thus it should not have come as a surprise when, in the summer of 1999, Klaus' ODS party ignited a debate about the proper meaning of Czech national identity. Countering the global aspirations of Havel's moral philosophy, Czech liberals (re-)introduced into the current political discourse notions like homeland, nation and nation-state, and underlined their importance as 'natural entities of human societies with which people can identify' (Klaus in *Lidové noviny*, 3 June 1999).

Klaus' defence of the legitimacy of national interests, voiced against the background of the policies of ethnic cleansing in Kosovo and the ensuing NATO intervention, provoked a critical response in the Czech media (Znoj 1999). Typical was the reaction of Jan Ruml, who was then leader of the

Freedom Union (US) party. He contrasted the idea of a nation-state with the superior principle of a state built around civil society. Recalling the heritage of Emanuel Rádl, Ruml embraced the idea of European integration which renders the concept of nation-state obsolete. 'We can only be truly national', noted Ruml, 'if we realize that the nation within us is Europe within us (*národ v nás [je] Evropou v nás)*' (Ruml 1999).

Despite Ruml's legitimate criticism, it can be considered Klaus' achievement that he turned the issue of national identity into a legitimate topic for mainstream political parties. The best outcome of the debate would be a synthesis which rejects both an undue reverence for the nation-state and its demonization. As the Czech journalist Václav Žák rightly argued, 'civil society, rather than being in sharp opposition to a nation state, should be a part of it' (Žák 1999). Moreover, there is no necessary contradiction between following a national interest and a foreign policy orientated towards open and friendly relations with others. As Emanuel Mandler suggested, 'the Czech national interest is full integration into the European Union' (Mandler 1999a). In fact, there is a wide consensus amongst the mainstream political forces in the Czech Republic about the need for this integration, even if some parties have reservations about the appropriate modalities of entry. The ODS of Václav Klaus, in particular, was fairly sceptical about the benefits of European integration. In March 2001 the party produced the so-called 'Manifesto of Czech Eurorealism', which advocated an intergovernmental, rather than a supranational vision for the European Union, and contemplated the alternatives to EU membership (Zahradil *et al.* 2001). The following section considers to what extent the different views of leading politicians and their parties were reflected by the sentiments within the broader sections of the population.

Feeling miserable *(*blbá nálada*)*

Whereas immediately after the end of communism there seems to have been unanimous agreement between both domestic and foreign observers that the Czechs (at that time together with Slovaks) were best positioned to master the challenges of transition thanks to their democratic traditions, ten years later the mood was considerably more pessimistic. Apart from the fact that even the economic reforms had not gone as smoothly as the former prime minister Václav Klaus would have had many people believe, Czech society proved to be far less immune to problems usually associated with postcommunist transition – such as corruption within both the political and economic spheres (a corruption scandal, in fact, led to the demise of Klaus' government in November 1997); growing disillusionment with the new elites (exemplified by the hugely popular civic initiative 'Děkujeme, odejděte' ['Thank you and leave'] of the former student leaders of the 1989 revolution who, in November 1999, called on all the leading politicians to step down); and expressions of chauvinism and extreme nationalism (especially directed towards the Romany minority). Characteristically, when Havel described the situation of the country in March 1997 with his unforgettable 'blbá nálada' (feeling miserable), the term became an instant catch-phrase (*Lidové noviny*, 18 January 1999).

Czech tradition as a liability

Writing on the tenth anniversary of the Velvet Revolution, Bohumil Doležal blamed this decline in public spirit not only on the new elites exemplified by Havel and Klaus, but also on Palacký and the Czech tradition of political thinking. According to Doležal, the crisis could only be overcome if the people gave up the 'obscure conviction that to be Czech means to be democratic' (Doležal 1999).

> Unreflected Czech chauvinism resulted in the first stage of the post-November [1989] development in the conviction that Czech society, due to its essentially democratic spirit, can do without the trappings of formal democracy and turn directly to its real content. This clearly echoes Palacký's delusions about 'ancient Slav democracy' and it is an attempt, typical of all immature nations, to sell one's weaknesses as strengths....This ideology was only modified during Klaus' rule, since it was claimed that Czechs had capitalism in their blood and therefore provide the best material for the creation of exemplary democracy.
> (Doležal 1999)

Doležal's criticism highlights the possible downside of the Czech liberal tradition, which aspires to equate Czech concerns with human concerns (that is, once again, *věc česká je věc lidská*). If the idea is understood as a descriptive account of the already existing situation, it can certainly lead to complacency – people who are democratic virtually by definition do not need to prove their credentials with corresponding behaviour. Furthermore, the overemphasis on the 'highly civilized and democratic Czech tradition' (or alternatively the more open-ended Central European tradition) can lead to a 'superiority complex' and intolerance of those who are perceived as lacking in these traits – whether they be 'the agitated people in the Balkans' (Havel cited in Todorova 1997: 156), more emotional Slovaks,[27] or disorderly Romanies. Hence, the notion of 'civilized Czechs' can only be helpful for the cause of liberal nationalism if it is understood as a normative goal that is worth striving for, rather than a description of the existing situation. As in the Polish case (see Chapter 3), the formulation must be conceived as a 'persuasive definition' which aims at 'a redirection of people's attitudes' (Stevenson 1944: 210).

Admittedly, the delimitation between the descriptive *is* and the normative *ought to be* is not always clear. In fact, it could be argued that some of Havel's concepts unwittingly add to the confusion. For example, as Gellner pointed out, the notion of 'truth prevails' is unhelpful and even misleading when used as a tool in analysing complex social processes. Thus, when Havel argued that communism in Czechoslovakia 'was defeated by life, by thought, by human dignity' (Havel 1991: 98), or in other words by 'living in truth', he misread the historic events which were far more determined by the overall decline within the communist world and the external circumstances than by the morally sound behaviour of large sections of the Czech population (as Havel himself partly conceded later – see Havel 1999c). One could even argue that the system was ultimately defeated by human opportunism, as at some stage people simply realized that the communist system of power was doomed and they therefore quickly abandoned the 'sinking ship', following their own personal interests rather than some higher responsibility. Furthermore, if the concept of 'truth prevails' implies a historic-deterministic view of the world, it is questionable even on moral and empirical grounds. 'Truth does *not* [always] prevail' (original emphasis, Gellner 1994: 128), and to assume otherwise could allow for the moral justification of *any* historic outcome – even criminal regimes were, after all, successful at certain times in history.

Czechs and Roma

Fortunately, 'truth *did* prevail' in the case of the notorious wall in Ústí nad Labem, which was built by the city council in 1999 in an attempt to segregate a small community of Romanies from their 'white' neighbourhood. The story of a two-metre-high wall, which threatened to become a new symbol of racial intolerance and ethnic division in the postcommunist world, exemplifies the problems of dealing with ethnic and cultural diversity of the Czech Republic. The municipal authorities defended the controversial project against persistent domestic and international criticism by arguing that its purpose was not to separate Roma and Czechs, but 'respectable and unrespectable people without regard for the colour of their skin' (Radio Prague). Only a few weeks after its completion in October 1999, the wall was dismantled as a result of successful government intervention. Still, the demolition of the wall did not eliminate the negative attitudes of mainstream society. According to the results of a 1999 survey by the STEM agency, 90 per cent of Czechs denied that the Roma community, in general, was discriminated against, but they were also convinced that 'ethnic minorities living in the Czech Republic should try and adapt to the local way of life' (Radio Prague, 29 December 1999). At the same time, and somewhat paradoxically, according to surveys repeated in 1994 and 1996, 83 per cent of Czechs believed that Romanies cannot really change as 'their race is unadaptable' (Gabal 1999: 85). These attitudes place Romanies in a no-win situation, as they have little chance of being accepted by mainstream society, whether they remain different – since their difference would not be tolerated, or attempt to assimilate – for hardly any one would trust their transformation.

As was demonstrated in Chapter 2, there are no easy, ready-made solutions for dealing with ethnic and cultural diversity. Yet any attempts at improving the situation of the Romany minority in the Czech Republic is predicated on a radical change of the prevalent attitudes of the dominant culture. Liberal nationalism could be instrumental in bringing about this change by expanding and redefining the notion of 'civilized Czechs'. As Karel Holomek argued, the negative attitude of Czechs towards Romanies was exacerbated by some aspects of the Czech tradition. Linguistic nationalism, for instance, which goes back to the nineteenth-century Revival Movement, is partly responsible for the discrimination against Romanies, whose knowledge of Czech seldom meets the demands of the mainstream (Holomek 1999: 158). The primary measure of civility in liberal nationalism, however, must not be a perfect command of the Czech language, but the values of tolerance and human decency. As Havel argued on many occasions, the culture of a nation should not be measured 'by the visit of rock stars to the Czech Republic or the display of wares by prominent fashion designers' but by the treatment of disadvantaged groups like Roma (Fawn 2001: 1214). Most people in the Czech Republic would agree with Havel that 'the best Czechs were always the Czech Europeans'. The crucial question is, as Pynsent remarked, whether 'the Czechs will let the Gypsies be Europeans as well' (Pynsent 1999: 231). So far, there is a wide gap between the Czech self-image, which sees its own nation as the embodiment of the values of liberalism and tolerance, and the reality of the Czech-Romany relationship, characterized by hostilities and racial discrimination (see also Chapter 2).

Conclusion

The enduring tension between the Romany community and the dominant Czech society clearly disproves all the simplistic accounts of postcommunist developments, which assumed that the Czechs are immune to extreme (i.e. exclusionary) nationalism by virtue of their culture (according to popular self-perceptions observed by Holy 1996: 189); or have succeeded in marginalizing nationalism (e.g. Vachudová and Snyder 1997); or that the Czech nation has suddenly become the epitome of a 'Western' type of nationalism (Kořalka 1994: 275). Hence, the application of theoretical concepts based on 'two types of nationalism' (see Chapter 1) leads to analyses which are not only incomplete, but seriously misleading. The assumption that the Czech transition could only have been successful thanks to the marginalization or even elimination of nationalist sentiments, fails to explain the positive as well as the negative impact of nationalism on recent developments in Czech society. Such an approach cannot account for the importance of the use of national symbols and attachments in the defeat of Czechoslovak communism, but equally it fails to explain the more recent expressions of chauvinism and xenophobia, such as the mistreatment of the Romany minority.

Still, it would be just as misleading and crudely reductionist to argue that the Czechs are a nation of racists. The analysis of different discourses of nationalism and their impact on the political processes within Czech society can offer a significantly more complex picture. While the forces of extreme nationalism must not be underestimated, liberal nationalism in the Czech Republic has a very good chance of positively influencing the political process. As has been demonstrated, there are numerous influential voices within Czech political discourse(s) which advocate ethnic tolerance. The crucial question remains whether different aspects of liberal nationalism expounded by some leading politicians and intellectuals can find support within wide sections of the population. As in the Polish case (see Chapter 3), the results of Q-methodology research conducted by Dryzek and Holmes, which aimed at measuring public perceptions, clearly indicate that this is possible. Liberal nationalists will be able to build on the pre-existing sentiments expressed in the discourse labelled 'civic enthusiasm', which stresses the importance of the active involvement of citizens in democratic processes and the need for 'a civic culture and an active civil society' (Dryzek and Holmes 1998: 16; see also Dryzek and Holmes 2002: 240–52). As Dryzek and Holmes observed, 'Czech discourse's enthusiasm for democracy and participation knows few bounds, in both its approval of the emerging post-communist political system, and in its hopes for a fuller and deeper democracy in the future' (*ibid.*). This is promising because it shows that it is possible to combine a strong sense of national identity (proudly recalling the best traditions of the Czech nation while critically evaluating its failures in history) with a strong commitment to the universal values of liberal democracy. This uneasy combination of particularist attachments and universalistic ideals is the defining element of liberal nationalism, which, as a very real societal force, can positively influence the outcome of the post-communist transition of the Czech Republic.

5 Nationalism in Slovakia

In contrast to the Czech Republic, which was usually seen as a forerunner in the process of postcommunist transition, predictions for the Slovak Republic were considerably less optimistic. The very circumstances of the creation of the independent republic boded ill for the future of democracy in the country. The push for separation was led by Vladimír Mečiar, a politician notorious for his authoritarian style. Moreover, the independence gained on 1 January 1993 was strongly supported by extreme nationalists who proudly recalled the heritage of the first Slovak Republic (1939–45), which was a nazi puppet state. Slovakia, 'which has negatively distinguished itself from other postcommunist, newly independent states' (OSCE 1997), was hence considered a textbook example of a postcommunist country in which the legacies of the past would be a serious impediment to the establishment of liberal democracy.

The largely unchallenged rule of prime minister Mečiar and his Movement for a Democratic Slovakia (HZDS), which dominated the Slovak political scene until October 1998, seemed to have confirmed all the pessimistic predictions. His autocratic government was characterized by a lack of respect for the democratic opposition, repeated attempts at obstruction of the free media, large-scale corruption in economic policies, and recurrent instigation of ethnocentric nationalism. Not surprisingly then, numerous studies have argued that these postcommunist developments were not just teething troubles, but went further, as they resulted from a deeply entrenched political culture hostile to the liberal democratic project (e.g. Carpenter 1997). A nation whose political ambitions have been frustrated for centuries was, in this view, by its very nature prone to extreme ideologies. Hence the appeal of extreme nationalism was explained usually 'by lack of a "usable" democratic past' (Boulanger 1999: 10; see also Wolchik 1997: 202), and 'the rise of illiberal democracy' (Zakaria 1997) in the country was presented as a logical result of Slovak national history. Whereas the Czechs could fall back on the democratic achievements of the Czechoslovak First Republic, the Slovaks had only the liability of their alliance with nazi Germany.

Other writers highlighted the agrarian character of Slovakia, and, relying on earlier findings of Barrington Moore ('no bourgeois, no democracy', Moore 1966: 418), saw it as a reason for the lack of democratic commitment of the Slovak people and their higher susceptibility to authoritarian forms of government. Elster *et al.* argued, for example, that traditional agrarian societies were in general more receptive to the communist system of power. Furthermore, the Soviet-style industrialization, in their view, resulted in the creation of 'industrialised and urbanised peasant society' which was not truly modernized and was thus not well suited for democratization (Elster *et al.* 1998: 299). Consequently, the authors contrasted the achievements of the Czech Republic, which was industrialized significantly earlier, with the failures of Slovakia and Bulgaria. They asserted that this 'may be due to the inhospitality of the society of the Czech lands with the Soviet type of communism, which after 1945 had to be imposed more or less coercively' (Elster *et al.* 1998: 304). But their assessment cannot be reconciled with the fact that predominantly agrarian countries like Slovakia or Poland did actually strongly resist the imposition of communism.[1]

Furthermore, all these accounts are, to various extents, vulnerable to two major criticisms. First, to deny the Slovak nation any experience of democracy means to disinherit it from the Czechoslovak First Republic. Curiously, this is predicated on the acceptance of the logic of those Slovak nationalists who have always regarded Czechoslovakia as a purely Czech state, and it ignores the historic realities of close links between the two nations which are still reflected in the widespread popular appeal in Slovakia of Slovak personalities who were associated with the creation of the Czechoslovak state (Štefánik), or later, in communist times, with the attempts at its democratization (Dubček).[2] Second, even a nation without 'a usable democratic past' is not doomed to remain illiberal and undemocratic. The past influences the present, but can never fully determine it. Liberal nationalism can be strengthened by a proud recollection of past achievements, but it can also develop as a counter-reaction to a totalitarian past. Even the past failings of a nation can serve as a point of reference for the elaboration of liberal values which people strive presently to achieve.

Moreover, to label a nation illiberal (or liberal for that matter) in inclination renders it a monolithic community with a single will, which is yet again an assumption typical for the logic of extreme nationalism rather than a suitable concept for social scientists. What is needed, instead, is a thorough examination of the different discourses of nationalism which compete for dominance in political processes. As will be demonstrated, even in Slovakia one can clearly identify not only chauvinistic conceptions of a nation espoused by the likes of Ján Slota, who led the Slovak National Party (SNS – Slovenská národná strana), but also the conception of liberal nationalism which seeks to reconcile particular ethnic allegiances with universal liberal values and was advocated, among others, by Peter Zajac, a founding member of the 1989 movement Public Against Violence (VPN – Verejnost' proti násiliu). Slovak society was deeply divided along the lines of two conflicting political directions represented by the two major political groupings. One side of the political spectrum (spanning the extreme nationalist SNS and the less radical but populist HZDS) alienated ethnic minorities and led to the country's increasing international isolation. In contrast, the anti-Mečiar coalition aspired to European integration and the policies of ethnic tolerance.

The September 1998 elections which brought the end of Mečiar's autocratic rule fundamentally challenged the theories which assumed (whether tacitly or openly) that the Slovak nation is inherently illiberal. The subsequent new government coalitions appeared genuinely committed to the principles of liberal democracy and the rule of law, and included representatives of the Hungarian minority, which marked a new beginning for dealing with ethnic diversity in Slovakia. The ethnic tolerance of the Slovak electorate was further manifested in the ensuing direct presidential election in May 1999, which resulted in Rudolf Schuster, of German ethnic origin, becoming the new head of state.[3] The new political constellation confirmed some isolated studies of Slovakia which had more accurately anticipated the changes already during Mečiar's rule, since they argued that despite the disappointing performance of the ruling elites, the country had 'an extremely lively civil society' (Kaldor and Vejvoda 1997: 80) and 'an active citizenry...which display[ed] democratic credentials comparable to their counterparts in the NATO and EU states' (Tétreault and Teske 1997: 139).

In fact, more recent developments in Slovakia clearly demonstrated that Slovaks were no less capable of adhering to liberal values than their Czech, Polish or Hungarian neighbours. This is also supported by evidence derived from serious studies of political cultures and attitudes, in contrast to the speculative accounts which extrapolate the character of a nation from the erratic behaviour of its political elites. As Stephen Whitefield and Geoffrey Evans showed in evaluating the political cultures in the Czech Republic and Slovakia, the differences between the attitudes of both people with respect to ethnic liberalism were 'only marginal – if anything, Slovaks are slightly more liberal than Czechs' (Whitefield and Evans 1999: 143). Similar conclusions were also reached by Sharon Wolchik who conducted a comparative study of Czech and Slovak popular attitudes towards politics (Wolchik 1998). Likewise, Plichtová and Erös, who examined the 'meaning of some political and economic terms in relation to the experience of two Slovak and Hungarian generations', identified 'more similarities than differences ... between Slovak and Hungarian respondents'. They found that 'Hungarians did not adopt a western type of democracy and individualism to a greater extent than Slovaks' (Plichtová and Erös 1997: 7). Hence the results of sociological surveys fundamentally undermine widely held assumptions about 'Slovak exceptionalism' (see also Kusý 1995: 139–55).

History

Sen je krátky, deň je dlhý

(Janko Král' – see translation below)

Yet while the Polish, Czech, or Hungarian people were able to see the transition towards liberal democracy as a logical culmination of their long historic struggle for freedom, in the Slovak case, the latest achievements seemed rather to defy the perceived 'logic' of national history. Peter Zajac, among others, observed that the decisive points in Slovak history were marked by unresolved tension between demands for national liberation and the advancement of personal liberties. Liberal values were repeatedly sacrificed for the national cause (as after 1848, 1938 and 1968), but in the end little was achieved, either for the liberty of the nation or the liberty of individuals (Zajac 1996: 100–27; cf. Kusý 1997: 460–481). As the Slovak romantic poet Janko Král' put it, reflecting on the experience of the 1848 revolutionary movement: 'the short dream was followed by a long day' (cited in Zajac 1996: 7). Slovak history could be seen as the illustration of a rule that high hopes were bound to lead to disappointments.

Hence, when the promised gains of democratization and the final end of authoritarian rule, which came with the Velvet Revolution of November 1989, seemed to have been hijacked by the populist nationalism of the ruling elites, who in turn created the independent Slovak Republic, not only Western analysts, but also many Slovak intellectuals (e.g. Martin Šimečka [1997]) accepted the logic of historical determinism according to which the current problems were interpreted as the inevitable results of centuries 'of strange history'. The legacies of the past, characterized by collaboration with the powers that be – 'a history of adaptation and outward loyalty to power regardless of its conditions' – inhibited the current democratic project (Šimečka 1997: 19). Martin Šimečka was not atypical in his pessimism about the future prospects of an independent Slovakia. He argued that although historically the country had been an integral part of European cultural and political space, the Slovak people on the whole were not capable of responding adequately to the current challenges, as they were lacking in any democratic tradition.

> Maybe the last eight years have been too complex an experience for the citizens of this country. For the first time in history, this nation experienced years of real freedom, and for the first time in history, it has to rely on itself in its own country. There is no experience it can lean on and no will to close a social agreement.
>
> (Šimečka 1997: 20–1)

Still others (like Zajac [1996]) believed that whatever the historical lega-cies, the Slovaks must not miss the unique opportunity of reconciling the goals of national self-determination with the advancement of liberal democ-racy. While past attempts at national liberation failed also because of hostile external circumstances (as in 1848, 1944 and 1968), currently Slovaks were experiencing a unique opportunity, where they themselves could decide their fate. The simple fact that Slovak independence was brought about by forces that endangered democratic developments did not mean that Slovakia could not become democratic. As Milan Šútovec suggested at the beginning of 1997, the Slovak state should be reinvented and endowed with a new and democratic content (Bútora and Bútorová 1999: 84). Moreover, an analysis of debates about the 'meaning' of Slovak history will show (as in the Polish and Czech cases) that different events and personalities have been appropri-ated for vastly different causes.

The origins of the Slovak nation and Gellner's theory of modernization

The emergence of the modern Slovak nation is a result of the radical processes of modernization within the Habsburg empire which culminated in the middle of the nineteenth century. As in the Czech case, Gellner's theory of nationalism, which states that modern nations are the products of nationalism rather than the other way round, accurately describes the histor-ical developments also in the Slovak context. This goes against the popular Slovak myth, which traces the beginnings of the Slovak nation back to the Greater Moravian empire of the ninth century, or even earlier.[4] Milan S. Ďurica, for example, described the people living on the current Slovak terri-tory during the first to eighth centuries as Slavs, but from the end of the eighth century as Slovak (Ďurica 1995: 9). He even reinvented the Greater Moravian empire by calling it 'Slovenská ríša' (the 'Slovak empire', Ďurica 1995: 15–20; cf. Lipták 1999: 265).[5] Such an understanding of Slovak history is anachronistic because it projects our contemporary conception of a nation back to the times when a sense of belonging to a national commu-nity was either nonexistent or irrelevant. There may have been people using different Slav dialects living on the territory of today's Slovakia for more than ten centuries, but neither they nor their rulers attached any importance to issues of ethnicity, let alone relied on nationalism as a political force (Kováč 1993).

In fact, there has been a growing consensus within contemporary Slovak historiography that those nationalistic accounts of Slovak history which assume that the nation is eternal, or at least that its history goes back to time immemorial, must be replaced with more academically sound approaches.[6] Dušan Kováč, among others, has convincingly demonstrated that issues of Slovak identity became important only at the end of the eigh-teenth century as a reaction to the attempts of the ruling classes to linguistically homogenize the ethnically diverse people of Hungary. In fact, before this, 'Latin [rather than Hungarian, or German] was for a long time in Hungary the language of public administration and even the literary language' (Kováč 1997: 38). Hence before the end of the eighteenth century, 'the Hungarian state and parliament strove for fair settlement and compromise in any conflicts which may have arisen between different ethnicities; the state was not yet an instrument of one single ethnicity' (Kováč 1993: 530).

Slovaks versus Magyars[7]

Before the forces of nationalism 'awakened' the Slovak national consciousness, the language of communication was determined more by class than by ethnic origin or place of birth. Social advancement was thus intimately linked with language. As Karl-Peter Schwarz put it, 'a Slovak who had risen into the ruling class also changed his linguistic and cultural milieu' (Schwarz 1993: 48).[8] With some simplification, one could say that until the second half of the nineteenth century, the multiethnic society of Slovakia consisted of 'a motley mix of nationalities...the Hungarian nobility occupied the castles and chateaux; the towns belonged to the Germans, Hungarians, and the Jews; and the villages and nature were left for the Slovaks' (Šimečka 1997: 15). Clearly, such an arrangement was inequitable and unjust. However, the disadvantages suffered by Slovak peasants were not caused by their ethnicity, or culture. Defying the beliefs of many nineteenth-century Slovak nationalist leaders, who claimed that the Slovaks had suffered some ten centuries of Hungarian oppression, the Slovak nineteenth-century liberal thinker, Štěpan Launer, pointed out that before 1848 their position was no worse than that of Magyar, German or Romanian peasants (Pynsent 2002: 11). All these people were oppressed as peasants, *not* as members of different ethnic communities. The issue of ethnicity only gained on importance towards the end of the eighteenth century. The Habsburg empire's drive for modernization, which was accompanied by attempts to homogenize the peoples of Hungary, undoubtedly disadvantaged its ethnic minorities. Slovak nationalists, led by L'udovít Štúr, were determined to change this by creating a Slovak literary language and securing more political rights for the emerging nation.

L'udovít Štúr: an archetypical liberal, Nazi or communist?

The aspirations of the Slovak nationalist movement clashed with the goals of the Hungarian fight for national emancipation, which culminated in 1848/9. Magyar insurgents led by Lajos Kossuth (1802–94) were passionate liberals following progressive goals in respect to social justice (they abolished statutory labour and the nobility's exemption from taxation), but their liberalism was somewhat lacking in respect to other nationalities of the empire. This reflected the European-wide failure of the progressive forces of 1848 to find a satisfactory solution to 'the problem [of] how to accommodate nationalist aspirations to the demands of political liberty' (Kohn cited in Sugar 1997: 92). For most liberals of the age, centralization was more important than a concern with ethnic diversity, which was seen as a hindrance to social progress. While Kossuth himself was against the forceful assimilation of ethnic minorities, he 'rejected all Slovak claims to cultural autonomy', and favoured Magyar as the only language of public administration in Hungary (Deak 1979: 45; for Magyarization see also Chapter 2). This attitude antagonized Slovak insurgents led by L'udovít Štúr (1815–56).

The figure of L'udovít Štúr, the intellectual 'father' of the Slovak nation, is as complex and paradoxical as the modern history of Slovakia. In fact, the conflicting views which Štúr held at various stages of his life anticipate all the major conceptions of the Slovak nation that would later dominate public debates. The ambiguous character of Štúr's heritage allowed its appropriation by pro-Western liberals (e.g. Hodža), Slovak national socialists (e.g. Mach), the ideologues of communism (e.g. Novomeský, Mináč), and contemporary anti-Western nationalists (e.g. Polakovič). While the Nazis were able to stress Štúr's German connections (he was educated in Halle, where he was influenced by German romanticism and the philosophy of Hegel and Herder), the communists utilized his pro-Russian sentiments. More recently, Štúr was recalled in order to argue the desirability of Slovakia's full integration into NATO and the European Union (Jurík 1998).

Štúr's major achievement was the codification of the Slovak literary language in the middle of the nineteenth century, which was based on the Central Slovak dialect and was thus easily accessible to a majority of the Slovak people. This accomplishment ended a long lasting division within the Slovak elites between Catholic intellectuals who used a language based on the West Slovak dialect, codified by Anton Bernolák at the end of the eighteenth century, and the Protestants who preferred the use of Czech. This codification of the Slovak literary language was not only a linguistic exercise but also an important political step, as only a people who had a common literary language could fight for more rights within the multiethnic empire. Thus the widely accepted codification of a literary language was not only a precondition for the internal unity of the nation, but also its acceptance by others. Yet even this accomplishment was not without controversy, as Štúr was criticized for separatism which destroyed the proclaimed unity – whether it be Czechoslovak (e.g. Jungmann, Havlíček, Palacký), or Slav (Kollár, Šafařík).[9]

These accusations of separatism were unjustified. First, despite some close links within Czech and Slovak intellectual circles, there was no unity to speak of amongst the common people. There was thus little use in contemplating the possibility of a common language for both 'branches' of 'one' nation (to use Kollár's terminology). Second, Štúr was initially a strong advocate of close brotherly links between the two nations. Notwithstanding his rejection of the idea of a common Czechoslovak nation, Štúr for some time explicitly opposed separatism. As he declared,

He who now seeks to sever himself from his brothers, will have to be taken to task by our nation. We want to remain in this bond with them, and keep sharing pride in their best achievements and uphold our spiritual connection. We want to help them whenever we can and expect them to do the same for us as befits good brothers.

(Štúr cited in Chmel 1997: 393)

Still, the creation of a common state of Czechs and Slovaks was not seriously considered an option in the middle of the nineteenth century. In fact, Slovak nationalist leaders originally aimed at autonomy within the Hungarian state. Only after the Magyar revolutionaries refused to accommodate Slovak aspirations did the Slovak elites turn to Vienna, hoping to gain more protection from the centralist state, this time against Magyar dominance. This tactic, which rendered Slovaks traitors of the revolution, did not pay off because the Austrian authorities failed to fulfil their promises.[10] Towards the end of his life, Štúr, in disappointment, radically reorientated himself towards Tsarist Russia, expecting the salvation of humanity from the most oppressive regime in Europe. He turned against the West, and explicitly rejected liberalism. This was also the reason why he could no longer sympathize with the Czechs, who were – in his view – corrupted by the overwhelming influence of Western values (Pynsent 2002: 17). Despite being a Protestant and virtually the 'creator' of the Slovak literary language, Štúr even urged his followers in his last work, *Das Slawentum und die Welt der Zukunft* (*Slavdom and the World of the Future*)[11] to adopt Russian Orthodox Christianity, and the Russian language and Cyrillic script.

Slovak liberals had to recall Štúr's earlier political activities if they wanted to present themselves as his legitimate heirs. His positions were initially remarkably pragmatic and aimed at the political emancipation of the Slovak people. Before 1848, Štúr understood the formation of the Slovak nation as going hand-in-hand with the transition of the common people into citizens aware of their rights and duties within the wider society. According to the contemporary Slovak philosopher, Tibor Pichler, Štúr's writings from this period can be regarded as 'the foundation of the Slovak liberal tradition' (Pichler 1998: 57). Thus, Milan Hodža (1878–1944), who was one of the most influential Slovak politicians in the Czechoslovak First Republic (and its last prime minister), was able to highlight Štúr's pre-1848 revolutionary ideas, in order to elaborate on his own version of liberalism. Writing in exile during the Second World War, Hodža contrasted Štúr's liberal credentials with the uncompromising attitude of Lajos Kossuth, who dismissed 'all non-Magyar claims for righteousness with his notorious: "The sword will decide" ' (Hodža 1942: 210). Štúr, on the other hand,

demanded the abolition of serfdom and the establishment of civil and national liberties without any distinction of race … Štúr was no radical....But he accepted many of the fundamental points of the contemporary Liberal programme and may, not unfairly, be regarded as the most genuine fighter for progress in the old Hungarian parliament before the March Revolution.

(Hodža 1942: 210)

Yet, at the same time as Hodža celebrated Štúr as an archetypical liberal, the chief ideologue of the Nazi puppet Slovak state, Alexander Mach, claimed that all the Slovak Awakeners from the late eighteenth century (starting with Bernolák) were actually national socialists and Štúr was to be seen as the 'Hitler of the nineteenth century' (Schwarz 1993: 150; cf. Chmel 1997: 27). Štúr's close connection with German culture and his cooperation with Vienna were presented as the anticipation of President Tiso's close links with Berlin. It is questionable whether the Slovak People's Party could legitimately claim its affinity with the nineteenth-century national move-ment, but its attempts certainly corresponded with the logic of a totalitarian state which aspires to total control of a nation, and therefore also its history. As the constitution of the Slovak wartime republic stated, 'the Slovak nation takes part in state power through the Hlinka's Slovak People's Party' (HSLS – Hlinkova slovenská ludová strana). Consequently, another leading ideo-logue of the Slovak wartime state, Štefan Polakovič, was able to argue that 'he who stands outside the party is outside the nation, which can easily be related to treason. To think correctly politically means to be in agreement with the party and its leader' (cited in Chmel 1997: 27; see also 279–90). This can be considered a classic statement of exclusionary nationalism which was to be echoed in the later developments of the nation. In fact, the very same Polakovič, who has lived since 1947 in Argentina, eagerly joined the post 1989 campaign for an independent Slovak state, publishing a book in 1991 called *Obnova národa duchom Štúra* (*The Renewal of the Nation through the Spirit of Štúr*) (see Pynsent 1994: 152).

The principle of a totalitarian party state was later also adopted by the communists (even if under different auspices – the enemy from within was now defined primarily by class rather than ethnic origin).[12] But the commu-nist regime had an uneasy relationship with Slovak nationalism. After all, nationalism in Slovakia was strongly associated with the wartime puppet state, and support for the communist party was never as widespread as in the Bohemian lands. In fact, some leading Slovak communists who were actively involved in the 1944 Slovak National Uprising (SNP) against the Germans, like the writer Ladislav Novomeský and the future president Gustáv Husák, were tried and sentenced in the 1950s for alleged 'bourgeois nationalism' (Schwarz 1993: 182). Nevertheless, as Pynsent observed, some aspects of Slovak nationalism were 'condoned, sometimes even encouraged, by the socialist state, especially in the wake of the 1964 anniversary of the Uprising' (Pynsent 1994: 151). Clearly, the communist regime needed its own version of 'glorious' Slovak history in order to strengthen its legitimacy.

The nineteenth-century Slovak nationalists did not fit neatly into a mould of prototypical communist revolutionaries. First, Marx and Engels explicitly criticized the attempts of the small Slav nations to take sides with Vienna, which amounted to an abandoning of the goals of the 1848 Magyar revolution (see Chapter 4). Second, it was difficult to accommodate Štúr's open hostility towards the ideologies of socialism and communism. 'He was not a socialist, he was a radical liberal who did not trust socialism', observed Vladimír Mináč. Notwithstanding his conservative inclinations, however, the 150th anniversary of Štúr's birth in 1965 brought his rehabilitation. In a poetic essay, Mináč exploited Štúr's pan-Slavism and downplayed his Austrian connections, which were only imposed on him by hostile external circumstances. 'In this sense, only the Uprising [rather than the puppet Slovak state] is consequently in line with Štúr's legacy: it delivered what Štúr really wanted, not what he was forced to do' (Mináč 1965: 352). In Mináč's interpretation, Štúr became a visionary who predicted that the liberation of nations would come not from the West (say from France), but from 'another nation which suffered more; a nation which harbours more love for mankind than those who boast of it without working according to its spirit' (Štúr cited in Mináč 1965: 353). As Mináč commented:

> We know which nation Štúr has in mind: it is – and it always will be – Russia. Russia is the backbone of Slovak politics, the first article of its faith; it is the force which allows for Slovak advancement even in the most hopeless situations: it is faith in the future.
>
> (Mináč 1965: 353)

In contradiction to his writing from the 1960s, after the collapse of communism Mináč reinforced his nationalist sentiments by celebrating the *liberation* of the nation from Russian influence. Still, he remained true to his original suspicion of the West by lending his sophisticated voice in support of isolationism. But other contemporary left-wing intellectuals, like Brigita Schmögnerová (a leading politician formerly from the Party of the Slovak Democratic Left), invoked Štúr's heritage to advance the cause of West European integration. Schmögnerová viewed his significance through the eyes of Ladislav Novomeský, who stressed the importance of Slovak tradition during the attempts to democratize communism in Czechoslovakia in the late 1960s. Novomeský wrote in 1966 that he was 'attached to [Štúr] in ever better agreement, since the more our society responds...to the call for democratization, even if it stems from other sources...Štúr is our – Slovak – measure of democratization and democracy' (Novomeský in Schmögnerová 1997: 206). Consequently, Schmögnerová attacked the attempts of Mečiar's coalition government to use Štúr to legitimize its policies of extreme nationalism leading to international isolation. Schmögnerová asserted that

Štúr was a convinced democrat, and that the current government is clearly trying to establish an authoritarian regime. And whereas Štúr fought for civic principles and national justice, the current government is attempting to base our state on nationalistic principles and on the enforcement of national egoism and national intolerance.

(Schmögnerová 1997: 207–8).

Schmögnerová was right to appeal to the democratic forces within the Slovak political spectrum not to leave national themes and symbols to the exclusive (ab)use of the extreme nationalists. But liberal nationalists must strive for more than just another (mis)interpretation of historical figures and events.[13] There is no need to falsify history. In fact, liberals must address serious weaknesses in nineteenth-century conceptions of the Slovak nation which can be found in Štúr too, such as his inclination to irrational anti-Western prejudices and strong anti-Magyar tendencies. A writer and an astute political commentator, Pavel Vilikovský, for example, was right to point out that even anti-liberalism has its roots in Štúr. 'There is a spectre haunting Slovakia', wrote Vilikovský, 'a spectre of liberalism...or in other words a spectre of the decadent, decayed and rotten West', and this spectre is more than 150 years old (Vilikovský 1998: 98). Henceforth, liberals are likely to be better served by invoking the wisdom of other critical thinkers of Štúr's generation (e.g. Ján Palárik and Jonáš Záborský), and by appropriating the heritage of the Czechoslovak First Republic, though the First Republic is no less controversial than the nineteenth-century nationalist movement.

Nineteenth-century liberal alternatives to Štúr: Ján Palárik and Jonáš Záborský

Even though Štúr is still regarded as one of the most influential figureheads of Slovak history,[14] Slovak political thinking in the nineteenth century was significantly more varied than the exclusive focus on Štúr's ideas would suggest. Worth mentioning are in particular the 'constitutional patriotism of Ján Palárik', and the 'critical nationalism of Jonáš Záborský' (Pichler 1998: 83, 98). In the 1860s, reflecting on the experience of the Slovak fight for national emancipation, Palárik developed a concept of Slovak liberalism that was situated politically within the constitutional order of the 'Hungarian fatherland' (*uhorská vlast'*). While Palárik was critical of the attempt of nineteenth-century Magyar liberals to demand 'linguistic assimilation in exchange for civic liberty' (Pichler 1998: 84), he did not seek a solution to the Slovak problem by the simple act of an autocratic ruler, but rather by the continuous political emancipation of Slovak-speaking citizens. Hence, 'Palárik was convinced that civic rights were the best and irreplaceable means for the realization of Slovak aims within [nineteenth-century] Hungary' (Pichler 1998: 90). In a similar vein, Záborský argued that the

Slovak cause could only be advanced by the education of the Slovak people, who had to change 'their slavish mentality into a civic mentality' (Pichler 1998: 105). Hence, Záborský saw a direct link between the project of national emancipation and the striving for social progress. He called on his compatriots 'to take active part in the process of modernisation in order to benefit from it privately and as citizens' (Pichler 1998: 106). To sum up, both Palárik and Záborský advocated a liberal nationalism, which stressed the importance of the cultivation of civic values within Slovak society achieved through the process of individual political emancipation.

Slovaks in the Czechoslovak First Republic

After the Austro-Hungarian Compromise (*Ausgleich*) of 1867, which gave Hungary an equal status with Austria, the policy of Magyarization of the Slovak people intensified to the extent that some historians were led to speculate that Slovak culture could have been eliminated (Leff 1995: 122). Consequently, the creation of the Czechoslovak Republic was a positive achievement, since it significantly improved conditions for the nation's development. The liberal democratic regime empowered individual citizens who could actively participate in the public sphere as never before. Moreover, Slovaks shared with Czechs, at least in theory, the privileged position of one of the two branches of a Czechoslovak nation; they were seen as official constituent nationalities of the new state (*štátotvorné národy* – see Chapter 4). The republic brought about a radical advancement of the national education system (including the creation of the first Slovak-language University – the Komenského Universita in Bratislava), and an unprecedented development of cultural life.

Less fortuitous was the impact of the unification of two very disparate economies. Slovak industry had difficulties coping with two major challenges. First, it had to deal with the severing of the close economic links with the 'Hungarian motherland' (Schwarz 1993: 112–13). Second, it had to compete with significantly more advanced Czech industry. This meant, in practice, that despite some attempts at alleviating the gap in economic development between the Czech and Slovak territories, it was the Slovak people who experienced more hardship (Kováč 1997: 67–9). Furthermore, even some well intentioned cultural assistance unwittingly contributed to the rising anti-Czech sentiments within some sections of the Slovak population. Whilst thousands of Czech teachers and middle-ranking public servants were sent to Slovakia to help to overcome the lack of educated Slovak elites, their help was increasingly perceived as a patronizing imposition, or even rejected as foreign domination.

Relatively soon after its creation, the Czechoslovak Republic had to confront the so-called Slovak question, which amounted to the satisfactory accommodation of Slovak ambitions within the multinational state. The problem was, to a large extent, caused by two fundamentally different conceptions of the desirable relationship between the two nations. In fact, the cause of contention was whether there were two nations to speak of. While a majority of Slovaks saw in Czechoslovakia a common state of Czechs and Slovaks, the vast majority of Czechs perceived Czechoslovakia as a Czech state, which rendered Slovaks just a slightly peculiar 'branch' of the Czech(oslovak) nation. Characteristically, Czech and Czechoslovak had been used interchangeably from the early stages of the struggle for a common state.[15] The reason for that was partly strategic. As the Western powers adopted the policy of national self-determination, it was easier to convince them of the legitimacy of a Czechoslovak nation-state than a new multinational state which would only replicate the problems of Austria-Hungary. Accordingly, when Štefánik, Masaryk and Beneš met in Paris in February 1916, they created the 'Conseil national des pays *tchèques*' – that is the Czech National Council; but the standard 'translation' in Slovak and Czech histories is 'československá národná rada', i.e. the Czechoslovak National Council (see Kováč 1997: 65). The concept of a united Czechoslovak nation may have been useful for international diplomacy, but domestically it led to the alienation of many Slovaks.

The differences in the understanding of the role of the Czechoslovak state increasingly exacerbated relations between the two nations. By questioning the very existence of the Slovak nation once again, the Slovak historical trauma was revived. Masaryk, who was himself partly of Slovak origin and entertained very close links with the Slovak intellectual elites well before the creation of the Czechoslovak Republic, was in the best position to understand Slovak sensibilities and national aspirations. However, it is still disputed to what extent he acknowledged that the Slovaks constituted an independent nation, rather than being just a part of a Czech (or Czechoslovak nation). Different and seemingly contradictory statements lend themselves to different interpretations. Miloš Tomčík, who argues that Masaryk did not question the very existence of the Slovak nations (Tomčík 1992: 33), quotes him as saying in Bratislava in 1921:

> The equality of Czech and Slovak half [of the common Czechoslovak nation] is expressed not only in the name of this state, but also in its constitution and the program of state politics which ensure the preservation of Slovak identity, language and culture, and the development of those qualities which constitute Slovak national character.
>
> (Masaryk cited in Tomčík 1992: 52)

In contrast, Carol Skalnik Leff cites a 1921 interview for a French newspaper, in which Masaryk stated explicitly:

> There is no Slovak nation....The Czechs and Slovaks are brothers. Only cultural level separates them – the Czechs are more developed than the Slovaks, for the Magyars held them in systematic unawareness. We are

founding Slovak schools. We must await the results; in one generation there will be no difference between the two branches of our national family.

(Masaryk cited in Leff 1997: 26)

Clearly, Masaryk's position was somewhat ambiguous, which may have been caused by the fact that he attempted to address different audiences with different aims. While the international community had to be assured about the unity and viability of the new state, the Slovaks feared domination by the Czechs. At any rate, the assumption that the Slovak nation would ultimately merge with the Czech nation proved unfounded, and no one would question the very existence of the Slovak nation today. But seen against the background of that time, in which most leading politicians felt compelled to stress commonalities between the two nations, it was not entirely unrealistic to expect that a conception of Czechoslovak unity that was primarily political could evolve further, and result in more cultural and linguistic convergence. The Slovak elites, on the whole, did not share this opinion. Nevertheless, even Andrej Hlinka, who would later become the most outspoken proponent of Slovak autonomy, originally stressed unity. Having received strong Czech support in his fight against Hungarian oppression, he declared in court in 1908 that 'whether our Magyar brothers like it or not, it remains an eternal truth that we, Slovaks, are with the Czechs one race, one culture, and one nation' (cited in Kováč 1997: 57).

As for the common people, many were significantly less concerned about their ethnic belonging than would be expected of a nation of fervent nationalists. Derek Sayer documented the frustration of Czech public servants, who in 1919 carried out a census in east Slovakia, and complained about the lack of a clearly formed national consciousness.

With the greatest eagerness we anticipated the response to the nationality question. 'Are you Slovak?' A blank stare. Excepting one village, the answer everywhere was: 'I speak both Slovak and Hungarian'. 'I did not ask which language you speak, but whether you are a Hungarian or a Slovak'....Often a horrifying answer would sound: 'It's the same difference! [*A to šicko jedno*] If the bread is buttered on the Hungarian side, I am Magyar, if it is buttered on the Czech side, I am Slovak'.

(cited in Sayer 1998: 175)

This perception may not have been typical for the whole territory of Slovakia, since the people in central Slovakia, for example, were certainly more aware of their nationality. But even allowing for significant regional variations, the statement is indicative of the fluid character of ethnic identities in the early stages of the Czechoslovak Republic. Ironically, the concept of Czechoslovakism, which aimed at achieving more unity between the two people (whether it was understood politically, or ethnically) unwittingly

facilitated the distinctiveness of the Slovak nation, as more nationalist political leaders in Slovakia were able to successfully mobilize large sections of
the population against the Czechs. Increasingly, the Slovak identity was
constructed not only against Magyars, but also against Czechs. The failure
of the Czecho(slovak) elites to accommodate satisfactorily Slovak aspirations within the multiethnic state paved the way for the rise of the Catholic
priest Andrej Hlinka (1864–1938) and his Slovak People's Party (HSL'S).
Tensions between the two nations were exacerbated by religious differences
and Hlinka's HSL'S increasingly mobilized popular support by contrasting
their own religious credentials – expressed in the programmatic call 'For
God and Country' – against 'a more secularly oriented central government
and against Czech "atheism/agnosticism" ' (Leff 1995: 114). Nazi Germany
exploited these Slovak grievances, and ultimately destroyed Czechoslovakia.
Paradoxically, the secular totalitarian regime of Nazi Germany helped to
sustain the ensuing Slovak 'parish republic', which legitimized its immoral
political practices with an exclusive nationalism which had a strong veneer
of Catholic faith.

The 'meaning' of the Czechoslovak First Republic (Slovaks and Czechs)

The meaning of the Czechoslovak First Republic is still a source of controversy in Slovakia as much as in the Czech republic (cf. Chapter 4). While
the ethnocentric Slovak intellectuals who interpret Slovak history as the
nation's ongoing fight for independence regard Czechoslovakia as a purely
destructive construct from the very beginning (e.g. Ďurica 1995: 117ff), the
more liberally minded historians usually stress that despite numerous failings, the creation of Czechoslovakia was a positive achievement as it
'rescued Slovaks from oppressive magyarization' and contributed significantly to their development (Kováč and Lipták 1997: 37). Contested is also
the meaning of Czechoslovakism.[16] Nationalist historians like Ďurica and
Kirschbaum understand Czechoslovakism as an attempt at the full assimilation of the Slovak people, which would even deprive them of their own
language (Ďurica 1995: 127; Kirschbaum 1995: 169–70). According to
Kováč, on the other hand, Czechoslovakism was merely a political concept
which did not practically affect culture and language. This can be
supported by the statement of the leading Slovak politician in the First
Republic, Milan Hodža, who argued in 1921 that 'we should not talk about
a Czechoslovak nation. We are either Czechs or Slovaks, but we cannot be
Czechoslovaks. We are the citizens of the Czechoslovak state and have a
common citizenship, but we are two nations' (Hodža 1997: 24). In fact, the
Slovak language was an official language of the state administration and
was taught in schools. Even Czech teachers who came to Slovakia in order
to alleviate the shortage of qualified personnel, learned Slovak and taught
in Slovak (Kováč 1997: 123–6).[17]

Furthermore, those who are critical of the heritage of the First Republic do not regard it as an important part of Slovak history and either ignore the leading Slovak politicians who served in various Czechoslovak governments and suspect them of some kind of treason (e.g. Hodža), or see them as the heroic defenders of Slovak rights. Thus, Milan Rastislav Štefánik (1880–1919), who is still one of the most popular historical personalities (despite being tabooed by the communists for more than forty years), is appropriated alternately by extreme nationalists who celebrate him as a hero who defied Czech dominance and became a victim of an elaborate Czech conspiracy, and by adherents of a more outward-looking Slovakia who present him as a modern European. Extreme nationalists exploit the fact that Štefánik perished in an aeroplane accident under circumstances which were never clarified. Ďurica, for example, goes so far as to suggest (without any supporting evidence) that Štefánik was murdered and that the most likely suspects would be Masaryk and Beneš, with whom Štefánik allegedly had some serious disagreements (Ďurica 1995: 123; cf. Kováč and Lipták 1997: 37). In contrast, Schmögnerová stresses the point that Štefánik, a well travelled astronomer who became a general in the French army, was true to both national *and* European values (Schmögnerová 1997: 209).

More recently, Slovak liberals have been rediscovering the intellectual heritage of Milan Hodža,[18] who is far less known and popular than Štefánik, although he was actively involved in Czechoslovak politics for considerably longer. During his Second World War exile in Great Britain, Hodža worked out a fascinating proposal for a Central European federation, which in many respects anticipated the current project of the European Union.[19] At a time when most politicians and theorists were primarily concerned with non-violation of national sovereignty, Hodža conceptualized the possibility of 'ordered sovereignty' which recognizes the limits to which a nation can and should be truly independent. It was hence in the interests of the small nations of Central Europe to accept the need for close cooperation, which would necessitate the pooling of particular national sovereignties. As Hodža put it, 'if there is an ordered freedom – to save freedom; and an ordered democracy – to save democracy; and an ordered economy – to save the economy, why not accept ordered sovereignty to save national existence?' (Hodža 1942: 161)

International cooperation, however, did not preclude nationalism. On the contrary, Hodža was convinced that 'the present whirlwind of hyper-nationalistic frenzy' could only be resisted by an alternative nationalism. As Hannah Arendt would demonstrate a few years later in *The Origins of Totalitarianism*, this type of nationalism is important as it provides 'a partial barrier against totalitarianism and its ability to mobilize political power' (Canovan 1999: 143). Similarly, Hodža, recalling the heritage of Mazzini, saw liberal nationalism (or in his terminology, 'democratic nationalism')[20] as a force necessary to counterbalance the challenges of Italian fascism and German Nazism. He argued,

When isolated, individuals are reduced to the incapacity to perform their moral duty to an over-national ideal unless they are an active part of that community which has been welded into an organic whole by affinities of natural conditions and purposes. That is the mission which nations have to fulfil....So, a democratic nationalist will do his best to develop his people's particular potential and to use it for the common cause of mankind.

(Hodža 1942: 157)

In contrast to the German integral nationalism of the day, which was based on the demand to 'subordinate the [individual will] to the national collective' (Hodža 1997: 55), Hodža's conception of nationalism stressed the importance of personal responsibility. 'In the final analysis, nationalism means responsibility – *my* responsibility for the contribution *my* nation can make in the advancements achieved by competition of nations' (Hodža 1997: 58). Against some fashionable ideas of the time which rendered cosmopolitanism the only possible alternative to the destructive forces of nationalism, Hodža defended liberal nationalism also on cultural grounds by stating that 'even cosmopolitan culture can only be real if it taps into the sources of national creations' (Hodža 1997: 54).

Being truthful to liberal nationalism, Hodža was able to separate the fight against German Nazism from the fight against the German people as such. He was one of the few politicians of his time who actually envisaged the transformation of Germany and its full integration 'into an international order based on co-operation' (Hodža 1997: 340). He was also far more sceptical about the democratic credentials of the Soviet Union than most of his contemporaries, and firmly opposed the blind pan-Slavism of his colleague and rival, President Beneš. In fact, the threat of Soviet domination of Central Europe was, in his view, an additional reason for the necessity of his project of a Commonwealth of Central Europe (Lukáč 1996: 70–1). As Stephen Borsody observed, 'had Edvard Beneš been as truly Masaryk's heir as he claimed to be, he would have endorsed the federalist reconstruction of Central Europe after World War II. Milan Hodža, pre-war Czechoslovakia's last democratic Prime Minister, did just that' (Borsody 1993: 289). Hodža died shortly before the end of the war, and the ensuing developments in Czechoslovakia were unfortunately influenced more by Beneš's anti-German and pro-Soviet policies than Hodža's vision of Central European cooperation (see Chapter 4). Yet Hodža appears to have been proven correct in his belief that some type of 'democratic nationalism' was needed for mobilizing resistance to Nazism. The defeat of the totalitarian regime of the wartime Slovak state (1939–45) was, after all, precipitated by the Slovak National Uprising of the summer of 1944.

Given that the ultimate goal of the SNP was the renewal of Czechoslovakia, although with significantly more rights granted to the Slovak part of the republic, it is understandable that people who cherish the heritage of the Czechoslovak First Republic are also proud of the SNP. But the SNP has also been celebrated by the defenders of national independence. 29 August, which marks the beginning of the Uprising, has been commemorated as a national holiday not only in Czechoslovakia (whether communist or postcommunist), but also after the creation of the independent Slovak Republic in 1993. Yet the meaning of the SNP is not less equivocal than any other event in Slovak history, and its interpretations are as manifold as the forces involved in the uprising. The communists claim that only they could have been 'truly antifascist', since the liberal democrats accepted capitalism which was by definition 'the father of fascism'.[21] Contrary to this, it has been argued that precisely the communists could not have been really antifascist as 'they were adherents of a totalitarian ideology strikingly similar to fascism in the first place' (Lipták 1999: 184). Both opposing views, however, were united in their evaluation of the SNP as a positive event, and both could agree with the official version of Slovak history published in 1994 by the Slovak department of Foreign Affairs:

The Uprising of 1944 is one of the key events of modern Slovak history. People of different political opinions participated in it with the goal of defeating the inhumane Hitler regime. The Uprising strengthened the national consciousness of the Slovaks. While the country was in the past mostly only an object of foreign interests – the Uprising meant that the nation took control in its own hands.

(Lipták 1994: 12)

The Slovak nation, however, could not keep control 'in its own hands' for long. First, the Uprising was defeated by the German army. Second, the ultimate liberation of Slovakia came with the Soviet army and the whole of Czechoslovakia was thereafter under strong Soviet influence. Since the Uprising was led predominantly by the Slovak communists, who closely cooperated with Moscow, it could even be argued that it paved the way for the communist takeover. In fact, the Uprising later became one of the main sources of legitimacy for the communist regime. Consequently, after the collapse of communism it would have seemed logical to some factions within society that the Uprising should be condemned as much as it was previously condoned by the communist functionaries. These sentiments led to a revival of interest in the puppet Slovak Republic and even to its glorification. Some groups went so far as to demand that the Catholic priest Jozef Tiso (1887–1947), who was president of the puppet state (and later sentenced to death as a war criminal), should be canonized as a martyr (cf. Pynsent 1994: 151).

It was not surprising that the confusion of the postcommunist transition caused by the sudden ideological vacuum produced such extreme claims. More of a cause for concern was the fact that such sentiments received, at times, support from the ruling elites. Paradoxically, Mečiar's establishment celebrated the Uprising and ostensibly distanced themselves from the 1939–45 Slovak Republic (Kamenec 1998b: 14), while at the same time supporting those extreme nationalist forces which condemned it on the grounds that it led to the destruction of the first independent state of Slovaks.[22] Mečiar's all-embracing populism could, in this way, accommodate the former communists as much as the newly emerging extreme right-wing nationalists. This can be illustrated by the 1995 publication of a history text-book, *Dejiny Slovenska a Slovákov* (*A History of Slovakia and the Slovaks*) written by a Slovak émigré historian, Milan S. Ďurica, which is eulogistic about Tiso and his regime. The publication sparked lively exchanges in the Slovak media, which clearly demonstrated that debates about the appro-priate meaning of national history are not only relevant for academics, but have bearing on contemporary political developments. In fact, as in Poland and the Czech Republic, arguments about the past were often primarily arguments about the current political aspirations of the elites with respect to the nation and the state. As the increasingly authoritarian regime of Vladimír Mečiar sought to use history as another source of legitimacy, disparate voices from within civil society resisted such a move.

Ďurica's study is based on the anachronistic assumption that the Slovak people have struggled for independent statehood for more than ten centuries. The logical culmination of this struggle is hence, apart from the short-lived republic during the Second World War, the Slovak state founded on 1 January 1993 by Vladimír Mečiar and his Movement for a Democratic Slovakia (HZDS). It is ironic that Mečiar and his ideologues (e.g. Hofbauer) keenly endorsed this reading of Slovak history, given that the HZDS originally opposed the move towards independence, favouring instead a reformed Czechoslovak federation. While there have been forces within Slovakia who had for a long time advocated the split of the Czechoslovak Republic (and Ďurica was one of their influential émigré supporters), Mečiar's move towards separatism was rather accidental. The Slovak journalist Marián Leško has presented compelling evidence that Mečiar's stance towards national independence was predicated on his deter-mination to hold on to power rather than some long-term vision for the nation (Leško 1996, esp. 47–89). Notwithstanding the fact that Slovak national independence was somewhat accidental, once established it was reinterpreted not only as a willed outcome of the ruling elites, but a neces-sary result of age-old developments.[23]

The meaning of the first Slovak state (Slovaks and Jews)

The high point of the controversy surrounding Ďurica's book was reached in 1997 after the Slovak ministry of education started distributing it free of charge to all primary schools in the country.[24] Apart from the media outlets sympathetic to Mečiar's administration, which praised the book as an important contribution 'in forming the national, historical and cultural awareness of future Slovak generations' (Letz 1996: 42), the study received widespread condemnation. The most comprehensive response came from the Historical Institute of the Slovak Academy of Science, which listed a vast number of factual errors, but above all objected to 'Ďurica's portrayal of the Holocaust of Slovak Jewry [which was] simply unacceptable, unethical and defie[d] present scholarly evidence'. Moreover, historians took issue with the presentation of 'the Slovak leadership, and especially Tiso, as the saviours of the Jewish population, when in fact they were directly responsible for the deportations' (Lipták and Kováč 1997: 37). The response concluded that the 'publication does not belong in schools, for both educational and moral reasons' (Lipták and Kováč 1997: 39).

In response, the HZDS protested against the efforts 'of certain political parties and religious institutions to disgrace the accomplished work of Professor Ďurica', and expressed 'the deepest respect for everything that Professor Ďurica has done for Slovakia and its well-being and for making Slovakia more visible abroad' (*Kritika & kontext*, vol. 2, no. 3 [1997] 63). Yet the (then) ruling party could not sustain this support as the controversy gained international dimensions. Since the book was partly funded by the European Union and its PHARE programme, the government was finally forced to respond to the pressure of the European Commission and withdraw the publication from schools (*ibid.*: 64).

The attempts to justify the moral legitimacy of the first Slovak state were not limited to domestic Slovak discourse. A more sophisticated version of a similar line of argument in the Western academic world was advanced by Stanislav J. Kirschbaum. Although Kirschbaum was more balanced in his evaluation of Tiso's role in 'the Jewish tragedy', he appears to accept Ďurica's claim that tens of thousands of Jews were actually saved by the presidential decrees and by 'Tiso's political courage [which] allowed him, for a time at least...to bring about an end to deportations' (Kirschbaum 1995: 199–200).[25] With respect to the very existence of the Slovak state, Kirschbaum argued that 'it is quite legitimate for [leaders of small nations] to seek the one [Hitler] that will guarantee the safety of their nation' (Kirschbaum 1999a: 15).

More important, Kirschbaum seems to be concerned exclusively with the 'safety and survival' of the Slovak nation (ethnically defined). Even though he writes on one occasion about 'the safety of all the inhabitants of Slovakia', his primary concern is with 'the life of the nation' (Kirschbaum 1999a: 14, 16; cf. Kirschbaum 1995: 276). Only in that way is it possible for Kirschbaum to conclude that the 'balance sheet [of the wartime Slovak state] is anything but negative'. It is not clear, however, how any achievements can be weighed against the death of some 60,000 Jews. Finally, Kirschbaum praises the political elites because they 'instinctively understood that their primary objective had to be the survival of their state' (Kirschbaum 1999a: 26). Yet, the primary objective of any legitimate state should be the survival of its people (regardless of their nationality!). Unless, that is, one subscribes to a political philosophy that puts the interests of the state and the nation above the interests of the individual. This seems to be dangerously close to the ideology of national socialism that was able to justify the elimination of the Jewish race on the basis of the 'interests' of the dominant nation.

Hence, Dušan Kováč was right to argue that to claim

> that small nations were destined to collaborate,[26] is to advocate shameless morality. The moral mire caused by collaboration inevitably weakens the spiritual health of a nation, because a nation cannot exist only for itself. The theory of national egotism developed in the nineteenth century failed because national egotism leads to isolation, and this in turn brings destruction.
>
> (Kováč 1999)

Communist Czechoslovakia: dissent and the emergence of liberal nationalism

Ďurica's illiberal anti-communism, which recalled the heritage of the first Slovak state, had a more liberal counterpart within the domestic opposition, which unambiguously condemned the crimes of the first Slovak state. A clear manifestation of this attitude was, for example, 'The Proclamation on the Deportation of the Jews from Slovakia', published by the Slovak dissidents in 1987. In the context of this book, the proclamation can be read as a manifesto of liberal nationalism, since it appeals to national sentiments in order to challenge not only the communist amnesia regarding certain parts of Slovak history, but also the communist system as such. The starting premise of the proclamation is the realization that it is important for 'nations, as much as individuals, to have a consciousness and a sense of historical continuity...[which] approves of good deeds and condemns the wrongs'. Consequently, the signatories of the proclamation acknowledged the responsibility and guilt of the nation and apologized to the Jewish people. They concluded:

> Anti-Jewish policies and especially the deportations of the Jewish citizens from Slovakia violated the principles which we would like to see as crucial in creating a Slovak future – equality for everyone regardless of race, tolerance, freedom of conscience, democracy, the rule of law, fraternity.
>
> (cited in Čarnogurský 1997: 124)

The official representatives of the communist regime had never released similar apologies, even as they continued to celebrate the defeat of Nazism in Slovakia. In fact, the proud recollection of the Slovak National Uprising was one of the few legacies of the Prague Spring of the 1960s which survived two decades of the post-1969 normalization. Another legacy usually stressed in the literature was the transformation of Czechoslovakia into a formal federation consisting of the Czech and Slovak republics. But as the authoritarian system of communist Czechoslovakia tended to be centralist by its very nature, the federation could never have had a chance to make a significant impact on the lives of citizens in both republics – only the implementation of radical liberal democratic reforms would have truly empowered the citizens. What the peoples of Czechoslovakia got instead was 'federalised totality' (Šútovec 1999: 120).

Prague (or Bratislava) Spring: nationalism or/and democratization

The Slovak concern for the federal reorganization of the state is usually seen as yet another instance of Slovak nationalism being in the way of democratization. A telling example of the Czech response was presented by Ludvík Vaculík in 1990, when he linked the new demands of Slovak political leaders with the 'treason' of 1968 by stating that 'when we [the Czechs] tried in 1968 to free ourselves from dictatorship, the Slovaks regarded it as our concern and went for autonomy' (cited in Leff 1995: 110). This attitude is also reflected in academic literature dealing with the Prague Spring. Sharon L. Wolchik argued, for instance, that while in the Czech lands the general pressure of the population was 'for further democratisation...in Slovakia, national issues took precedence for the population as well as for many party leaders' (Wolchik 1992: 137). Similarly, J. F. Brown stressed that 'the Slovaks had seen the Prague Spring as a national rather than a democratic opportunity – one with anti-Czech overtones' (Brown 1994: 54). Such generalizations are unhelpful. It may well be argued that for many Slovaks (as well as Czechs) there was no contradiction, at least originally, between the revival of national sentiments and the urge for liberalization. In fact, the drive towards a 'socialism with a human face' was spurred by (liberal) nationalism in both parts of the country.

Furthermore, it is misleading to present the move in the late 1960s towards more liberalization as a solely Czech achievement. Indeed, some writers claim that the beginnings of the Prague Spring are to be found in the political developments of Slovakia. Not only was the leader, Alexander Dubček, a Slovak reforming communist but, as Karl-Peter Schwarz argued, 'in the early sixties there was much more open discussion within the party organisations, editorial offices and the universities in Slovakia than in the Czech lands' (Schwarz 1993: 191). The most prominent example of such activities was the publication of a monthly, *Kultúrny život (Cultural Life)*, renowned for its critical and daringly open articles, that were eagerly circulated amongst both Czechs and Slovak intellectuals. The monthly 'took the position that it was important to achieve democratisation before federalisation rather than the other way round' (Kirschbaum 1995: 243). Synthesizing both views, Daniel Rapant, a prominent Slovak historian, argued on the pages of *Kultúrny život* that 'we [the Slovaks] have to realise that the only reliable basis for the future of our state and nation is neither federation on its own, nor democracy on its own, but them both in a close connection' (Rapant 1968: 9). A competing newspaper *Nové slovo* (*New Word*), founded by Gustáv Husák, espoused reversed priorities and was ultimately vindicated by the developments which followed the Soviet-led invasion of Czechoslovakia in 1968. Husák was able to use the new situation to his own advantage, and, after replacing Dubček as the new leader of the Czechoslovak Communist Party, he sought to legitimize the repressive policies of 'Normalization' by realizing the Slovak demands for federalization (Čarnogurský 1997: 110). But even if the result of the ensuing 'Normalization' was formal federation *without* democratization, the defeat of the ideals of the Prague Spring cannot be attributed solely to Slovak nationalism.

The Czech perception that the goals of democratization were undermined by Slovak nationalism seemed to have been validated by marked differences in the extent of post-1968 repressions. The policies of 'Normalization' affected the Czech lands significantly more than Slovakia. Correspondingly, Czech opposition to the communist regime appeared to be more pronounced than its Slovak equivalent – the signatories of the human rights organization Charter 77, for example, were almost exclusively Czech. This is not to say that 'no effective opposition movement had existed [in Slovakia]' (Vachudová and Snyder 1997: 6). Rather, it took different forms and manifested itself predominantly in the religious realm (Pauer 1999: 16). While the demands of religious communities and their leaders in Slovakia were more moderate than some claims with which Czech dissidents challenged the authoritarian state, their reach was arguably much broader.

The most visible testimony to the popular appeal of religious movements were numerous pilgrimages to sites of religious significance (such as Levoča), which were attended in the late 1980s by hundreds of thousands of believers. These religious pilgrimages often turned into quiet demonstrations against the communist regime, and created opportunities for the formation of alternative associations which were able to escape state control. According to one of the main protagonists of the religiously inspired resistance against communism, Ján Čarnogurský, 'the Church in the totalitarian state became one of the last islands of freedom which allowed for the survival, or the new emergence of civil society' (Čarnogurský 1997: 85). In contrast to the experience of the wartime Slovak Republic, when the traditional religious sentiments of the vast majority of the Slovak people were (mis-)used as a source of xenophobic state-sponsored nationalism, the religious nationalism which emerged in the 1980s was reminiscent of Mazzini's.[27] As Čarnogurský stressed, the pilgrimages fostered not only a sense of spiritual and national unity, but were also meeting grounds for mutual understanding that transcended national boundaries, as they were attended by Czech, Polish and even Austrian visitors (Čarnogurský 1997: 60).

But even in predominantly Catholic Slovakia, not all opposition to the communist regime was religiously inspired. The more lenient approach of the authorities towards official culture allowed for some proliferation of non-conformist voices. For example, the late 1980s brought about a renewal of undeferential political satire in the theatre, consisting of re-emerging stars from the time of the Prague Spring such as the comedian duo Lasica and Satinský (popular as much in Slovakia as in the Czech lands), or successful new entrants like Milan Markovič. It is worthwhile noting that their satires usually targeted not only the communist authorities, but also state-spon-sored, narrow-minded, ethnocentric nationalism.[28] Among the few Slovak signatories of Charter 77 were the lawyer Čarnogurský (see above), the eminent Slovak writer Dominik Tatarka, and the political scientist Miroslav Kusý, who was one of the most outspoken critics of the discrimination against ethnic minorities in communist Czechoslovakia. Kusý argued that 'the general denial of rights [was] inherent in a totalitarian system, in which the interests of all groups, including the nationality groups, were subordi-nated to the "superior interests" of those in power, whether Czech or Slovak' (Skilling 1989: 92).[29]

Still, the dissident movement in Slovakia was far less numerous and influ-ential than in the Czech lands. Not surprisingly then, it was the Catholic Church which organized the largest demonstrations which preceded the Velvet Revolution of November 1989. The first open confrontation with the communist system was the 1988 signature campaign which demanded freedom of religion, and was signed by some 300,000 people in Slovakia (out of 500,000 in the whole country). In March 1988, the communist authorities 'repressed brutally a peaceful candlelight religious rally organ-ised by František Mikloško' (Kirschbaum 1995: 248), and many more similar demonstrations followed. Thus, while the November 1989 revolution was triggered in Prague and reached Slovakia only some five days later (Pauer 1999: 16), Slovak society was arguably as willing to bring about the end of the communist system of power as Czech society was. Once again, Czechs and Slovaks 'made' common history, even if their experiences of those common (or similar) developments differed significantly.

Slovaks without history?

There were also significant differences among the perceptions of this recent history within Slovak society. Those Slovak intellectuals who were primarily concerned with national independence rather than democratization were also critical of the common heritage of the Czechoslovak dissident move-ment. Reflecting on Charter 77, Vladimír Mináč noted that 'Slovak intellectual dissidence was not independent, did not even take a step without the consent of Prague, was Czechoslovak, and in its political consequences, it was even Czechoslovakizing' (cited in Kirschbaum 1995: 248). This view corresponded with the strong tendency in the more ethnocentric history writings (e.g. Ďurica) and literature (e.g. Ferko, Jaroš, Mináč) to 'expatriate' the Slovak nation from the histories of Austria-Hungary and Czechoslovakia by arguing that Slovaks, a quintessentially peaceful people, do not really have their own history and were always just innocent victims of the powers that be. As Mináč wrote in the late 1960s,

> If history is understood as a history of kings and emperors, commanders and princes, military victories and conquered territories, if history is thus a history of violence, plunder and exploitation, then we [the Slovaks] have no history, at least not in the sense of being the subject of such a history. But if the history of civilisation is a history of work, a history of discontinued but ever again and again resumed and victorious construction, then this is our history. We [the Slovaks] are a nation of constructors, builders, not only in the metaphorical, but also literal sense of the term.
>
> (cited in Kováč 1993: 535–6; cf. Pynsent 1994: 154)

Mináč's understanding of Slovak history goes back to Štúr's idealistic conception of Slovaks as 'a nation of farmers and builders' (Pynsent 1994: 154) who allegedly had civilizing effects on such 'uncultivated warriors' as the neighbouring Magyars. More recently, however, this traditional philosophy of Slovak history has been challenged for being anachronistic and misleading. In a direct response to Mináč, a distinguished Slovak biochemist, Ladislav Kováč (unrelated to the historian Dušan Kováč), argued in 1989 that the Slovaks should free themselves from inferiority complexes about their past, because they lead to aggressive nationalism directed against others (whether they be Magyars or Czechs). As he put it,

> We do have history – Central European history is our history and Central European culture is our culture. It belongs to us all who now speak Slovak, as much as we used to speak for generations Slovak, *and* German, *and* Hungarian, being a part of one political, economic and cultural community in Upper Hungary.
>
> (Kováč 1989: 511)

The lesson derived from this 'multicultural' perspective of history is Ladislav Kováč's call on the people to positively contribute to the present and future developments of Central Europe (not against but with the neighbours). Similarly, Dušan Kováč warned against Mináč's mythopoeic reading of history because it engendered nationalism emptied of moral responsibility. 'The "liberation" of the nation from Hungarian history is its apologia. The nation [according to this view] bears no responsibility for wars and bloodshed' (Kováč 1993: 536). In line with this, Rudolf Chmel, who is currently (since September 2002) the minister of culture, argued that the myth about Slovaks without history amounts to a 'castrated history'. As he said, 'we [the Slovaks] need to repopulate our history by adding to it histories which we share with Hungarians and Czechs' (Chmel 1996: 376). Chmel also called for the Slovak version of *Vergangenheitsbewältigung* (coming to terms with the past) with respect to Hungarians (Chmel 1996: 461).[30]

The debates about the 'meaning' of Slovak history which preceded the fall of communism set out the points of reference for an exploration of the values of a liberal democratic society, but they also created the ideological framework for an ethnocentric conception of the nation. While the ideas of a handful of intellectuals did not determine the ensuing political developments, they were certainly influential; whether by lending legitimacy to the emerging authoritarian regime of Vladimír Mečiar, or by mobilizing support for the democratic opposition. One of the most contentious issues that impacted on political developments after 1989 was the question of the appropriate relationship between the state and the (ethnically defined) nation – first within the Czechoslovak state, and later in the context of the newly created, independent Slovak Republic.

From Velvet Revolution to Velvet Divorce (1989–92)

It has been argued that the process of democratic transition in Czechoslovakia has been complicated by the protracted 'disputes over constitutional issues, both between the national elites of the two republics and among the Slovak elite itself' (Szomolányi 1997: 9). The democratizing impetus of the 1989 revolution brought to the fore deep-seated differences about the role of the new state, not only between many Czechs and Slovaks, but also within Slovak society. Although such differentiation was desirable, as it reflected the pluralist character of the society, the divisions also led to some radicalization of Slovak politics. It appeared, at times, that the original goals of the Velvet Revolution had been hijacked in Slovakia by extreme nationalists who seemed to be more concerned with the fate of the nation (defined in exclusionary terms) than with the freedom of the individual citizens constituting this nation. Many faithful servants of the communist regime, such as Dušan Slobodník, reinvented themselves as nationalists, by substituting the logic of class struggle with the language of chauvinism, which saw the Slovak nation threatened by 'the anti-Slovak conspiracy of Prague and Budapest' (Slobodník 1998) supported by the dubious interests of the West.[31]

One of the main sources of Mečiar's enduring popularity was the widespread perception that he has consistently been the best defender of Slovak national interests, whether it be against 'traditional enemies' like Hungarians and Czechs, or new challenges from the West. While many analysts have rightly argued that Mečiar's policies were not based primarily on the ideology of ethnocentric nationalism (see e.g. Kusý 1998: 25–9), as a gifted populist politician, Mečiar certainly appealed to such sentiments whenever it suited his purposes. In fact, it can be argued that the very creation of the independent Slovak Republic was as much the result of the political ambitions of

Mečiar and his acolytes as it was a consequence of historic legacies and the rising economic discrepancies between the two republics.

Very soon after the Velvet Revolution, it became clear that a majority of Slovaks had very different expectations of Czechoslovakia from those of their Czech counterparts. 'Many Slovaks were of the opinion that the existing state was dominated by the Czech part, and that Slovakia was entitled not only to a more equal and visible position but also to more political self-rule' (Hilde 1999: 649). This was demonstrated as early as the spring of 1990 in the notorious 'hyphen war' about the appropriate name for the new postcommunist republic. While the Czech politicians wanted to simply retain the name Czechoslovak Republic (without the addition of 'socialist'), the Slovak members of the federal parliament demanded that the new state be called the Czecho-Slovak Republic: a name which would reflect the distinct nature of both nations as well as their equal status. The hyphen was unacceptable for the Czechs as it reminded them of the short-lived post-Munich Second Republic Czechoslovakia without the Sudetenland (which was called Czecho-Slovakia in 1938–9). For the Slovaks, on the other hand, the Czech unwillingness to accept such a symbolic change seemed to vindicate their fears of Czech domination.

As Milan Šútovec showed in a fascinating book-length study of *The Politics of Semiotics, or Hyphen-War*, the failure of the political elites to reach a consensus that would satisfy all parties in the conflict ultimately led to the disintegration of the country (Šútovec 1999).[32] The first compromise solution adopted after a series of protracted disputes was to name the country in two different ways, following (allegedly) different grammatical rules in both respective languages. The Czech name of the country, *Československá federativní republika* (Czechoslovak Federative Republic), was to be 'translated' into Slovak as *Česko-slovenská federatívna republika*. Not surprisingly, this 'grammatical' solution met with fierce resistance in Slovakia, where the hyphen was seen as an important symbol of the recognition of equality of both nations in the federation. Finally, another compromise was found in the name of the Czech and Slovak Federal Republic, but the bitter dispute exacerbated relations between the two constituent nations of that federation, and paved the way for a split that no one seems to have wanted.

Hence, it is ironic that Mečiar and his HZDS ultimately derived a great deal of political legitimacy from the creation of an independent state which was never desired by a majority of the Slovak people.[33] In fact, while the republic's split is usually seen as a Slovak imposition on the Czechs (see Chapter 4), Paal Hilde concluded that it was not a result of Slovak secessionist nationalism. Rather, the split was caused by those Czech political forces which

> put the value of continued economic reform, stability and rapid 'reintegration' into Europe above that of preserving the common state. The

break-up ... was a result of the promotion of what the political right saw as Czech national interest, over those of the Federation. Interpreted like this, the key to the break-up of the CSFR lies in Czech rather than in Slovak nationalism.

(Hilde 1999: 663; cf. Leff 1997: 131)

Whether Czechs or Slovaks, or in fact both nations (or their inexperienced political leaderships) are to be blamed for the split of the republic, what seems clear is the fact that the event was rather accidental. Nevertheless, very soon after the realization of national independence, the event was reinterpreted as a logical and more or less necessary result of Slovak history.

The strongest political party in Slovakia did not originally aim at separation. As Mečiar unambiguously stated ahead of the 1992 elections, 'an independent Slovak state is not the programmatic goal of the HZDS' (Leško 1996: 81). In accordance with this, he also claimed that his party was pushed into independence by the Czech political leaders, who were not prepared to make compromises in seeking a new model for the common Czech and Slovak state, such as a confederation which would better accommodate the Slovak demands for more control of their own affairs. Furthermore, Mečiar explicitly distanced himself from those 'jingoists [*huránárodniari*] who want to return to conceptions which are obsolete'. In contrast, he stressed that 'the Slovak national interest lies in European integration and respect for European standards...If we accepted the national principle, this would lead to self-isolation and it would damage the interests of Slovakia' (cited in Leško 1996: 206).

Slovak independence and the rule of the HZDS (1992–March 1994, October 1994–1998)

It is one of the paradoxes of recent Slovak history (made possible by the tergiversations of Mečiar) that the country was, in fact, led to self-isolation by the very same politician who earlier opposed the national principle. The fact that neither the HZDS nor Mečiar actually desired national independence did not prevent the party from claiming its monopoly as the only truthful defender of the interests of the Slovak nation and its state. As the party's deputy chairman, Augustín Marián Húska, claimed in 1996, 'Mečiar and the HZDS have become the hope of Slovakia and the main authors of Slovak statehood' (cited in Fisher 1996a). Despite such claims, the party never succeeded in representing the hopes of all the people living in Slovakia, and it also failed in its attempts to impose its own vision on the whole of Slovak society. If anything, the creation of the independent republic deeply divided Slovak society. The first clear manifestation of this divide was the parliamentary crisis of March 1994, in which Mečiar's government lost its majority in parliament. It was replaced by an interim government led by Jozef Moravčík (March–October 1994), which comprised a wide coalition of political parties, including a splinter group of the HZDS created by a number of dissatisfied detractors.[34] This event clearly demonstrated that there were influential forces within Slovak society which had not accepted the HZDS' vision of a Slovak state. Moravčík's government, on the other hand, aimed at 'implementation of the values of western civilisation characterised by parliamentary democracy, political pluralism, freedom of thought and information, the state of law, civil society and respect for minority rights' (Žiak 1996: 146).

Mečiar's elites and their supporters refused to acknowledge the legitimacy of the alternative government on the grounds that it represented those 'anti-Slovak' forces who were 'against national sovereignty, against the emergence of the new state, and against the dissolution of the federation' (Mečiar 1994). In a programmatic speech, Mečiar formulated the main strategy of the ensuing political struggle by stressing that it was thanks to the policies of the HZDS that the Slovaks had gained, 'as a gift after a thousand years', their own nation state. Any attack on the policies of his party was consequently deemed illegitimate, as it represented an attack on the nation as such. 'Whenever this state is challenged – or, if not the state then its functions and institutions – it equals challenging the very essence of Slovaks as a nation' (Mečiar 1994). Mečiar and his ideologues (e.g. Húska, Hofbauer) sought to equate the interests of their party with the interests of Slovak nation and the state. This strategy was not without success, as it arguably contributed to the HZDS's return to power in the October 1994 elections. Only this time the HZDS was forced to enter into a coalition with the extreme right-wing Slovak National Party (SNS) and the far-left Association of Slovak Workers (ZRS).

In stark contrast to his anti-nationalist stance in 1992 (see above), Mečiar reversed his position with respect to the role of the new state by accepting the national principle. He stated explicitly that it was 'correct that we are building a nation state' (cited in Leško 1996: 206). Such a state, moreover, was to be protected from criticism and was, in that way, beyond 'good and evil'. In fact, Mečiar put the interests of the state above conventional morality. As he said in 1995, attacking the President of Slovakia Michal Kováč: 'whoever heads a state and is in the public service, has to protect the interests of his state, whatever they are, they are his. They can even be bad, but they are his' (cited in Leško 1996: 149).

In 1996, the coalition government followed an initiative of the radical Slovak National Party and sought to implement the 'Law for the Protection of the Republic', which would allow the prosecution of individuals who 'spread false information' that might be seen as damaging Slovakia's interests, however these were defined (Fisher 1996b). According to the official propaganda campaign accompanying the controversial legislation, the law was directed against 'internal enemies'. As Mečiar put it, 'we will not allow our republic to be subverted, and thus the government will adopt an amendment to the penal code...that will make such activities unlawful and punishable' (cited in Mesežnikov 1998: 11). The law and its justification were reminiscent of communist times,[35] and hence met with fierce protests from all sections of society. Strong concerns were voiced by a wide section of the public – not only opposition parties and journalists, who would both have been directly affected by the new legislation, but also the Catholic Church, trade unions, judges, and a number of civic groups. Ultimately, the ruling coalition bowed to this immense domestic and international pressure and shrank back from implementing the new law (Mesežnikov 1998: 12).

The incident was instructive in two respects. First, it clearly demonstrated the intention of the ruling coalition to strengthen its position of power. The government's authoritarian tendencies, especially in relation to the electronic media, the economy and the parliamentary opposition, were not just some accidental excesses of erratic politicians (e.g. Mečiar), but corresponded with a genuine desire to build a nation-state dominated by the political power of the HZDS and its coalition partners. Second, the incident showed the determination of large sections of Slovak society to defend the freedoms gained by the Velvet Revolution, and to resist by peaceful means the monopolization of the state by Mečiar's coalition.

Another controversial piece of legislation was the 'Law on the State Language', adopted in 1995, which severely restricted the language rights of ethnic minorities by 'requiring the use of Slovak in virtually all aspects of public life' (Dostál 1998: 39). The law was clearly directed against the Hungarian minority. This is evident from the justification that recalls the Slovak national grievances of the past, and purports to aim at the protection of the Slovak language against the persistent danger of Magyarization:

> From the end of the eighteenth century, the Slovak language had to withstand the increasingly aggressive pressure of the Hungarian language….Forced Magyarization during the time of historic Hungary, as well as between the years 1938 and 1945 when Hungary occupied a large part of Southern Slovakia, inflicted wounds that remain open to this day.
>
> (cited in Brusis 1997: 420)

Since the invoked fear of Magyarization of the Slovak population cannot be rationally justified in a country with a clear Slovak majority, the law might rather be seen as an act of revenge for past injustices; only this time the disadvantaged national group was not to be Slovak but Magyar. As Lájos Grendel commented, 'the politicians of the current [1997] ruling coalition in effect emulate those policies (of the old Hungarian empire) which they condemn as unjust' (Grendel 1998: 111). Grendel pointed out that national problems could only be addressed satisfactorily when both Slovaks and Magyars in Slovakia avoided 'fundamentalist nationalism' in favour of liberal principles. 'A modern democratic state in Slovakia cannot be built on paranoid phobias, infantile nationalism, never ending recrimination of past injustices, distrust and the inhibition of difference' (Grendel 1998: 112). Similar criticism was also voiced by Slovak intellectuals and political leaders (e.g. Kusý 1998: 124–5). Although these objections did not prevent the ruling coalition from adopting the restrictive language law, the debate provided a good opportunity for the exploration of liberal values in Slovak society, and paved the way for the adoption of a more liberal law by the subsequent government in 1999.

It is important to note that not only national minorities, but also large sections of Slovak society never accepted the vision of an ethnically exclusive Slovak state which would disregard basic liberal principles (Fisher 1996c). The HZDS's vision of a homogenous nation-state produced a society which was deeply divided, not only along ethnic lines, but even within the Slovak community. This division could only be overcome by endowing the state with a new meaning which would be less exclusionary. As Svetoslav Bombík argued,

> The idea of Slovak statehood should not be derived from an exclusive ethnic-cultural principle, but rather from a pluralist understanding of Slovakia based on democratic principles of civil society and the rule of law. Our coat of arms should be Pluralism – Solidarity – Central Europeaness [*Stredoeurópskost'*]. If Slovakia failed to follow this vision, it would, to its own detriment, repeat the mistakes of the previous states on the same territory (Hungary and Czechoslovakia). Both states attempted to equate the national interests of an ethnic majority with the interests of the multitude of nationalities living within those multinational states.
>
> (Bombík 1995: 186)

A Q-methodology study conducted in Slovakia in 1998 provided evidence that different views on the role of the state divided not only the elites, but also the whole society. The study, which is based on the evaluation of a variety of sources (newspapers, electronic media, and discussion groups of representative cohorts of the population), identified two competing discourses of democracy, labelled 'developing pluralism' and 'unitary populism'. Although the exponents of unitary populism, who supported Mečiar's HZDS and/or the far-right Slovak National Party (SNS), claimed to believe in democracy, it was 'democracy of a decidedly illiberal and anti-pluralist sort', which was based on 'a unitary conception of the public interest as defined by the will of the majority and its implementation by government' (Dryzek and Holmes 2002: 187). Clearly, this discourse was unable to accommodate satisfactorily the legitimate demands of ethnic (or, indeed, of any other) minorities. In contrast, the exponents of developing pluralism, who were largely supporters of the anti-Mečiar opposition parties in the 1998 elections, explicitly endorsed the principle that 'the majority must accept that minorities too have rights, and that democracy is not simply majority rule'. In line with this, the adherents of developing pluralism believed that the important features of democracy are not only 'liberal freedoms, constitutional government, and the rule of law', but also 'respect for the rights of national minorities' (Dryzek and Holmes 2002: 179).

While the Q-methodology study did not determine which of the two competing discourses exercised more influence within Slovak society, the result of the September 1998 elections indicated strong support for the ideas of developing pluralism. The electoral success of more liberal political forces, combined with the political isolation of the HZDS, made it possible to radically change the meaning of the new Slovak state, not only on a symbolic level, but also in various practical policies. The new coalition government consisting of the Slovak Democratic Coalition (SDK), the Party of the Democratic Left (SDL), the Hungarian Coalition Party (SMK), and Schuster's Party of Civic Reconciliation (SOP) had a comfortable three-fifths majority in parliament, and was able to introduce new legislation which better accommodated the demands of ethnic minorities (e.g. the language law). But the polarization of society did not simply end with the inauguration of the new government.

The end of 'Mečiarism'

One of the divisive issues that lasted far beyond the September 1998 elections was the evaluation of the role of Mečiar in the context of Slovak history. Interestingly, the radically different interpretations of his achievements and failures are not limited to accounts originating in Slovakia, but are also reflected in English-language academic literature. While those observers who were primarily concerned with the emancipation process of the Slovak nation construed Mečiar as a founder of Slovak democracy, others argued that Mečiar's rule seriously undermined the emerging liberal democratic order. Stanislav Kirschbaum, in line with his concern for the heroic struggle of the Slovak nation for survival (Kirschbaum 1995: 10), condoned Mečiar's era, since 'for all its confusion, [it] was also characterized by policies, often described as nationalist, that allowed Slovaks to take control of their state and its destiny' (Kirschbaum 1999b: 601). According to Kirschbaum, Mečiar should be credited for 'many post-independence achievements' and his 'mistakes and errors of judgement...should be viewed rather as the growing pains of Slovak independence' (Kirschbaum 1999b: 596).

In contrast, most Western reports were highly critical of Mečiar's administration. Typical was the assessment of the Economist Intelligence Unit:

> His nationalist-populist government curtailed the cultural rights of the large Hungarian minority, repeatedly ignored constitutional court decisions, and subordinated most key public institutions – including the

intelligence service, the state-owned broadcasting media, the police, the prosecutor's office and most branches of the state administration – to direct political control.

(EIU Country Report, 4th quarter, 1998: 10)

The list of 'growing pains of Slovak independence' (Kirschbaum 1999b: 596) could easily be extended. While the EIU report attempted to identify political goals and strategies (however questionable they may be), Steven Fish pointed out that conventional political wisdom does not suffice in understanding 'Mečiarism', that is '*ochlochracy*, or rule by the rabble'. In his view, 'Slovakia was governed [until September 1998] by a coalition of misanthropes and harlequins, headed by a politically wily but mentally unbalanced prime minister...[who] established a regime based on thuggery, incompetence, and the contempt for law' (Fish 1999: 47). Fish argued that Mečiar sought to establish a unique regime which lacked any programmatic goals and coherence, but was aimed simply at maintaining and enhancing his political power. 'In organizational and institutional terms, Mečiarism was characterized by personalization and de-ideologization of the party and by partyization of the state' (Fish 1999: 47).

Fish's vivid account of the role of Mečiar in Slovak history is certainly more accurate than the evaluations of those nationalist-minded analysts who do not hesitate to justify the failures of the new Slovak state as the inevitable growing pains of a 'young' nation, while arguing, at the same time, that Slovaks are the oldest people in the whole of Europe. Clearly, liberal democracy in Slovakia developed, if anything, in spite of the rule of Mečiar, thanks to the incessant activities from within civil society which defied the authoritarian tendencies of the state administration. But it has to be acknowledged that even Mečiar and his ruling coalition adhered to *some* basic rules of the democratic game, and accepted their defeat in the September 1998 elections.

Yet the end of 'Mečiarism' did not end all the political problems. In fact, some legacies of Mečiar's authoritarian rule are still able to adversely affect the process of postcommunist transition. Not only have widespread corruption and the recurring abuse of political power undermined the people's trust in the newly created institutions of the democratic state, but some of the opportunistic legislative measures of the previous government have had a lasting impact on the political structures of Slovak society. Mečiar's administration sought to weaken the political influence of the opposition parties by adopting a new election law in 1997, which rendered the conventional coalition agreements meaningless by multiplying the 5 per cent threshold by the number of parties entering the coalition. In response, the opposition forces strengthened their unity by the creation of the Slovak Democratic Coalition (SDK) led by Dzurinda, which comprised 'the centre-right Christian Democratic Movement (KDH) and Democratic Party (DS), the centrist Democratic Union (DU) and two small centre-left parties, the

Slovak Social Democratic Party (SDSS) and the Slovak Green Party (SZS)' (*EIU Country Profile, Slovakia 1998–99*: 13). While the new coalition party proved successful in securing victory over Mečiar and his Movement for a Democratic Slovakia, the artificially enforced unity has significantly altered the existing party structure. This development was partly reversed in November 2000, when the KDH split from the SDK, 'while some representatives of the Christian Democratic platform merged with the liberal platform of the SDK to create a new political entity – the SDKU' (Slovak Christian and Democratic Union) led by Dzurinda (Mesežnikov 2002: 33).

On the more positive side, the fragmentation of parties led also to the weakening of those political parties which openly expounded extreme nationalist views. The Slovak National Party failed to secure sufficient support in the September 2002 elections, due to the emergence of a splinter group, the Real Slovak National Party (PSNS). And even Mečiar's HZDS has been considerably weakened through various infighting between dissatisfied party members. Yet, despite the various achievements of the new ruling coalition led by Dzurinda (see below), the prevalence of liberal democratic forces can still be challenged. The most formidable opponent is possibly Robert Fico, leader of the populist political party Smer ('Direction'), whose views, particularly with respect to Romanies, are a cause for concern. Whatever shape the party-political landscape in Slovakia may take, there is still a significant body of public opinion in favour of populist and extreme nationalist alternatives to the more liberal democratic policies. These views correspond with some aspects of traditional Slovak culture, which support hostility towards ethnic minorities and could exacerbate the problems associated with the cohabitation of different ethnic communities. Two case studies will demonstrate that some problems both preceded and outlived the rule of Mečiar.

Gabčíkovo-Nagymaros: the nation of builders in a struggle for electricity

One particular source of animosity between Slovaks and Hungarians has been the project of a hydroelectric power plant on the Danube. The project, which involved a redirection of the river stream, received a remarkable degree of consensus in Slovakia which defied the traditional political cleavages. The plant, which originated as an idea in the 1950s and the construction of which started in the late 1970s, was supposed to cement the 'brotherly' relations between the two neighbouring communist countries. After the demise of communist power in both countries, the hydroelectric scheme gained fundamentally different meanings in Slovakia and Hungary, and led to mutual distrust rather than brotherhood. While most Hungarians saw it as a legacy of the Stalinist obsession for megalomaniac projects which resulted in the ruthless exploitation of nature, the Slovaks saw the project as a powerful demonstration of their creative potential. In both countries the project was inseparably linked with nation-building, and hence became a source of political legitimacy which transcended its purely economic purpose (Hood 1998). In fact, the conflict could be seen as a validation of Mináč's philosophy of Slovak history (see above). Throughout the 1990s, his 'nation of constructors and builders' was engaged in a peaceful struggle against its traditional enemy (the Hungarians) for a new source of electricity. In this interpretation, the ambitious project was yet another manifestation of the creative spirit of a nation which had to defy, over centuries, hostile forces from within and without. While the construction of the power plant was supported by a wide spectrum of political forces, there can be little doubt that Mečiar's popularity was boosted by his uncompromising attitude towards Hungarian opposition to the project.

Slovaks versus Romanies

Apart from their historical bias against the Hungarians, many Slovaks have traditionally been prejudiced against Romanies and Jews. Although the extent of hostility and the pervasiveness of anti-Roma sentiments within Slovak society were no different to what they were in the Czech Republic, the Slovak political elites (particularly from within the HZDS and the SNS) were more outspoken in voicing racial prejudice. A telling example of anti-Romany rhetoric used by Mečiar was his argument voiced in a televised debate that questioned the legitimacy of the Slovak Hungarian demands by stating that half of them were actually Roma. As a report of the European Roma Rights Centre commented,

> Being tainted by Gypsydom is, evidently, according to Mečiar, a suitable cause for having one's political demands rejected. Anti-Romani statements are extremely effective politically because most Slovaks simultaneously hold two beliefs. One is that Roma are bad (criminal, degenerated, stinking, too rich, too poor, ill-adapted, disgusting) and the other is that they are treated too well by the state and other Slovaks.
>
> (Cahn and Trehan 1997: 49)

Even more blatant were the statements of the consecutive leaders of the Slovak National Party (SNS), Ján Slota and Anna Malíková. While Slota stated that the only way to deal with Gypsies was with 'a big whip and a small yard' (cited in Cibulka 1999: 126), Malíková openly advocated the policies of segregation as a possible solution to the 'Roma problem' (Schutz 2000a). Regrettably, such opinions resonated with large sections of the Slovak population. According to an opinion poll conducted by *Focus* in September 1999, 87 per cent of the Slovak population would prefer not to have a Romany neighbour (Schutz 2000a).

The political situation post-September 1998

Although the simple fact of removing Mečiar's coalition from power did not bring about the end of all hostilities directed against ethnic minorities in Slovakia, several policies of the subsequent coalition governments created the preconditions for significant improvements. A promising step was the creation of the position of deputy prime minister responsible for human rights issues and the protection of minorities. The position was filled by Pál Csáky, a senior member of the Hungarian Coalition Party. Moreover, the very fact that a Hungarian party was represented in the coalition governments was significant. First, it secured more direct influence for the representatives of the larger national minority in Slovakia on legislation that would affect it. Second, it allowed for the proliferation of leading Slovak Magyar politicians who were able to participate in administering problems affecting the whole of society, not only their ethnically defined constituency. As Bútorová *et al.* suggested, 'the common efforts of Slovak and Magyar politicians within the ruling coalition to solve broad social, economic and environmental problems could contribute to the strengthening of mutual trust and improve the attitudes of the democratically orientated Slovaks towards the Hungarian minority' (Bútorová *et al.* 1999: 263).

One of the first practical measures aimed at improving the situation of the Hungarian minority was the adoption of the long-awaited minority language law in July 1999. The main purpose of the law was to alleviate the negative impact of the previous legislation of Mečiar's government, which had imposed serious restrictions on the use of minority languages in public administration. The adoption of the bill was preceded by fervent disputes. The opposition, consisting of the HZDS and the SNS, objected to the new law, and claimed that it amounted to an act of treason. The Hungarian Coalition Party (SMK), on the other hand, rejected the law (despite being a member of the governing coalition) because it did not go far enough in protecting the language rights of minorities. In particular, the Magyar representatives criticized the provision according to which the use of minority languages in official contacts was guaranteed only in those cases where the minority group makes up 20 per cent of a particular municipality. But while the final result did not meet with the approval of the SMK, it was endorsed by the European Union and the Organization for Security and Cooperation in Europe, since it was based on their recommendations (*The Slovak Spectator*, 19–25 July 1999). Thus, even if the resulting compromise was far from ideal (and it is doubtful whether an ideal solution which would satisfy all parties can ever be found – see Chapter 2), it clearly showed that improvements in the situation of national minorities were possible.

Although the situation of the Hungarian minority has improved considerably since October 1998, there has been less progress in the treatment of the Romany minority. The repeated waves of emigration of the Slovak Romanies to the countries of Western Europe have increased international attention to their problems. Partly as a reaction to this, Dzurinda's first government coalition adopted a new strategy 'for the Solution to the Problems of the Roma National Minority and a Set of Measures for Its Implementation'. The *European Roma Rights Centre* criticized some paternalistic elements in the new strategy, but it also acknowledged that 'the program is an improvement over measures taken by the former government' (*Roma Rights*, 4/1999). Yet, even the best measures of a government take time to impact on the societal culture, which needs to be changed radically if lasting improvements are to be achieved.[36] The trend so far has not been very encouraging. While the mistrust of Slovaks towards Hungarians and Jews has declined in the 1990s, it significantly increased towards Romanies (Vodička 2003: 16). The changed political circumstances resulting from the political isolation of the extremist forces such as the SNS and the HZDS, which have considerably strengthened the forces of liberal nationalism in Slovakia, are yet to be reflected in a change of the general attitude of the majority towards Romanies.

Concluding remarks

A new Slovakia: a chance for liberal nationalism?

> Slovakness has certain content, good and bad. The good one has heroic elements defying misfortunes; it is a trust in truth and the rule of law, a thirst for them; justice not only for me and for us, but for everyone; humanity.
>
> (Matuška 1946: 322)

As has been demonstrated, postcommunist developments in Slovakia were strongly influenced by two diametrically opposed conceptions of nationalism. At one end of the political spectrum were those extreme nationalists within the SNS and the HZDS who sought to monopolize the nation and the state, and showed little concern for those citizens of the republic who did not support their vision (whether they were ethnic Slovaks or members of national minorities). At the other end of the divide were those politicians and intellectuals who stressed the importance of civic values, and saw the role of the state primarily as serving all citizens rather than serving a nation defined in exclusive terms. Yet such a classification of the divide is somewhat misleading, as it implies that civic and national concerns are by necessity in conflict. As Peter Zajac commented,

> It is only meaningful to talk about a sovereign nation in a democratic society, if it is a nation of free citizens; a nation which is based on the principles of human dignity; a nation respecting the basic human rights of individuals and minorities; a nation which is prosperous, educated

and cultured; a nation respectful of other nations and ethnic groups. That is, it must be a nation with an unambiguously civic basis.

(Zajac 1996: 130)

Hence, the real distinguishing mark between the two conceptions of a people are not 'whether it is *national*, or *anti-national* [Slovak, or anti-Slovak], but rather whether it is *democratic* and *pluralistic*, or *totalitarian* and *monolithic*' (Zajac 1996: 131). Paradoxically, many journalistic accounts, as well as a number of academic studies on recent Slovak developments, accepted the reductionist logic which renders the nation a monolithic community. Only in that way was it possible to suggest that Slovak nationalism was illiberal virtually by definition. The approach presented in this chapter, which has sought to examine different discourses of nationalism within Slovak society, offers a more complex picture. It makes clear that even in times when Slovak politics was dominated by forces inimical to the ideals of liberal democracy, alternative forces were espousing radically different sets of principles. Whether those principles were labelled 'democratic nationalism' (Hodža, Zajac), 'patriotism' (Lukáč), 'constitutional patriotism' (Bútora and Bútorová), or 'pluralism – solidarity – Central Europeaness' (Bombík), they could all be accommodated within the concept of liberal nationalism (see Chapter 1), which seeks to reconcile particular national traditions with the universal values of liberalism. Schmögnerová, recalling the heritage of Štefánik (and relying on the liberal thoughts of the influential literary critic and societal commentator Alexander Matuška), succinctly formulated the ideal of liberal nationalism in the Slovak context: 'We have to express, in accordance with European standards, our own Slovak modification of universal values' (Schmögnerová 1997: 212; see also Chmel 1996: 378; Pichler 1998: 125).

Possibly the best symbolic expression of the new content with which the Slovak state was endowed was a new reading of the Slovak national anthem. As Bútora and Bútorová observed, all demonstrations against the authoritarian tendencies of the government in the early stages of independence were also directed against extreme nationalism, and were hence usually devoid of national symbols. Thus, while the anti-communist demonstrations in November 1989 were usually concluded by singing the Czechoslovak national anthem, anti-Mečiar gatherings used popular protest songs rather than 'the Slovak anthem, which at the time was a source of embarrassment to many Slovak democrats' (Bútora and Bútorová 1999: 94). The anthem, which in its second stanza alludes to the long historic struggle of the Slovak nation, seemed an inappropriate tool for the defence of liberal values (see note 23 for the text of the anthem). But this has changed, as can be seen in Bútora and Bútorová's dramatic description:

After a while, however, participants at such rallies began to sing the Slovak anthem. It was sung by Slovak politicians, students, NGO representatives, actors, members of the Church, academics, representatives of the Hungarian parties....This represented a symbolic turning point, demonstrating the seriousness of the struggles being waged by the opposition in the name of constitutional patriotism....Awakening Sleeping Beauty no longer meant awakening Slovakia to national independence. That has already been achieved. It meant awakening Slovakia to freedom, democracy, and an open society.

(Bútora and Bútorová 1999: 94)

The contest between different conceptions of nationalism in Slovakia is not over. But if the second Dzurinda-led coalition sustains its determination to fight off any renewed attempts at the monopolization of the Slovak state, the chances of liberal nationalism becoming a dominant force in society are good.

6   Conclusions

The principle aim of this book was to investigate whether nationalism in Central Europe poses a threat to the liberal democratic project, or whether under certain circumstances it can, in fact, enhance the chances of consolidating the new political order. This question proved to be more difficult to answer than many conventional theories of nationalism imply. The stereotypical notions which divide the nations of the world and their nationalism(s) into liberal or illiberal; Western or Eastern; progressive or backward – whether this be on the basis of 'two types of nationalism', 'two types of civilization', or even 'two types of postcommunist transition' – were proven to be too simplistic, and hence unhelpful in understanding the role of nationalism in the countries of this study: Poland, the Czech Republic and Slovakia. As was demonstrated in the first chapter, the character of nationalism is not determined by geography, nor by the political history of a nation. A careful analysis of particular case studies showed that the role of nationalism is more ambiguous than these theories suggest.

Instead of designing new divisions of Europe, this study sought to identify different conceptions of nationalism that compete for dominance within each nation, and to assess their influence on political developments. This is not to say that the conceptual map of Europe should by redrawn by assigning the Czechs, the Poles (and now even the Slovaks?) to the West, just because they appear to be less illiberal than was originally assumed. Although the claim that the nations of the former Eastern Bloc are illiberal by inclination is wrong, its complete negation would not be correct either. I have argued, instead, that a new theoretical framework is needed to replace the reductionist schemes (along the lines of 'two types of nationalism') which resulted in descriptive accounts that were not only incomplete, but seriously misleading.

Not surprisingly, the case studies demonstrated that none of the societies in focus were immune to the appeal of ethnocentric nationalism, which puts one's own nation above all others. The likes of Tadeusz Rydzyk in Poland, Miroslav Sládek in the Czech Republic, and Ján Slota in Slovakia sought to mobilize popular support by espousing ideas of extreme nationalism and inciting ethnic hatred. A serious cause for concern was the fact that they were able to present themselves as the legitimate heirs to their respective national histories and traditions. As the brief historical surveys showed, in each country there were aspects of national tradition hostile to the liberal democratic project. Whether it was Dmowski's integralist vision of the pure Polish nation, traditional Czech chauvinism against the Germans, or the heritage of Tiso's Slovak state, some legacies of the history of the Central European nations seemed to be a serious impediment to liberalism.

However, the case studies also showed that each nation can boast influential spokespersons for ethnic tolerance and a more inclusive conception of their nation, which are defining elements of liberal nationalism. While the likes of Adam Michnik, Václav Havel and Peter Zajac do not explicitly describe themselves as liberal nationalists, they all aspire to formulate universal values of liberalism within their particular national context, and were also able to strengthen the legitimacy of their call by relying on liberal aspects of their respective national histories. The Czech liberals recalled the heritage of Masaryk, the Slovaks rediscovered Hodža, and the Poles prided themselves on liberal aspects of their 'Noble Democracy'. But liberal nationalists can also be critical of their own nation, and, on many occasions, it may be appropriate for them to condemn the darker parts of their national history. The debates about the moral implications of the expulsion of the Germans from the Czech Republic, traditional anti-Semitism in Poland, or Slovak collaboration with Nazi Germany, provided useful points of reference for exploring more general liberal values.

Yet liberal nationalism is not the answer to all the problems facing the societies of Central Europe, which are experiencing a radical transition from the communist system of power to some form of liberal democracy. In fact, as I have argued in Chapter 2, the theoretical framework of liberal nationalism cannot even provide clear-cut solutions for accommodating ethnic difference. While liberal nationalists are best suited to understand and support the claims of national minorities for special treatment, ethnic diversity can generate situations which cannot be resolved to the satisfaction of all competing demands. In many cases, the best one can hope for is the amelioration of conflicts, rather than their elimination. The exploration of the conflicting imperatives for the treatment of the Romany minority showed, for example, that their demands for cultural recognition are sometimes incompatible with demands for social justice. Hence liberal nationalists have to accept that what is morally desirable is not always feasible in the political realm.

This is not to question the importance of normative ideals. In fact, this study is normative as much as it is descriptive. While it seeks to describe the changing meaning of national identities and nationalism(s) as observed in Poland, the Czech Republic and Slovakia, it also openly advocates a certain conception of nationalism. It endorses those ideas and traditions within the respective national discourses which approximate the ideal of liberal nationalism explored by classical theorists such as Herder, Mazzini and Mill, and contemporary political theorists such as Yael Tamir and David Miller. Thus the study seeks to assess the prevalence of liberal nationalism in all the three countries; but by highlighting the strengths and weaknesses within the various nationalist discourses, it also prescribes what is desirable for the advancement of liberal democracy. These prescriptions are often close to the political thoughts of intellectuals, past and present, who have lived in the countries in focus: ranging from Adam Mickiewicz to Marcin Król and Adam Michnik in Poland; from Emanuel Rádl to Václav Havel and Petr Pithart in the Czech Republic; from Milan Hodža to Miroslav Kusý and Peter Zajac in Slovakia.

Three corrections: Poland, the Czech Republic, Slovakia

The applied methodology brought results which seriously challenged widespread assumptions about the role of nationalism in the postcommunist development of Poland, the Czech Republic and Slovakia.[1] Despite the expectations that nationalism would 'contribute to undermining the best chance of building democracy that Central and Eastern Europe has ever had' (Schöpflin 1995: 65), its impact was not so one-sided. The predictions derived from the theories of 'two types of nationalism', which implied that the political processes in all the postcommunist countries would be domi-nated by a resurgence of aggressive nationalism, were not fulfilled. Rather, there is some evidence suggesting that the postcommunist transition was also affected by the forces of liberal nationalism, although their influence varied considerably in each country.

In the case of Poland, it was demonstrated that the initial impact of illib-eral religious nationalism was less significant than was originally anticipated. First, I have argued that religious nationalism need not be illib-eral by definition. By identifying those aspects within Polish religious thought which were compatible with liberal values (represented prominently by Józef Tischner), it was shown that even Polish Catholicism does not need to be an insurmountable obstacle to the establishment of a liberal demo-cratic order. In fact, many Polish intellectuals argued, in line with Alexis de Tocqueville, that religious attachments can be useful for the development of civic virtues, and may be considered valuable as an ultimate source of morality. Second, the assumption that all Poles are ardent Catholics indif-ferent to individual political rights, proved to be unfounded. The various aspects of the constitutional debate (such as the legality of abortion) clearly demonstrated that the vast majority of the people, including many Catholics, resisted the interference of the Catholic Church in political life. Although the Catholic Church in Poland had played an important and honourable role in the fight against communism, its role in Polish society had to be redefined after 1989. It was promising that this was advocated not only by church outsiders (like Michnik), but also by some leading figures from within the Catholic intelligentsia (like Tischner) who argued, for example, that the separation of church and state served the best interests of Polish democracy as well as the needs of the Catholic Church. The appeal of extreme religious nationalism was, however, not the only challenge to liberal nationalism in Poland. The same anti-communist sentiments that made liberal democracy possible threatened to become a new source of exclusion by opposing the inclusion of former communists in the newly defined Polish nation. Characteristically, Adam Michnik showed a great deal of generosity and opposed the blind anti-communism of the 1990s as much as he had opposed communism in the earlier years. His conciliatory gesture towards the former communist ruler General Jaruzelski was a practical example of an inclusive notion of Polishness that transcended the previous political divide.

Yet a number of Polish intellectuals have also argued that the (largely unjustified) fear of extreme nationalism after 1989 prevented many liberal thinkers (including Michnik and Król) from fully appreciating the importance of national symbols and tradition. Zdzisław Krasnodębski, for example, criticized the widespread tendency of intellectual elites after 1989 to distance themselves from 'the political vocabulary of Solidarność in which national solidarity, participatory freedom and integration by common heritage and values were stressed' (Krasnodębski 2003). This, according to Krasnodębski, could partly explain the lack of political engagement of the wider masses (as demonstrated, amongst others, in the declining participation in successive postcommunist elections), and the general decline in ethical standards in politics. However, this is not to say that there was no such a thing as liberal nationalism in Poland after 1989, but rather that more of it was needed. At any rate, the more recent debates about the implications of recent and not-so-recent Polish history provided a useful point of reference for the ongoing contest about the desired nature of Polish national identity. The contributions of Cichocki, Gowin and Krasnodębski reinvigorated the calls for a kind of nationalism that would be compatible with the demands of liberalism. In view of these debates, and against the background of more general observations of postcommunist developments in Poland, my conclusions about the role of nationalism in Poland were more optimistic than the expectations of some previous studies.

In contrast, my study of nationalism in the Czech Republic showed that the country was not as devoid of ethnocentric nationalism as has often been suggested (e.g. Kořalka 1994: 275; Bollerup and Christensen 1997: 131; Vachudová and Snyder 1997). The methodology applied offered a more complex picture. The exploration of various conceptions of nationalism within Czech society showed that the Czech understanding of the nation is not immune to chauvinism (especially in respect to the Romany minority) despite the popular perception to the contrary. At the same time, it was possible to identify conceptions of liberal nationalism which were in line with the Czech tradition of liberal thought expressed succinctly by Havel in the notion *věc česká je věc lidská* ('the Czech concern is a human concern').

In fact, more than any other nation of Central and Eastern Europe, the Czechs were able to call on their historical experience of liberal democracy. The political and intellectual legacy of the first Czechoslovak president, T. G. Masaryk, for example, served the former president Václav Havel as a source of inspiration. Yet even Czech tradition and political history has been more equivocal than many Czechs would like to believe. The very idea of a Czechoslovak nation, for instance, proved problematic, since it led to the exclusion of the large German minority and, arguably, also to the political marginalization of the Slovak people. What was encouraging, however, was the critical approach of many leading intellectuals and politicians to those legacies of Czech history that could undermine the cause of liberal nationalism. This goes back to the ideals of dissidents such as Jan Patočka and Václav Havel, who firmly believed that the overcoming of the totalitarian political system was predicated on the renewal of moral decency in Czech society. The disputes about the historical failings of the Czech nation were, hence, not only of intellectual interest, but also had serious political implications. Being true to his convictions, Havel became the most outspoken supporter of reconciliation with the Germans by apologizing for the violent expulsion of the German population after the Second World War, and repudiating the principle of collective guilt. The election of Václav Klaus (March 2003) as Havel's successor can be seen as a setback to this process. Klaus, architect of the Czechoslovak (and Czech) economic transition, may be seen as an outspoken defender of liberal values, but when it comes to Czech-German relations he has shown himself to be more nationalist than liberal.

On the face of it, Slovakia was the country that offered the best opportunity for validating the theories of 'two types of nationalism'. Because the establishment of national independence was closely linked with the political ascendancy of the populist demagogue Vladimír Mečiar, political developments in Slovakia seemed to have confirmed the assumptions that the nations of Eastern Europe were prone to succumb to extreme nationalism; only the west-east borders needed to be adjusted to fit the new equation. Thus scholars were able to argue that while the Czechs and the Poles were now to be considered a part of the West which has overcome the temptations of ethnocentric nationalism, the Slovaks were doomed to remain illiberal for considerably longer (e.g. Carpenter 1997; Vachudová and Snyder 1997). This argument was always difficult to sustain because it grossly underestimated the societal forces which opposed the authoritarian and extreme nationalist policies of the government; but after the repeated success of different anti-Mečiar coalitions in the elections of 1998 and 2002, the argument could only have been upheld by ignoring these political developments.[2]

Yet this study did not seek to play down the danger of the extreme nationalist forces in Slovakia. Indeed, unlike in Poland and the Czech Republic, extreme nationalism in Slovakia became a part of the political mainstream, exemplified by the admittance of the notorious Slovak National Party to the 1994–8 coalition government, and the numerous policies directed against the Hungarian minority. Moreover, the discourse of liberal nationalism has probably not been as pervasive as in the other two countries. But even if the country seemed to have lacked influential figureheads of comparable moral standing to Havel and Michnik, the assumption that the Slovak nation as a whole was illiberal by virtue of its history and political destiny could never be justified.

Given the considerable success of the Polish, Czech and (after September 1998) Slovak elites in marginalizing the impact of extreme nationalism, which could be contrasted with the political ascendancy of Haider's extreme-right Freedom Party in Austria, it would be tempting to redefine the old East-West division by assigning Austria to the troublesome postcommunist East and the three countries of this study to the politically stable West.[3] This could give some late satisfaction to all those Czech intellectuals (such as Kundera) who repeatedly stressed, even before the end of communism in Central and Eastern Europe, that Prague was actually west of Vienna. Such a classification would, however, only replicate the previous misconceptions. Rather, the case illustrates that the methodology used in this study, which is based on the examination of different discourses of nationalism competing for dominance within a nation, can even be usefully applied to 'Western' nations. Instead of indiscriminate condemnation of the Austrians as a nation of racists, an unbiased analysis of recent Austrian developments would have to consider not only the views and the deeds of the new ruling administration, but also the corresponding reactions from within civil society.

The meaning of liberalism East and West[4]

The rise of extreme nationalism in Austria underlines the fact that challenges to liberal democracy are not restricted to the postcommunist countries of Central and Eastern Europe. Still, political extremism in any form is arguably more dangerous to postcommunist countries, which have not yet established a robust institutional framework to ensure that a change of government and its policies does not result in a change of political system. This is also the reason why many intellectuals in Central Europe resist those influential theories of liberalism which, in their concern for state neutrality with respect to conflicting political values, are rather hesitant in endorsing liberalism as a comprehensive political doctrine. It seems that while the well established liberal democracies in the West can afford themselves the luxury of a 'procedural republic' in which justice is maintained simply through the just procedures of an (allegedly) strictly neutral state, the countries of postcommunism are in need of liberalism as a 'fighting creed'.

But it may well be that the fiction of a neutral state is damaging even to the West. As has been discussed in this book, the notion of state neutrality is vulnerable to objections raised by liberal nationalists, who exposed the concept of strict state neutrality as an unhelpful fiction with respect to ethnicity and culture. This criticism could be extended by arguing that 'the version of liberalism that renounces the formative ambition and insists government should be neutral toward competing conceptions of the good life' (Sandel 1996: 322) is self-defeating, as it undermines the very freedom that it seeks to protect. As Michael Sandel argued in *Democracy's Discontent*, 'the public philosophy by which we live cannot secure the liberty it promises, because it cannot inspire the sense of community and civic engagement that liberty requires' (Sandel 1996: 6). Sandel's aspiration to revive the spirit of republicanism in the United States by renouncing 'both the theory and the practice of the procedural republic' has many affinities with the ideals of those intellectuals in Central Europe whom I have labelled liberal nationalists.

Marcin Król, for example, cautions against the current vogue for a 'liberalism of fear' which is afraid of espousing some fundamental values, and proposes instead his concept of a 'liberalism of courage' (referring to more traditional liberals such as Alexis de Tocqueville) which does not shun comprehensive conceptions of the good. Other writers in Poland argued that even religious sentiments could be usefully employed as the ultimate source of morality, which contributes to the consolidation of liberal democracy. Similarly, Václav Havel has sought to reconstruct the foundations of liberal democracy by employing concepts like 'transcendence' and 'the order of being' that point to an older tradition of moral philosophy. Havel's understanding of politics, which developed in opposition to the communist regime, was driven primarily by moral considerations. As he put it, 'our absolutely basic experience [has been] that, in the long run, the only thing that can be meaningful politically must first and foremost be a proper and adequate response to the fundamental moral dilemmas of the time' (Havel 1999b: 4).

Although the focus of this study was not liberalism as such, even the occasional references to debates about its meaning in Poland, the Czech Republic and Slovakia warrant the assumption that arguments developed in response to the challenges of the postcommunist transition could also inform debates in the West. This should not come as a surprise for those who are aware of the fact that the liberal democratic project itself is as ambitious as it is fraught with difficulties and inherent tensions – whether in the East or the West. Hence, if the progress of postcommunist transition in Central Europe is measured against the failings and achievements of existing societies in the West (rather than some lofty ideals), the prospects appear to be very promising. One of the main contentions of this book has been that the multifarious facets of nationalism pose not only a threat to this process, but can, under certain circumstances, advance the cause of liberal democracy in Central Europe.

Notes

1 Nationalism in Central Europe

1   As Gellner admitted, his theory was vulnerable to one simple objection, 'if industrialisation was the motor of national mobilisation, then how come that pre-industrial nations could come into being?' (Schöpflin 2002: 1). This question points to the limits of the theory of modernization when applied to Slovaks and Poles, since their countries were modernized extensively only in the first half of the twentieth century; that is well after the emergence of their national movements. In both cases, the rise of nationalism went hand-in-hand with modernization (for a concise and persuasive criticism of the weaknesses of Gellner's theory see also Poole 1999: 20–3).
2   Smith made an important qualification of this ideal-typical classification by asserting that 'every nationalism contains civic and ethnic elements in varying degrees and different forms' (Smith 1991: 13). For a more comprehensive critique of civic/ethnic dichotomy see Brubaker 1999.
3   But as Hobsbawm shows, the Americans and French were not the only people

> freely offering membership of a 'nation' to anybody who wanted to join it, and 'nations' accepted open entry more readily than classes. The generations before 1914 are full of great-nation chauvinists whose fathers, let alone mothers, did not speak the language of their sons' chosen people, and whose names, Slav or Magyarized German or Slav testified to their choice.
>
> (Hobsbawm 1990: 39)

The potential flexibility of ethnic loyalties in Central Europe was exemplified by the history of Rusyns. At different times Slovak Rusyns were seen and saw themselves as Ukrainian, Slovak, Ruthenian, or Russian. As was observed in a study of this ethnic group in Slovakia:

> When we compare the rubric 'nationality' in census [sic.] from different dates we find an incredible fluctuation: inhabitants of the same village are mentioned once as Rusyns, ten years later as Slovaks, a further ten years later as Russians, later still as Ukrainians, then again as Slovaks.
>
> (Mušinka 1992: 224; see also Burgess 1997: 133)

Even nationalisms in Central Europe were thus not always exclusionary. See also note 22.

4　In a speech at the Central European University in Budapest in 1992, Hobsbawm appealed to the moral responsibility of young students of history from Central and Eastern Europe, who by pursuing their search for historic truth could prevent the rise of nationalism (Hobsbawm 1997: 1–10).

5　This is not to say that the current political system in Germany reflects Habermas' views. In fact, German citizenship law is, despite some recent liberalization, still largely based on ethnicity, making it difficult for foreigners to acquire German citizenship.

6　This is one of the fundamental paradoxes of liberal democracy which, although based on universalist ideals, can only function in the particular context of a nation-state. As Margaret Canovan noted in her study of Arendt's republicanism,

> barriers against immigration and special rights for citizens contradict the ideal of human rights. But without bounded nations or quasi-national republics, *no one* would enjoy human rights. This is so because powerful political structures able to mobilize the consent of their citizens are necessary not only to guarantee rights inside their own borders, but also to try to protect human rights across the world.
>
> (Canovan 1999: 148)

7　As is often the case with the theories of nationalism, however plausible the theory in question, there is always a counterexample that can challenge its universal applicability. The often made link between language and nationality, which can be traced back to Herder, Fichte and Wilhelm von Humboldt, seems to be undermined by the existence of a nation that speaks four different languages (the Swiss), and a number of different nations sharing a virtually identical language (the different varieties of English). The most intriguing counterexample to the validity of linguistic nationalism is the experience of the Irish, whose attempts to revive the Gaelic language have largely failed, yet no-one can seriously doubt the existence of a separate Irish identity. (Despite the considerable efforts of the Irish Republic and its state-sponsored education system, only a minority of the Irish people have active command of the Gaelic language, and most people clearly prefer English as their primary means of communication). Further limitations of Herder's linguistic nationalism are also discussed in Chapter 2.

8　The widely spread claim that the war in Yugoslavia was caused by primordial ethnic hatred is seriously flawed. As Hardin argued, 'nothing that must be socially learned can be primordial'. Thus the war in the former Yugoslavia preceded ethnic hatred (as distinct from mere hostility) rather than the other way round (see Hardin 1995: 150).

9　See also an earlier study by Hans Kohn, who used the distinction between a 'voluntaristic' and an 'organistic' idea of a nation to contrast Western and Eastern nationalism. According to Kohn, one is 'based upon liberal middle-class concepts and pointing to a consummation in a democratic world society, the other based upon irrational and pre-enlightened concepts and tending towards exclusiveness' (Kohn 1944: 457; on Kohn's dichotomy see also Walicki 1989: 4–7, 119–120; Snyder 1990: 173–6; Tamir 1993: 83; Brubaker 1999). As Walicki pointed out, the typological distinction between the conceptions of the 'cultural nation' and the 'political nation' was developed even earlier, at the beginning of the twentieth century in Meinecke's *Weltbürgertum und Nationalstaat* (Walicki 1989: 4; 1997: 227).

10 'With one or two exceptions, the democratic systems were able to deal with these [nationalistic] movements [in the West] fairly successfully – Northern Ireland and the Basque country represent the main failures' (Schöpflin 1995: 46). Virtually identical was the assessment of Daniel Chirot: 'Yet in Western Europe, internal nationalist disputes are the exceptions, not the rule: Only in Northern Ireland and over the Spanish Basque issue is there much violence' (Chirot 1995: 51). In fairness to Schöpflin, it is important to point out that he more recently moved away from his earlier position. In his book *Nations, Identity, Power*, he explicitly rejected 'a kind of residual "Hans Kohnism", the proposition that there is a Good Western nationalism (civic, democratic, peace-loving etc) and a Bad Eastern nationalism (nasty, brutish and anything but short)' – as representing a 'truly lazy' attitude (Schöpflin 2000: 5).

11 In contrast, people wary of the extreme nationalist forces in Central Europe use Fichte as a conversation stopper. Aviezer Tucker, for example, dismissed the attempt of Václav Havel 'to find a philosophical position that would allow him to combine his universalism with nationalism' by referring to Fichte who 'invented modern nationalism at the beginning of the nineteenth century in response to the invading French. Since then, nationalism has ruled all other identities out of order' (Tucker 1999: 197–8). For a more sophisticated exposition of Fichte's influence on Masaryk see Pynsent 1997.

12 Herder explicitly rejected every form of colonialism. He was exasperated about the presumptuous attitude of Europeans, who believed that they were able to export progress to all corners of the globe, and who in that way sought to justify the political and economic subjugation of 'inferior' peoples. 'If there were such a thing as a European collective spirit...it could not but feel ashamed of the crimes committed by us, having insulted mankind in a manner such as scarcely any other group of nations had done' (Herder cited in Barnard 1965: 100).

13 As Brian Porter argued in the conclusion to his compelling account of the nineteenth-century history of Polish nationalism, 'the ideal of multiculturalism is not an American invention of the late twentieth century, but a quintessentially East European dream of the early nineteenth' (Porter 2000: 237).

14 The British anthropologist of Polish origin, Bronisław Malinowski, demonstrated that it is rather the other way round: the present creates history. Historical figures and events are appropriated (by a nation) for current purposes and are true or 'valid in virtue of – and only in virtue of – satisfying a current need' (cited in Gellner 1987: 62). According to Malinowski, beliefs about the past should be seen as 'charters' of current practices. In line with this, Adam Michnik asked rhetorically: 'Do we not often argue about the past, thinking that we are arguing about the truths of the present?' (Michnik 1985: 333).

15 This did not, however, prevent Kymlicka from labelling a number of national cultures as illiberal. In his attempt to explain why some nationalisms became virulent and others not, Kymlicka referred to the political culture of the country in question and suggested that 'Serb, Ukrainian, and Slovak nationalisms are illiberal because they emerged in illiberal states' (Kymlicka 1997: 64). Not only is this explanation circular (is the state illiberal because it reflects the desires of an illiberal nation, or the other way around?), but it also ignores the above finding that 'the liberality of a culture is a matter of degree' (Kymlicka 1995a: 94).

16 As early as 1956, when Russian troops were poised to suppress the revolutionary upheaval in Hungary, the director of the Hungarian News Agency sent a memorable telex to the outside world: 'We are going to die for Hungary and for

Europe' (Kundera 1984: 33). The short statement expressed loyalty to the nation as connected with an allegiance to the ideals of freedom and democracy (i.e. Europe).

17 Curiously, this is an inversion of the perception of Jan Kollár, who in the nineteenth century celebrated nationalism as 'a product of reason and cultivation' and contrasted it with

> dull, intolerant, hate-filled patriotism; [which] is often merely an excuse for the blackest deeds; beyond his fellow-countrymen the patriot knows only enemies; patriotism often serves only for the ostensible justification of injured human rights and for misused violence against weaker neighbours or fellow countrymen who belong to other people.
>
> (cited in Pynsent 1994: 59)

18 Michnik, whose political thoughts are deeply embedded in the tradition of Polish national culture, considers himself to be a proud Polish patriot, but certainly not a nationalist. However, in our private conversation at the University of Melbourne (17 November 1997), Michnik conceded that his patriotism could be described in English as liberal nationalism. The Polish use of 'patriotism' instead of 'liberal nationalism' is somewhat misleading, since patriotism is derived and refers to territory rather than to a nation (see Walicki's attempt 'to rescue' the neutral meaning of nationalism in the Polish language in Walicki 1997b: 33–5; for a similar argument see also Krasnodębski 2002).

19 Mark Mazower challenged the myth of 'European civilizational superiority' by producing a gloomy account of Europe's twentieth-century history. In his *Dark Continent*, Mazower reminds his readers that Europe was *not* destined to become free and democratic. 'Though we may like to think democracy's victory in the Cold War proves its deep roots in Europe's soil, history tells us otherwise'. In the first half of the twentieth century, 'dynamic non-democratic alternatives to meet the challenges of modernity' emerged in Europe, which were 'no more foreign to its traditions, and no less efficient as organizers of society, industry and technology' than liberal democracy (Mazower 1998: 3–4). 'Fascism, after all, was the most Eurocentric of the three major ideologies, far more so than either communism or liberal democracy' (Mazower 1998: xiv).

20 While in 1994 Čarnogurský advocated closer links to NATO through the Partnership for Peace programme, since NATO extended its invitation for full membership, he has been adamantly opposed to Slovakia entering the alliance.

21 A witty polemic from an 'outsider' was published under a subheading that says it all:

> Why do many Western scholars, including Samuel Huntington and his much discussed *The Clash of Civilizations and the Remaking of World Order*, still insist that non-Western means 'inferior', asks [Aleksa Djilas], who makes his home in the non-European, non-Protestant, non-Anglo-Saxon state of Serbia.
>
> (Djilas 1997: 33)

The assumption that the Serbian people were intrinsically illiberal was challenged by subsequent developments. Characteristically, when Slobodan Milošević was defeated in the September 2000 elections by a more moderate nationalist leader Vojislav Koštunica, many observers feared that this would not result in any significant change in Serbia. In contrast, Dušan Djordjevich defended Koštunica and his democratic credentials: ' "Liberal nationalism" may seem like an oxymoron, but in Serbia, as elsewhere, it is much more productive to welcome moves in that direction than to condemn all nationalist sentiment in the vain hope for some leap to cosmopolitanism' (Djordjevich 2000).

22 Ethnicity itself is not exclusive by definition. Lichtenberg accurately observed that 'the same questions that are raised about nationality – whether it is open or closed, dependent on birth, or not – can be raised about ethnicity' (Lichtenberg 1997: 56). Smith reached a similar conclusion, stating that '*ethnies* are not inherently exclusive'. He cites Czech and Catalan nationalism as good examples 'of an ethnic culture that is assimilatory and inclusive, and its ethno-linguistic nationalism has, on the whole, been open and peaceful, even under oppressive circumstances' (Smith 1995b: 16). Other writers, however, who see liberal and national values as inherently contradictory, have problems in interpreting Czech history. Thus Bollerup and Christensen argue that the Czech liberation movement against Soviet and communist dominance in the late 1980s 'was liberal rather than national in its aim and scope', even though 'the ethnically based common Czech identity was at least as important to the majority of the Czechs' as it was to Slovaks (Bollerup and Christensen 1997: 131; see also Chapter 3).

23 As Rogers Brubaker observed, 'ethnonational violence [in Central and Eastern Europe] is neither as prevalent, nor as likely to occur, as is often assumed' (Brubaker 1998: 273). These surprising findings call for explanation. The often-posed question about the causes for the escalation of ethnic conflicts in the region needs to be complemented by addressing the reasons for the *absence* of these conflicts (Brubaker 1998: 282).

24 This is not to say that it was not possible to mobilize public support along extreme nationalist lines. While the Republican Party disintegrated after the failure of the 1998 elections, the success of the Czech Communist Party in the June 2002 general elections (it won 18.5 per cent of the vote) indicated that nationalist rhetoric (in this case anti-German) can still pay off.

2 Reflections on minority rights in Central Europe

1 The implementation of this ideal can, however, be very difficult. The promotion of religious tolerance goes against any fundamentalist religious belief systems for which the assumption is central that *their* and *only their* belief is correct. When children, for example, are exposed to a variety of religious doctrines, they can come to doubt the doctrine promoted by their parents and in that way a religiously tolerant state inevitably undermines some religious communities. (For a legal case in the United States, in which some fundamentalists and evangelical religious families saw their religious freedom violated by the existing state school system, see Macedo 1995.)

2 The dispute between contemporary liberal theories, represented by Rawls, and contemporary communitarians, represented by Taylor, was to some extent predated by the philosophical dispute between Kant and Herder.

3 I am aware of the fact that this term is being contested. As far as communitarianism denotes a concept that is in opposition to liberalism, neither Kymlicka nor Taylor can be thus labelled, since they both tried to accommodate insights of the communitarians *within* the liberal theory. But to the extent that they shifted the

focus of theorizing from individuals to groups, they certainly adopted some basic tenets of communitarians. In fact, it can be argued that at least occasionally they leave the platform of political liberalism whenever they put the interests of groups above the interests of individuals (see for example the critique of Kymlicka in Laitin 1998: 221–36, esp. 232).

4   The language of public administration in eighteenth-century Hungary was Latin. This was to change according to the 'language ordinance of 1784, which stipulated the introduction of German as the official language in all parts of the Monarchy' (Deak 1979: 42). A few years later, Joseph II's successors dropped the demand, and Hungarian nobles returned to the use of Latin. Hungarian replaced Latin as the main language of public administration only in the 1830s and 1840s, much to the displeasure of many representatives of the Hungarian nobility.

5   The importance of the perceived threat to the Czech culture changed over time. 'Czechoslovakism was perhaps more a matter of culture than politics up to the Ethnographical Exhibition of 1895 and the formation of periodical *Hlas*. Thereafter the politics became ever more important'. The actual creation of the Czechoslovak First Republic was, hence, primarily motivated by political and strategic militarily considerations. (I am indebted to the anonymous reviewer at Routledge for this addition). But as far as the goal was to ensure the dominance over other ethnic groups, such as Germans, Hungarians, Poles and Ruthenes, this political project certainly had cultural dimensions.

6   Incidentally this is the title of a nationalistic account of Slovak history, *A History of Slovakia: The Struggle for Survival* (Kirschbaum 1995). The notion of the 'struggle for survival' was also invoked by Dmowski's National Democrats in Poland at the turn of the nineteenth and twentieth century. As Brian Porter clearly demonstrated, the idea of 'an eternal struggle for survival' of the Polish nation *vis-à-vis* its perceived enemies from without and within resulted in rabid anti-Semitism, the heritage of which still troubles Polish society (Porter 2000: 227–32; see also Chapter 3).

7   As a journalist supported by Mečiar's government, Hofbauer was awarded the 1994 L'udovít Štúr Prize following a nomination from the Association of Slovak Journalists that had very close links with the ruling coalition (Schmögnerová 1997: 203), which strongly suggests that his views would then have been widely shared within the ruling elite.

8   I concur with the view of Alexander Ossipov, who identified the crucial problem in the arguments that defend special rights for ethnic minorities:

> All arguments in favour of preferential treatment for minorities can be used to justify the protection of an ethnic majority, as it can also be described as a non-dominant community whose culture is at risk of alien influences and requires defensive measures.
>
> (Ossipov 2001: 182)

9   Jerzy Zubrzycki, who was a spiritual father of the Australian policy of multiculturalism, stated explicitly that 'because some minority values are totally inconsistent with fundamental values of the dominant Australian culture...*it would be nonsense to say that multiculturalism means that every culture is equally valued and equally legitimate*' (my italics, in Hirst 1994: 29). In other words, whenever a conflict arises between different values espoused by various migrant groups, the Australian values override the values of migrant cultures.

10 Kymlicka's distinction is plausible, but not without dangers. The competing claims on territories of the ethnic communities of the former Yugoslavia are, after all, based on their historic right to live on a certain piece of land. Similarly, Slovak extreme nationalists try to invalidate claims of Hungarians for more cultural autonomy, or minority rights, by referring to a thousand years of the history of Slavic inhabitation of Slovakia. In that sense Slovak nationalists consider themselves more 'indigenous' than the Hungarian tribes. 'Are the Slovaks [who allegedly inherited their territory from their Slavic forebears] in any way better than Hungarians only because they came earlier?', asked Slovak historian Eduard Krekovič rhetorically, questioning the ethical validity of political arguments based on different readings of histories (Krekovič 1998: 6) (see also the criticisms of Kymlicka's differentiation between national minorities and immigrants in Ossipov 2001: 179–81).

11 The claim that denial or negligence of identity equals oppression could turn grotesque if applied too widely. An important part of my identity is constituted by my profession. I am what I am doing. And being an academic and a political scientist, I have to believe that I can make a real contribution to our understanding of societies; that my work is useful and important. I derive from my work a great deal of personal satisfaction. Yet the vast majority of Australians probably think that academics are useless 'wankers' (as a letter to the editor of the *Australian*, 24 July 1998, put it). This is very disturbing and causes me to doubt not only the meaning of my work, but my personal worth. It seriously violates my right that my identity (as a political scientist) be duly recognized. Should I expect the state to step in and end this oppression?

12 It is telling that the term 'od-rod-ilec' is derived from the Latin 'de-gen-erate'. In other words, it was seen as a sign of degeneration when a Czech spoke German (I am indebted to the anonymous reader at Routledge for this point). It is one thing to oppose enforced assimilation, yet another to condemn those who chose to assimilate into another linguistic group.

13 For example, the Romanies did not have the status of ethnic minority in communist Czechoslovakia, and gained it in Slovakia only in 1991 (Vašečka 2002: 152–3). This improvement in formal status has had significant implications, and arguably benefited the Romanies. When the Slovak Republic signed the *European Charter of Regional or Minority Languages* in 2001, it accepted also its responsibility to protect nine minority languages, including the Romany language (Vašečka 2002: 152).

14

> The 1952 Dictionary of the Czech Language defined 'gypsy' as a 'member of a wandering nation, a symbol of mendacity, theft, wandering jokers, liars, imposters, cheaters'. This was a definition, as Josef Kalvoda observed, that was issued just 2 years after the Czechoslovak communist regime outlawed any discrimination based on colour.
>
> (Fawn 2001: 1214)

In Slovak the word *cigániť* also means 'to lie'. Another revealing fact is that the Czech language has 'cikáně' for Gypsy child (a noun form used only for animals except in the case of Gypsies and Jews, 'žídě') – I am indebted to Routledge's anonymous reviewer for alerting me to this point.

15 Maria Theresa's attempt to enforce such a change may seem fanciful today. In 1761 the enlightened despot 'outlawed use of the word *Cigány* and decreed that

Gypsies in the future be called "new citizens", "new peasants", or "new Hungarians"' (Crowe 1994: 38).

16 This is not to suggest that this sort of incident could only happen in the Czech Republic. For numerous cases of state institutions failing to counter racism (or even themselves being racist) against the Romany minorities in Slovakia, see for example a report by the European Roma Rights Centre, *Time of the Skinheads: Denial and Exclusion of Roma in Slovakia* (Cahn and Trehan 1997).

17 The same law was previously interpreted the other way round. Karel Peřina, a judge from Hradec Králové, decided in a case investigated in 1997 that 'the attack of Skinheads against the Romanies cannot be considered racist since both the Romas and the Czechs are of the same Indo-European race' (Macháček 1997).

18 In 1773, the Habsburg empress issued a decree which

> forbade marriages between Gypsies and ordered Roma children over age five to be taken away to state schools and foster homes, resulting in the virtual kidnapping of approximately 18,000 Gypsy children from their parents. The intention behind this edict was to dilute Romani bloodlines and to speed up their assimilation.
>
> (Barany 2002: 93)

The communist authorities in Czechoslovakia introduced another method of 'diluting' Romani bloodlines. The Ministry of Health's 'Decree on Sterilization' from 1972 was used 'to encourage the sterilization of Romany women in order to reduce the "high unhealthy" Romany population' (Crowe 1994: 60).

19 Fraser uses the term 'post-socialist condition' to describe the tendency of ever more left-wing intellectuals in America after the 1989 revolutions in Central and Eastern Europe to focus more on the politics of recognition while neglecting (the often related) problems that stem from social injustice in societies (Fraser 1997).

20 In stark contrast to this achievement, most Romany children do not even enjoy the 'privilege' of being admitted to regular primary schools. The widespread practice of exclusion of Romany children from regular Czech primary schools by assigning them to 'special schools for the mentally handicapped' is a gross example of institutionalized racism. On the basis of purportedly ethnically neutral assessments, a Romany child is approximately 'fifteen times more likely to have been judged to have "intellectual deficiencies"' than his or her Czech counterpart (Cahn and Chirico 1999: 14). In a recent case, the European Roma Rights Centre sued the Czech Ministry of Education and the local school authorities on behalf of eighteen children from the town of Ostrava. After the claims were rejected by the Czech Constitutional Court, the Centre filed an application with the European Court of Human Rights in Strasbourg, challenging 'systematic racial segregation and discrimination in Czech schools' (*Radio Prague*, 19 April 2000).

21 In fact, a recent comprehensive sociological survey in the Czech Republic indicates that many Romanies themselves opt for assimilation. The survey showed that the number of respondents who declared themselves as Romanies rather than Czechs had fallen by nearly two thirds over a period of ten years: from 33,000 to 12,000. According to Jan Spousta, these results cannot be explained simply by the fear of Romanies to declare their ethnicity (though this may have been a factor in individual cases). Instead they reflect a genuine attempt of many Romanies to become a part of the majority Czech culture. As Spousta argues,

the Czechs should welcome this development and broaden their definition of Czechness. 'To be Czech should be equated with the willingness to participate in Czech affairs and to consider this country to be one's homeland, regardless of the colour of one's skin, and the ability to pronounce the ř correctly' (Spousta 2002).

3 Nationalism in Poland

1　One of the legacies of communism was the sense of alienation of the 'common people' from their political elites. The dividing line between *us*, the people, and *them*, the illegitimate communists rulers, pertained even after the collapse of communism, even though the rulers were then legitimized in free elections.

2　See the witty polemic about the age of nations entitled 'Do Nations Have Navels?' (Gellner 1997: 90–101).

3　American democracy has often been a point of reference for the Polish people. 'The American rather than the French revolution inspired the eighteenth century enlightened reformers in Poland' (Krzemiński 2003: 38). Tadeusz Kościuszko (1746–1817), who was a hero of the liberation struggle both in Poland and in North America, is the very embodiment of a Polish-American connection. There is an ironic twist to the friendship between Kościuszko and Jefferson that shows that the Polish patriot was possibly a 'better democrat' than the author of the Declaration of Independence. 'When the American Congress handed him his back pay of $12,208.54, Kościuszko, in spite of his currently (1798) difficult financial circumstances, donated the whole sum to the purchase, freeing and education of Negro slaves' (Walicki 1989: 96). Subsequently, in his own homeland, Kościuszko defended a political nationalism that embraced different ethnicities of the Polish-Lithuanian Republic (Walicki 1989: 98).

4　Mickiewicz and his work served as a powerful source of inspiration in the fight against communism. The best example of the subversive potential of his literary work was the reception of the play *Forefathers' Eve* (*Dziady*) staged in Warsaw's National Theatre in January 1968. The politically sensitive audience enthusiastically endorsed the passages directed against the Russian autocracy, as it drew parallels with the excesses of the communist system of power. Not surprisingly, the Polish communist authorities suspended the performance. The restriction triggered large-scale student protests, which were brutally suppressed in March 1968 (Vetter 1998).

5　Szacki maintains that there is no tradition of liberalism in Poland, not even in the sense of 'practical history, that is...what really influences the attitudes of people today', and that consequently the prospects for liberal democracy in post-communist Poland are bleak. He states correctly that there is no reason to 'associate every fight for freedom with liberalism' (Szacki 1995: 49). But when people do associate them – as they do – then their beliefs (that Poland was destined to become both free and liberal-democratic) do 'influence their attitudes'. This is not to say that Szacki is not right to criticize misrepresentations of Polish history. Rather his critique is a welcome contribution for the Polish people and their understanding of political liberalism. As Michnik rightly suggested (in a different context) 'a noncritical stance toward one's history is...incomparably more detrimental to honest patriotism than the most severe and uncompromising criticism' (Michnik 1993: 151).

6　They did this, however, in different ways. While the romantics firmly believed that there was no contradiction between the fight for one's own nation and humanity at large ('For Your Freedom and Ours!'), the Positivists were concerned with the chauvinistic potential in the romantic idea of national messianism. The influential Warsaw Positivist, Aleksander Świętochowski, ridiculed Mickiewicz's vision of Poland as the Christ of Nations.

> Songs praising our greatness and deriding the pettiness of the Germans, the English, the Americans, the French, the Italians, etc. sound most beautiful to our ears. The first do not have enough faith, the second feeling, others higher pleasures, others finally morality. We and only we are the embodiment of all virtue according to this theory....Possessing such a privilege, we base our political, social and intellectual careers upon it. We do not die, because we sleep and dream.
>
> (cited in Porter 2000: 49)

7 This is not to say that the nationalist aspirations of the Polish elites were widely shared by the common people. As Porter observed, 'until the very end of the [nineteenth] century, the "Polish question" concerned only a minority of those we might categorize as Polish, with few peasants demonstrating any interest in independence' (Porter 2000: 15). While it is 'difficult to be precise about the degree and extent of the Polish-speaking peasantry's national sentiments' (Lukowski and Zawadzki 2001), it is safe to assume that it was not very widespread.

8 Even though most Polish historians usually argue that Dmowski's aim of ethnic homogeneity was to be achieved in a smaller Poland that would not include 'Kresy' in the east (today's Lithuania, Belarus and Ukraine), Brian Porter convincingly challenged this widespread misconception. Even if Dmowski and his supporters accepted that not all their ambitious goals could be achieved at once, 'the *Endecja*'s vision of the future Poland was indeed expansive, including East and West Prussia, Poznania and Silesia in the west, and extending as far as the Dnieper River in the east' (Porter 1992: 651). However, in contrast to Piłsudski, who aimed at the creation of a multinational confederation, Dmowski saw the east as a space for national expansion (Porter 2003a).

9 Dmowski's *Thoughts of a Modern Pole* 'was a best-seller when it first appeared in 1902, and it went through numerous editions during Dmowski's life and gained a renewed popularity and topicality during the 1980s, as the Polish nation came together in Solidarity' (Sugar 1995: 267).

10 It is important to remember that the Western Allies endorsed the expulsion of Germans and generally supported measures that aimed at ethnic homogenization of the countries of Central Europe. As Kersten observed, 'after World War II ended, even democratic societies decided that the resettlement of ethnic groups did not contradict accepted moral standards (especially when applied to the Germans)' (Kersten 2001: 77). Forced migration was seen as a necessary price for ensuring peace and stability in Europe.

11 This is not to suggest that the Polish communists bear the sole responsibility for the expulsion of Germans. The policy was widely popular and endorsed by other political parties and their leaders, including the likes of Stanisław Mikołajczyk, leader of the opposition (Kersten 2001: 79). See also note 33.

12 Still, current Polish-Ukrainian relations are not without problems. To come to terms with unpleasant truths about one's national history is a painful and lengthy process. See, for example, Kuroń's critical analysis of current advances in dealing with darker aspects of Polish history (Sadowski 2001).

13 A September 2002 opinion survey by the Warsaw-based research institute CBOS (Centrum Badania Opinii Społecznej) showed a dramatic increase in positive responses to the prospect of improved Polish-German relations. While

in 1990 only 47 per cent of Poles believed that Polish-German reconciliation was possible (50 per cent believed it was impossible, 2 per cent found it difficult to say), in 2002, 80 per cent of Poles agreed with the statement (19 per cent did not agree, and 1 per cent found it difficult to say). Similar improvements were registered also with respect to the possibility of friendly Polish-Ukrainian relations – in 2002, 73 per cent of Poles believed that reconciliation was possible (25 per cent believed it was impossible, and 2 per cent found it difficult to say) (Strzeszewski 2002). In the same period of time there was also a significant increase in positive attitudes towards both nations, though a disturbingly large number of Poles still confess their dislike for the Ukrainians (Strzeszewski 2003).

14 As Cichocki pointed out,

> today the Endecja is seen above all as a camp of national hatred....What is often forgotten is the fact that the Endecja was also a revolt against romantic tradition and an attempt to formulate a modern patriotism linked with national and state interests; the patriotism of responsibility for the state. For some representatives of this national movement, such as Wojciech Wasiutyński and Adam Doboszyński, this aspect of Endecja's program remained dominant, independently of the evolution of National Democracy towards brutal national egoism and xenophobia.
>
> (Cichocki 2002)

15 According to the Centre for Public Opinion Research, '7 per cent of Poles listen to Radio Maryja regularly' (Głuchowski 1999: 74). Furthermore, Father Rydzyk and his Redemptorist order produce a monthly magazine, *Przyjaciele Radio Maryja* (*Friends of Radio Maryja*), as well as the national daily *Nasz Dziennik* (*Our Newspaper*) with a circulation of 250,000 (Głuchowski 1999: 72). Even though Rydzyk has repeatedly showed disregard for the legality of his activities, state authorities have been been very hesitant in interfering with Radio Maryja. In fact, the broadcaster was recently (February 2003) granted the licence for a television channel (*BBC News*, 13 February 2003).

16 According to Zdzisław Krasnodębski, this is what happened with an earlier apology that Kwaśniewski offered on the thirtieth anniversary of the anti-Semitic campaign instigated by the Polish communist leadership in March 1968. While Kwaśniewski was willing to acknowledge the responsibility of the Polish people for the anti-Semitic excesses of 1968, he failed to mention the political responsibility of the communist party and its members. The fact that the leader of the party of former communists did not see the need to address the historic responsibility of his party is revealing. As Krasnodębski wryly commented, 'it is a telling paradox that the voluntary membership in a totalitarian movement has no moral and political consequences whatsoever, while the belonging to a nation attained through birth has' (Krasnodębski 2001: 3; for a similar argument see also Gowin 2001). According to Porter, even discussions about Jedwabne 'have been inadequate because they have failed to grasp the contributions of specific anti-Semitic institutions (the Endecja and the Church, mainly). It is actually much easier to say "we Poles are guilty" than to seek the specific roots of violent anti-Semitism' (Porter 2003a).

17 A CBOS survey that focused on the relationship between Poles and other nations showed, in January 2003, that '23 per cent of Poles liked Jews, 23 per cent were indifferent, 46 per cent disliked them and 8 per cent found it hard to say' (Strzeszewski 2003: 2). Another survey, which specifically targeted young people,

188 *Notes*

brought more promising results. The findings revealed that 'anti-Semitic clichés [were] not deeply rooted among Polish adolescents' (Ambrosewicz-Jacobs 2000: 588). 'When asked directly, the majority of the surveyed students (77.7 per cent) stated they have positive feelings toward Jews' (Ambrosewicz-Jacobs 2000: 578).

18 It is important to note that I am describing the prevalent *perceptions* of the historic role of the Catholic Church in Poland. As Brian Porter recently demonstrated, the role of the Catholic Church in Polish history was much more ambivalent than is usually assumed. Throughout the nineteenth century, the church authorities were, in fact, largely supportive of the status quo in partitioned Poland. As a result, 'there was always a great deal of tension between the patriotic activists and the institutions of the Catholic Church'. The importance of religion to 'national survival' is often exaggerated. 'Even during the worst years of denationalisation, the Church was never the *only* space within which Poles could express and cultivate the myths, customs, or practices of their ethnicity' (Porter 2003b: 5).

19 The relationship between the Polish Catholic Church and the leaders of the opposition was at times ambivalent (see for example Tighe 1997). Understandably, the goals of the anti-communist dissident movements were not always identical with the goals of the Polish Catholic Church, which despite its fundamental opposition towards communist ideology, occasionally sought compromise with the communist state. Arguably, there are even some similarities between the formal structures of both organizations: the Catholic Church as well as the communist state were both hierarchical and elitist, while professing certain egalitarian principles. In fact, Dieter Bingen argues that the Church 'had contributed in critical moments (1945, 1956, 1980) to the stabilization of the existing system of power by de-escalating the conflicts' (Bingen 1997: 129). But while Bingen is rather critical of the role of the Polish Catholic Church *vis-à-vis* the communist state, other observers, like Bogdan Szajkowski, praise the, at times, conciliatory attitude of the church hierarchy as a sign 'of political realism' (Szajkowski 1997: 161). Accordingly, Szajkowski stresses that 'there can be little doubt that the Roman Catholic Church played an immensely important role in anti-communist resistance and the final demise of the communist system' (Szajkowski 1997: 162).

20 Even though the Catholic Church has traditionally had an uneasy relationship with political or economic liberalism, serious attempts have been made to find a more conciliatory position. The 1991 *Centesimus Annus* encyclical by John Paul II on religious aspects of socialism and liberalism, for the first time acknowledges some positive aspects of a free market economy. Moreover it stresses the importance of a 'legally governed country' and 'appreciates democracy' (see the topical special supplement of *National Review*, 24 June 1991).

21 In the 1990 election campaign Wałęsa himself tried to strengthen his position by chauvinistic remarks highlighting his ethnic 'purity'. He claimed publicly 'that unlike his opponents he was "a true Pole, a Slav and a Catholic", "a full blooded Pole with documents going back to his great grandfathers to prove it", "a pure Pole, born here"'. In that election he competed against Tadeusz Mazowiecki, who was accused by Wałęsa's supporters of being 'a crypto-communist subject to Jewish influence' and 'descended from converted Jews' (Tighe 1997: 360).

22 It should be noted, however, that these findings are somewhat undermined by the good performance of the League of Polish Families in the September 2001 elections.

23 A survey published in *Gazeta Wyborcza*, 24 June 1998 (p. 2) showed that Jacek Kuroń was the most popular politician, supported by 73 per cent of the people,

followed by Kwaśniewski with 70 per cent. The CBOS agency's opinion poll was conducted in May 1998 and involved 1,652 people.

24 One of the main messages the pope conveyed on his visit to Poland in June 1999 was to stress the importance of reconciliation. As Bishop Pieronek put it during the official press conference in Thoruń: 'The holy father talked about reconciliation and who wants to profit from his talk must take part in the process of reconciliation'. He added that it is certain that some of the broadcasts of Radio Maryja do not comply with this imperative. In this light, the fact that John Paul II declined the invitation to visit Father Rydzyk and his religious broadcaster were seen as a symbolic gesture (see *Rzeczpospolita*, 8 June 1999). According to some critics, however, the pope should have been more outspoken in the criticism of the extreme attitudes of the broadcaster (see for example *Myśl Polska* cited in *RFE/RL Report*, 29 June 1999).

25 This is not to say that a majority of Polish priests is openly anti-democratic, even if one would certainly wish that their support for democracy were stronger. According to a recent survey (January 2003) published by the Catholic Information Agency (Katolicka Agencja Informacyjna), 59 per cent of Polish priests agreed with the statement that 'democracy is the best possible political system' (Porter 2003a).

26 Consider, for example, to what extent John Paul II's comment resembles Tocqueville's reasoning.

> The alliance between democracy and ethical relativism is dangerous because it deprives civil society of a stable moral reference point and, in this way, radically weakens its ability to determine the truth. For if there is no ultimate truth that guides political activity…it is easy to instrumentalize ideas and convictions according to the goals that authority sets for itself. History teaches us that democracy without values easily turns into open or camouflaged totalitarianism.
>
> (cited in Michnik 1998)

This message was also one of the main themes of the June 1999 visit of John Paul II to Poland (see for example his speech to the Polish parliament reproduced in *Rzeczpospolita*, 12 December 1999).

27 In Rawlsian terminology, 'liberalism of courage' could be labelled a comprehensive doctrine of liberalism. It is worthwhile noting that Król does not ignore the inherent tension between religious values and liberalism. He states, in fact, that 'a fundamental agreement between Christianity and liberalism is not possible, although some forms of cooperation are possible' (Król 1999: 151). But the experience of the Polish dissidents who were united with the Catholic Church by their common enemy, communism, should not raise unrealistic expectations about the role of the church in a liberal democratic society.

28 This could only be achieved by strictly following the ideal of public reason.

> This ideal is that citizens are to conduct their public political discussions of constitutional essentials and matters of basic justice within the framework of what each sincerely regards as a reasonable political conception of justice, a conception that expresses political values that others as free and equal also might reasonably be expected reasonably to endorse.
>
> (Rawls 1996: 1)

29 'According to a CBOS poll conducted in February 1993, 58.2 per cent of respondents opposed the Church's position on abortion, and only 33.2 per cent supported it' (Eberts 1998: 827). This is yet another indication of the fact that not all Polish Catholics uncritically endorse all the views of the Catholic Church.

30 Although the period of five years is not a long time in the constitutional history of a nation, it is worth noting that Winczorek saw his initial optimistic assessment of the 1997 constitution largely validated in 2002, especially when assessing the constitution's performance against the historic background. As he put it,

> the constitution of May 3, 1791 was in force only for a year, the constitution of March 17, 1921 was in essence finished already after five years, the constitution of April 23, 1935 functioned only until September 1939. Should the longest lasting constitution in the Polish history thus far be the [communist] constitution of July 22, 1952, which lasted until 1992 (and partly until 1997)? Let's give the present constitution a chance.
>
> (Winczorek 2002)

31 A recent opinion survey published in *Rzeczpospolita* (15 March 2003) showed that even those Poles who describe themselves as Catholic, do not necessarily subscribe to all the dogmas of Catholic faith. Instead, the prevalent tendency has been to adopt 'religion *à la carte*', that is to choose just certain aspects of the prescribed religious beliefs according to one's own personal preferences.

32 See, for example, a case study by Warmińska, who showed that a tiny minority of Polish Tartars could develop an identity that was Polish and Muslim (despite the fact that Polish national identity has traditionally been linked with Catholicism). 'Polish Tartars...consider themselves Muslims with a common origin but at the same time stress sameness with Poles' (Warmińska 1997: 343). It is also worth noting that Józef Buzek, prime minister in 1997–2001, is a Protestant (Lukowski and Zawadzki 2001: 286).

33 Attempts to extricate the Polish nation from the responsibility for all evils in its history by blaming the communists are arguably as fallacious as the attempts of Polish communists to shift the burden of responsibility onto the Polish nation. (See, for example, the discussion of the role of wider Polish society in the March 1968 anti-Semitic campaign in Szczypiorski 1998).

34 I am aware of the fact that Michnik is not very popular in Poland today. He is also an easy target for attacks by extreme nationalists, who often stress his Jewish background (I am indebted to Brian Porter for alerting me to this). But this is not to say that the ideas expounded by the likes of Michnik, Kuroń and Tischner cannot be influential in Polish society. It is worth considering that Michnik, for example, is the founder and the editor in chief of the largest Polish daily, *Gazeta Wyborcza*.

35 An opinion poll from 1994 indicates, for example, that the exclusionary understanding of the Polish nation and citizenship is not as widespread as is usually assumed. The respondents in the survey were asked who, in their view, was Polish.

> The leading answers were someone who speaks Polish (cited by 96 per cent of respondents), whose citizenship is Polish (92 per cent), whose parents were Polish (82 per cent), or who lives in Poland (80 per cent). Surprisingly, not much more than one-half of the sample (57 per cent) said that a Pole was someone who was Catholic. These answers on national identity indicate a considerably more liberal orientation that those warning us of Polish

nationalism and xenophobia would lead us to believe. If political culture reflects the types of relationships that prevail between members of different groups, then we can say that tolerance, a core concept of Western liberalism, has grown in the 1990s. On the other hand, Poland's affliction, a stubborn anti-Semitism that refuses to disappear, puts into question society's real commitment to tolerance.

(Taras 1999: 382)

4 Nationalism in the Czech Republic

1   As Masaryk stated in the introduction to his influential study on the 'meaning' of Czech history, 'the Czech question is for me a question about the fate of mankind, it is a question of conscience' (Masaryk 2000: 11). This programmatic statement served as a point of reference for a collection of essays entitled *Sto let Masarykovy České otázky* (*One Hundred Years of Masaryk's Czech Question*), in which Havel stressed the contemporary relevance of Masaryk's work. 'To consider Masaryk's book to be merely a historic document would show not only a poor understanding of an important part of Czech history, but also a poor understanding of our present times' (Havel 1997a: 7).

2   The various strategies of communist propagandists to alienate Palach from his supporters included the attempt to interpret his martyrdom as motivated by Buddhism (in those times self-immolation as a form of political protest was notorious for its use by some Buddhists in Southeast Asia) rather than being in line with Czech tradition. As Holy observed, 'the symbolic significance of Palach's act was thus to be devalued by being construed as something totally alien to Czech and, indeed, European culture' (Holy 1996: 45).

3   Difficult but not impossible. The spin-doctor of communist propaganda, Zdeněk Nejedlý, simply stressed Hus' revolt against the feudal establishment and his concerns with the common people 'rather than his piety and pursuit of truth'. Consequently, Nejedlý was convinced that if Hus had been alive in the 1940s he would have been a communist politician rather than a priest (Kemp 1999: 107). Still, the communist regime, glorifying the tradition of revolutionary violence, saw itself possibly more indebted to the Hussite military leader Jan Žižka.

4   Kukral speculates that the story could have been 'a clever piece of propaganda of the Voice of America' (Kukral 1997: 79). In fact, it was the last desperate ploy of the Czechoslovak secret police (StB) to preserve the existing regime. Ironically, the secret police who sought to provoke unrest and thus hoped to create a pretext for a firmer reaction of the communist leadership, achieved precisely the opposite. As Timothy Garton Ash remarked, this was 'one of the relatively few cases where behind a conspiracy theory you find a real conspiracy – although one that went rapidly and gloriously wrong' (Garton Ash 1999: 16).

5   This image was something of a myth, given the fact that the East Germans were among the first peoples in Europe to rebel against the communist system of power. Their June 1953 anti-communist uprising actually predated similar events in Hungary and Poland in 1956, let alone the Prague Spring of 1968. Furthermore, the dissident activities of the 1970s and 1980s, organized in the GDR mostly under the auspices of the evangelic church, were comparable with the movements in Czechoslovakia (even though they were considerably weakened by the forced expulsion of many East German dissidents to West Germany).

6   Herder undoubtedly exerted a strong influence on the intellectual leaders of the Czech national movement in the nineteenth century (such as Kollár, Jungmann, Šafařík, Palacký). 'It is an irony of fate', commented Masaryk, 'that German philosophy provided the groundwork for an anti-German national movement. In order to build a Czech culture, our awakeners used German philosophy, and even French and English thought came to us primarily through German mediation' (Masaryk in Kovtun 1990: 63). Yet, as Pynsent observed, the notion of 'peace-loving Slavs' predates Herder and originates with the early seventeenth-century Czech Protestant priest Adam Hartmann (Pynsent 1999: 213). Furthermore, Josef Zumr argues that because Herder himself was influenced by a number of seventeenth-century Czech thinkers, including John Amos Comenius (1592–1670), the Czech revivalists in the nineteenth century were, through their interest in Herder, in effect restoring the broken links with the Czech reformation movement (Zumr 1997: 61).

7   Pynsent argues that the term *jazyk*, used in the chronicle to describe the Czech nation, indicates an early form of linguistic nationalism, which sees language as the defining feature of a nation. The word *jazyk*, which means tongue and language, is used in the chronicle also in the meaning of nation (*populus, natio*) (Pynsent 1999: 205). In contrast, Tilman Berger cautions against this seemingly plausible interpretation. According to Berger, the author of the chronicle was primarily concerned with the emerging class divisions between lesser nobility and burghers rather than with nationalist mobilization against the Germans (Berger 2001: 189). Contested is not only the meaning of the chronicle, but also its authorship. As James Naughton noted, 'the one thing quite certain about the author of the slightly later so-called Dalimil Chronicle, is that his name was not Dalimil, which is a later misapprehension' (Naughton 2001).

8   The myth of the White Mountain as a symbol of the 'age-long' Czech-German struggle distorts the actual history. The fact that 'the armies of the King of Bohemia and Roman Emperor Ferdinand II (1617 [1619]–37), together with the division of the League of the Catholic states, defeated the forces of the rebellious estates of Bohemia and their allies from the Protestant Union' (Petráň and Petráňová 1998: 143) cannot be seen simply as the German defeat of the Czech aristocracy. The conflict was primarily political rather than ethnic. 'Some of the foremost Czech aristocrats…remained staunchly Catholic' while 'some leaders of the Protestant nobility were German' (Sayer 1998: 44). In fact, it can even be questioned whether this ethnic division can be clearly defined along these lines. As Holy pointed out, 'the noble families of Bohemia who rebelled against the Habsburg monarchy can hardly be classified as Czech when the notion of what it means to be Czech became established only in the last century' (Holy 1996: 112).

9   The ethnically neutral term 'Böhme' made it possible for the nineteenth-century noble inhabitant of 'Bohemia', Joseph Mathias von Thun, to declare:

> daß ich weder ein Čeche noch ein Deutscher, sondern nur ein *Böhme* bin, daß ich, von inniger Vaterlandsliebe durchglüht, das Unterdrückenwollen einer dieser beiden Nationalitäten – gleichviel welcher – als das unheilvollste Mißgeschick betrachte und daß ich für meine čechischen Brüder das Wort ergreife, weil ich es für Ritterpflicht halte, auf der Seite der Schwächern zu stehen.

> (my italics, cited in Berger 2001: 191–2)

10 To be fair to Palacký it should be noted that the Czech language does not have an equivalent for *Böhmen*. The same applies to the corresponding adjective *böhmisch* (Bohemian), which is clearly more inclusive than *český* (Czech) as it refers to all the inhabitants of Bohemia regardless of their ethnic origin. Petr Pithart may have gone to far when he argued that this 'linguistic problem' somehow anticipated Czech excesses in chauvinistic policies, starting with the discrimination against Germans in the first Czechoslovak Republic to the expulsion of the German population of Bohemia after the Second World War. 'Were we not able to, or did we not want to be able to express this?', Petr Pithart asked rhetorically, implying that the Czech language just reflects the unwillingness of Czech people to accommodate the Germans in Bohemia (Pithart 1993; for a more comprehensive survey of the implications of the missing term for Czech history writings, see Čaněk 1996: 19–24; for an example of the usage of the (non-existent?) term 'Czechia' in contemporary academic literature and the short etymological survey of both terms, see Sláma 1998: 37).

11 To give an example – while the Czech edition of the first book dealing with the years 451–894 explicitly states that the government of the Slavs 'was thoroughly democratic' ('vláda jejich byla veskrze demokratická') the corresponding place in the older German edition does not include such a direct statement (cf. Palacký 1939: I, 58–59; 1844: I, 58–9).

12 It is open to debate whether this position was based merely on tactical considerations (which took into account the balance of power between the seemingly omnipotent state and the relatively small groups of dissidents), or whether it reflected a genuine desire to accept the existing system of law.

13 Clearly, this was inconsistent with the fraternal relations which Czechs were supposed to have with the 'better' Germans living in the GDR. But propaganda does not need to be consistent. More importantly, it should tap into prevailing popular sentiment. According to Milan Uhde, a common humorous interpretation of the German acronym for DDR ('Deutsche Demokratische Republik'), was 'Dočasně Dezorientovaní Revanšisté', meaning 'revanchists who are temporarily disorientated' (Uhde 1995: 215).

14 Palacký's friendly gestures towards the Germans can be contrasted with the vitriolic attacks on Czechs by Friedrich Engels. One of the spiritual leaders of the communist movement despised Czechs (as well as other small Slavic nations of Central Europe) for their lack of revolutionary fervour. He keenly awaited their annihilation:

> These remnants of a nation, mercilessly crushed, as Hegel said, by the course of history, this *national refuse*, is always the fanatical representative of the counter-revolution and remains so until it is completely exterminated or de-nationalized, as its whole existence is in itself a protest against a great historical revolution.
>
> (Engels 1973: 221–2)

15 The concept of Czechoslovakism also had some serious implications for the Czech-Slovak relationship. But since it seems to have affected Slovaks more than Czechs, I will deal with it more explicitly in the following chapter.

16 This is very much in line with more recent formulations of the liberal justification for individual rights. In the words of Michael Sandel,

> what justifies the rights is not that they maximize the general welfare or otherwise promote the good, but rather that they constitute a fair framework within which individuals and groups can choose their own values and ends, consistent with a similar liberty for others.
>
> (Sandel 1996: 11)

But there is also an important difference between Rádl and certain types of contemporary political liberalism. While thinkers like Rawls and Rorty explicitly deny the need for a philosophical and/or metaphysical grounding of this notion of justice (in Rawls' terminology, 'comprehensive liberalism'), Rádl firmly believed that the need for just procedures is ultimately derived from a universal moral law. In this respect, Rádl's liberalism is more traditional and Kantian.

17 The only exception, according to Hrabal's witty novel *Closely Observed Trains*, was grandfather Vilém, who, as a professional hypnotist, attempted to halt the German invasion of March 1939 with his magic powers. His hypnotic powers worked for a while and halted the first tank of a long convoy.

> The whole army stood still. Grandfather touched the leading tank with his outstretched fingers, and kept pouring out towards it the same suggestion: 'Turn round and go back, turn round and...' And then the lieutenant gave a signal with his pennant, and the tank changed its mind and moved forward, but Grandfather never budged, and the tank ran over him and crushed his head, *and after there was nothing standing in the way of the German army'*.
>
> (my italics, Hrabal 1990: 12)

Obviously, Hrabal's fiction cannot be read as a serious historical study, but it sheds some light on the Czech self-perception of the past achievements and failings. The meaning of national history is not an exclusive domain of historians, philosophers or politicians.

18 What changed with time was the enemy. Originally, during the Czechoslovak First Republic, the enemy was defined by class – the bourgeoisie; later, the deciding characteristic became ethnicity – German; and after 1948, when there were hardly any Germans left in Czechoslovakia, the victims of revolutionary violence were the enemies from within – once again the 'bourgeois' (although this label was often used in an arbitrary manner).

19 This is clearly in line with Engels' argument explored above (note 14). But while for Engels the advanced German nation was to fight against the backward and conservative Slavic nations (excluding revolutionary Poles, but including Russia – see Walicki 1995: 153–66), in Stalin's view, the historic mission of the revolutionary Russians was now to destroy Germans.

20 Challenging the widespread view of the expulsion as the inevitable outcome of the Second World War, the Czech historian Milan Churaň argues that 'even though the expulsion could not have happened without the world war, the war was not the reason for the expulsion, but rather "the unique historic opportunity for ethnic cleansing"' (Churaň 2001: 37). Furthermore, it is surprising that despite the fact that the Czechs did not suffer nearly as much as their Polish counterparts during the war, their reprisals were no less violent. As Norman M. Naimark observed,

the Czechs were treated much differently [from the Poles]. Relatively few died during the war; Czech industry prospered, as did its workers; and direct attacks on Czech nationals were sporadic and rare. Yet the Czechs were as brutal as the Poles, if not more so, in taking revenge on the Germans.

(Naimark 2001: 14)

21 A compromise solution was adopted by a joint Czech-German historical commission, which was established by the German and Czechoslovak governments to advance the process of reconciliation. Its report differentiates between two different stages of 'transfer' and refers to the first, 'wild' period from May until August of 1945 as 'an "expulsion" (*vyhnání*), with its connotation of violence', and to the second, organized transfer of 1946 'as a "forced expatriation" (*nucené vysídlení*)' (Glassheim 2001: 205).

22 Yet the 1939–89 timeframe does not apply to the legalities of restitution, since it is not possible to reclaim property lost before 25 February 1948. This leads, among others, to the exclusion of all those German Czechoslovak citizens expelled immediately after the Second World War. While the government has repeatedly defended its controversial policy by advocating the need for a pragmatic solution which minimizes the potential for conflicts, some critics (e.g. Mandler 1999a) see it as an expression of chauvinism and an unwillingness to address the darker aspects of Czech history.

23 This critical attitude towards one's own national history is yet to be fully reflected in the Czech school curriculum. As a comprehensive study of standard post-1989 history textbooks revealed, Czech children are still taught in a very one-sided manner which celebrates the Czech nation as peace-loving and largely ignores those aspects of Czech nationalism which were directed against others (whether they be Germans, Jews or Romanies – see Čaněk 1996). But the very fact that the teaching of history is being criticized is a promising sign that its content may change with time.

24 Admittedly, this was partly caused by the reaction of the Sudetendeutsche Landsmannschaft, which responded to Havel's apology by making unrealistic demands for financial compensation (for a critical evaluation of initial German responses see Pauer 1999: 21–2).

25 The undeferential treatment of Havel seems to have become a burgeoning industry, replacing previous attitudes which bordered on idolatry (e.g. Kriseová 1991). The best-selling Czech biography by Přemysl Svora's, *Sedm týdnu, které otřásly Hradem (Seven Weeks Which Shattered the Castle)*, for example, presented Havel as the helpless victim of his second wife, the actress Dagmar (Svora 1998). Written for a wide audience is also the recent critical and somewhat unbalanced study by John Keane, *Václav Havel: A Political Tragedy in Six Acts*. The most fanciful analysis of Havel's political philosophy in academic literature is possibly the study by Marie L. Neudorfl, who criticizes Havel for being influenced by Patočka. Neudorfl does not seriously explore Patočka's philosophy, but simply dismisses it on the grounds that he was 'a student of the German Nazi philosopher Martin Heidegger' (Neudorfl 1999: 119). (It is worthwhile noting that applying the same logic to other influential students of Heidegger would result in questioning the democratic credentials of the likes of Hannah Arendt and Richard Rorty.) Similarly, Neudorfl seems to be paying little attention even to Havel's own writings. She asserts, for example, that Havel failed to recognize the relevance of culture and national history in political processes, which clearly ignores all the evidence to the contrary (see above). (For a more

sophisticated appraisal of Patočka's philosophy and his influence on Havel see Findlay 1999.)
26 This criticism seems exaggerated, especially given that Havel openly endorsed the principles of a free market economy (Havel 1991: 46–8). In fact, by critics from the other end of political spectrum, Havel was accused alternately of accepting 'the ideology of extreme economic liberalism' (Neudorfl 1999: 125), or even of 'cynically appropriating the knaves of capitalism' (Žižek 1999: 6). More accurate and unbiased is the description by Isaiah Berlin, who held that Havel is simply 'a type of a left-wing liberal' (*Lidové noviny*, 15 November 1997).
27 Robert B. Pynsent noted that even Havel was not always free of this type of prejudice. He commented on Havel's New Year's Day address of 1 January 1991 thus: 'Like characters in a medieval dispute, the Slovaks represent Emotion and the Czechs Reason: the Slovak Republic "will be a republic of love and pride", but the Czech Republic "will be a republic of wisdom and tolerance for all its citizens"' (Pynsent 1994: 153).

5 Nationalism in Slovakia

1 In fact, if anything, there was significantly more domestic support for the Communist Party in the Czech lands than in Slovakia. In the last semi-free election in 1946, the Czechoslovak Communist Party gained '43 per cent of the votes in Bohemia, 35 per cent in Moravia, and 30 per cent in Slovakia' (Leff 1997: 47; see also Chapter 4 in the present volume). As the German historian Jan Pauer accurately analysed, 'because the non-communist forces dominated the 1946 election in Slovakia, the establishment of the communist power monopoly was only possible with the help of Prague' (Pauer 1999: 15).
2 According to a 1999 public opinion survey carried out by the Institute for Public Affairs in Bratislava, 89 per cent of respondents in Slovakia evaluated the historical contribution of Alexander Dubček positively, or rather positively. Milan Štefánik gained the support of 73 per cent of the respondents (Gyárfášová 2001: 255).
3 The significance of Schuster's German origin should not be overestimated, since his ethnicity was not really an issue in the election campaign. But it is worthwhile noting that his party, the Party of Civic Reconciliation (SOP), paid most attention to the protection of minority rights of all the parties, apart from the Hungarian Coalition Party (Kusý 1999: 176).
4 This interpretation of Slovak history found its expression in the preamble of the 1993 Slovak constitution:

> We, the Slovak nation, mindful of the political and cultural heritage of our forebears, and of the centuries of experience from the struggle for national existence and our own statehood, in the sense of the spiritual heritage of Cyril and Methodius and the historical legacy of the Greater Moravian Empire, proceeding from the natural right of nations to self-determination, together with members of national minorities and ethnic groups living on the territory of the Slovak Republic...that is, we, citizens of the Slovak Republic, adopt through our representatives the following Constitution.
> (http://slovakia.eunet.sk/slovakia/history-politics/slovak-constitution.txt)

5 In contrast, the Czechoslovak mythopoeic history writings regard Greater Moravia as the first common state of Czechs and Slovaks.

6 The archeologist Eduard Krekovič, for example, ridiculed such approaches by arguing that if the logic of extreme nationalist historians were accepted, one could claim that the first *homo sapiens* must have been Slovak too (Krekovič 1998: 5).

7 The problems of fair accommodation of ethnic minorities within the Hungarian state are reflected in the language, since it is not possible in Hungarian to express the difference between a citizen of Hungary and a member of a Hungarian ethnic community (Pithart 1993). The same is true of the Slovak language in respect to its own national minorities, but in respect to Hungary and its people it is possible to distinguish between Uhorsko (the pre-1918 Hungarian state which does not imply any ethnicity) and Mad'arsko (the Magyar nation state). Whenever attempting to stress the issues of ethnicity, I will follow convention and employ the term Magyar rather than Hungarian.

8 This can be nicely illustrated by a poem written by Pavol Ország Hviezdoslav (1849–1921), *Mňa kedys zvádzal svet* (*I Was once Lured by the Wide World*). Hviezdoslav alludes in the poem to his early beginnings, in which he, as a talented young writer, naturally wrote in Hungarian. Having realized that his own mother of Slovak ethnic origin could not understand his poetry, he gave up on the opportunity to become a part of the Hungarian mainstream and became one of the most significant Slovak writers. In contrast, Sándor Petöfi, of Slovak ethnic origin, became the most influential *Magyar* poet, celebrated as a hero of the 1848/9 Revolution. Similar claims about the Magyar revolutionary leader Lajos Kossuth, who is supposed to have been of Slovak ethnic origin (e.g. Schwarz 1993: 48), appear to be unfounded (see Deak 1979: 10).

9 Even on the territory of the current Czech Republic, individual national identities in the first half of the nineteenth century were often very fluid. This is exemplified by Jan Kollár and Pavol Jozef Šafařík, who were both of Slovak ethnic origin but considered themselves Czechs, Czechoslovaks, or simply Slavs. Kollár, in particular, was firmly convinced of the existence of one Slav nation and called for the cultural unity of all Slavic tribes. This confusion is reflected in the contemporary categorization of their ethnicity. Thus Kollár is described as a 'Slovak poet' in both the *Encyclopaedia Britannica* and a standard Slovak Encyclopedia (EU-SAV 1993: 345), but as a 'Czech poet of Slovak origin and the main protagonist of Czech national classicism in poetry' in a standard Czech Encyclopaedia (*Academia* 1972: 531). Similarly, Šafařík is labelled as a 'leading figure of the Czech national revival' in the *Encyclopaedia Britannica*, but as a 'Slovak scholar' in the Slovak Encyclopaedia (EU-SAV 1993: 701), and a '*Czech and Slovak* scholar and poet' in the Czech equivalent (my italics, *Academia* 1972: 1196).

10 However, the bleak view of the so-called Bach's 'neoabsolutist' period in Slovak history (1849–67) has been recently revised. The time of neoabsolutism is no longer associated exclusively with repressive centralization of the empire and police terror, but also with the economic, social and cultural development of the Slovaks. See, for example, the edited volume *Die Habsburger Monarchie und die Slowaken* (Kováč *et al.* 2001, esp. 145–8).

11 Written in German in 1853; published first in a Russian translation of 1867; German original 1931; but in a Slovak translation only in 1993 (Pynsent 2002: 9).

12 Two marching songs attest to the similarities in logic of two different state ideologies. The supporters of Tiso's regime were mobilized by the lyrics of extreme nationalism: *Kto je Slovák, s nami nôti / kto nie s nami, ten je proti. / Kamaráti, na stráž, kamaráti na stráž!* ('He who is a Slovak, sings with us /

who is not with us, is against us / friends be on guard! [the fascist greeting]'). Some ten years later, strikingly similar lyrics celebrated the road to a communist society: *Kto nie je s nami, je proti nám / ale nás nesmie z cesty zviesť / dvíhame hlavy až k výšinám / voláme, Práci česť* ('He who is not with us, is against us / but he must not lead us astray from our path / we raise our heads to the heights / and call, [the communist greeting] Honour to work!') (Lipták 1999: 219).

13 The most fanciful interpretation so far has come from a highly respected financier, the erstwhile Deputy Governor of the Slovak National Bank, Marián Tkáč, who claims Štúr is in fact the chief inspirer of national banking, since he

> had been the first to write about saving banks in Slovak....Štúr did not found our banks, but without him these banks would not have come into being as they did. They would have been less Slovak....At the beginning was the word, and the word was Štúr's.
>
> (cited in Pynsent 1998: 281)

14 Opinion surveys from 1990, 1996 and 2000 show that Štúr, together with Dubček and Štefánik (see note 2), are seen by most Slovaks as historic personalities to be proud of (Gyárfášová 2001: 252).

15 Causing much Slovak frustration, this approach was readily adopted abroad and persisted, at least in many journalistic accounts of Czechoslovak developments, into the late 1990s. An instructive illustration of this terminological confusion is the short study *The Czecho-Slovaks: An Oppressed Nationality* by the eminent British historian of Polish origin, Lewis B. Namier. Written at the height of the Second World War, the study argued that the unity of 'these two branches of one single nation' was only being undermined by external enemies (Germany and Hungary). 'Both speak the same language ... Slovak is, in fact, merely a more archaic form of Czech' (Namier 1942: 3). Consequently, Namier suggested that this 'unique [nation] among the Slavs' may be called the 'Czech nation' for short (Namier 1942: 5).

16 Different ideas about the nature of Czech and Slovak coexistence were also reflected in the different names used for the description of the common republic. The so-called Pittsburgh agreement of 30 May 1918, which envisaged the creation of autonomous Slovak administrative structures including a Slovak parliament, talked about the establishment of a Czecho-slovak state (notice the hyphen). The actual official declaration of 28 October 1918, which marked the establishment of the new republic, talked, in contrast, about the Czechoslovak state (without a hyphen). Until 1920, when the only correct form was determined by law as *Republika Československá*, both written forms were commonly used (Šútovec 1999: 186–9). As discussed below, the hyphen became again a point of contention in March 1990.

17 Kováč does not dispute, however, that the idea of a political Czechoslovak nation was not an attractive ideological construct for the Slovaks, since it revived their historic anxieties. In the second half of the nineteenth century, the Hungarians originally claimed that *Natio Hungarica* was also just a political concept. But in reality, the Hungarians used the idea as a pretext for harsh assimilation policies (Kováč 1997: 123).

18 The crucial step was the publication of the first Slovak translation of *Federation in Central Europe* written originally in English in 1942 for British and American readership (Hodža 1942; 1997; for examples of contemporary Slovak evaluation

of Hodža see Chmel 1996: 448; Lukáč 1996: 70–2; Kusý 1998: 212–4; Pekník *et al.* 2002).

19 But while Hodža envisaged that the movement for ever closer federative links between the European nations would start from Central Europe, possibly expanding later to the West, the actual postwar development was the other way round. As it turned out, the nations of Central Europe are now to be admitted to the EU, that is a (West) European federation.

20 It is worthwhile noting that nationalism has been discredited to such a degree that the very term has a negative connotation in the Slovak language (as in Czech and Polish). Hence, Pavol Lukáč has suggested that 'at the end of the twentieth century Hodža's democratic nationalism should rather be called patriotism' (Hodža 1997: 25; cf. Chapters 3 and 4).

21 Fascism is often distinguished from German Nazism in Western historiography since, despite some similarities, there are also important differences between the two movements (i.e. Italian fascism was not as anti-Semitic as German Nazism). But in the communist interpretation, Nazism is just one of the various representations of fascism; it is its 'most reactionary and most aggressive variety' (*Malá encyklopédia Slovenska* 1987: 130).

22 The most outspoken supporters of the heritage of the wartime Slovak Republic were to be found in the ranks of the Slovak National Party (SNS). Marking the fiftieth anniversary of the Slovak National Uprising, Ján Slota, chairman of SNS, defended the wartime fascist state as a 'Slovak miracle' and condemned the anti-fascist uprising as a 'national shame' (Ulc 1996: 348). But similar claims came also from within the Movement for a Democratic Slovakia (HZDS). At the party congress in March 1996, Gabo Zelenay, a journalist closely associated with the HZDS, compared the present achievements of the (then) ruling coalition with the good economic results of the wartime Slovak state with the comment: 'During [World War II] we were in third place in Europe economically. Right behind Switzerland and Sweden, third was Slovakia. And such a miracle was achieved today by our leadership and finance minister' (cited in Fisher 1996a).

23 This found its expression also in the national anthem *Nad Tatrou sa blýska* (*Lightning Flashes Over the Tatra Mountains*), which was amended by an addition which reiterated the theme of the destiny of the nation and its rebirth: *To Slovensko naše posial' tvrdo spalo / Ale blesky hromu / Vzbudzujú ho k tomu / aby sa prebralo* ('Our Slovakia was so far sound asleep / But thunder and lightning / Encourage her / To wake up'). For a critical evaluation of the Slovak anthem see Kusý 1998: 181.

24 The book was actually published in 1996 by the Slovak Ministry of Education through its pedagogical publishing division as a supplementary text for history courses in primary and secondary schools. This was the second, expanded edition which had a print run of 100,000 (!) copies.

25 In a recent comprehensive study of Tiso, the Slovak historian Ivan Kamenec convincingly challenged such claims. First, to present Tiso as a saviour of the Jews cannot be reconciled with his openly displayed anti-Semitism. Second, there is an uneasy question that the defenders of Tiso cannot satisfactorily address:

> How was it possible that the President could stop the deportations in summer 1942 (although there is no direct or indirect evidence available in support of this claim), but he was not able, and did not attempt to stop the transports from the very beginning, or at least earlier than 1942?
>
> (Kamenec 1998b: 96)

Tiso, in fact, defended the policies directed against the Jews in the face of strong criticism from the Vatican as late as November 1944:

> The Slovak government took action against the Czechs and the Jews not because of their nationality and descent, but out of duty to protect the nation against enemies that have been destructive for centuries....We owe thanks and loyalty to Germans, who not only accepted the natural right of our nation to exist and be independent and free, but who supported us in our [fight] against the enemies of our nation, the Czechs and the Jews.
>
> (Stehle 1991: 58; see also Kamenec 1998b: 114)

26 While the word 'collaborate' can be value-neutral in English, in Slovak it has a distinctly negative connotation and stands for traitorous cooperation with an enemy. Hence Kováč obviously does not oppose cooperation between the nations *per se*, but only that which helps to sustain criminal regimes such as the Nazi.

27 It would be difficult, however, to describe Čarnogurský as a liberal nationalist, since he has consistently opposed liberalism. In a lecture presented at an international conference in New York (October 1991), for example, Čarnogurský called for the Catholic Church to fight against liberalism (Čarnogurský 1997: 146). It needs to be taken into consideration, however, that Čarnogurský's understanding of liberalism is rather one-sided, as he seems to equate liberalism with moral relativism. As I have discussed in Chapter 3, liberalism is not incompatible with religious beliefs. (On Čarnogurský's attitude to liberalism, see also his interview in *Lidové noviny*, 23 October 1991, reprinted in Čarnogurský 1997: 276–86).

28 The influence of the artistic community in Slovakia (or in any other country of Central Europe) should not be underestimated. The 1989 revolution was driven not only by students but also by intellectuals and artists. After 1989, some popular actors became skilful politicians (i.e. Milan Kňažko), others retained their artistic careers while becoming at the same time active publicists and political commentators (e.g. Milan Lasica and the late Július Satinský both regularly wrote about political issues for influential newspapers like the daily *Sme* and the weekly *Domino fórum*). For an excellent example of literary satire see the novel of Pavel Vilikovský, *Večne je zelený... (Ever green is...),* which ridicules the myth of the Slovak's thousand-year subjection to Magyar rule (Vilikovský 1989, esp. 65–9; cf. Pynsent 1994: 192). For an example of underground literature, consider *Reminiscencie* by Peter Konkoly (Konkoly 1986).

29 In November 1989, Kusý was released from political imprisonment and took part in the Velvet Revolution. Between 1998 and 2002 he was a senior adviser to the deputy Prime Minister Pál Csáky, responsible for minority issues, and his political thoughts would, therefore, have had a direct impact on the policies of the broad coalition government led by Dzurinda.

30 There was virtually no debate in Slovakia about the attempted expulsion of Hungarians from Czechoslovakia after the Second World War (and even Chmel did not refer to it in the article cited above). This may partly be due to the fact that the plan was never fully implemented.

> The Czechoslovak government did not acquire international backing or the approval of Hungary to dispose of its entire Hungarian minority; nevertheless, 89,660 Hungarians were forced to migrate from Slovakia to Hungary

from 1945 to 1948. In exchange 73,273 Slovaks, or almost three-quarters of the Slovak minority, left Hungary for Slovakia.

(Ther 2001: 57)

Considering this largely unknown event in Slovak history, Miroslav Kusý challenged those Slovaks who expected the Hungarians to apologize for Lajos Kossuth and Appónyi, who are seen as responsible for the enforced Magyarization of Slovaks. 'Who should apologize to whom?', asked Kusý rhetorically (Kusý 1998: 225–30).

31 In the wartime Slovak state Slobodník was a member of the Hlinka Youth that emulated the Hitler-Youth, and later, after a term in a Soviet labour camp in communist times, he became a well published propagator of socialist realism in literature and the translator of official Soviet literature. In 1991 he became an active member of the Movement for a Democratic Slovakia (HZDS) and served as minister of culture in 1992–4. As Peter Zajac observed, the numerous metamorphoses of Slobodník's political affiliation (fascism, communism, extreme nationalism) show only one consistency – 'the syndrome of loyalty to the totalitarian regime' (Zajac 1996: 192). Similarly, Vladimír Mináč, who was one of the most prolific and revered writers of socialist realism, transformed himself into an influential spokesman of extreme nationalist forces, and became an active supporter of the Slovak push for independence. He stated that although 'he failed as a communist, as a Slovak he stands at the threshold of a new future' (Štrasser 1996).

32 Šútovec wrote his book in order

to commemorate an unhappy state, which was called Republika Československá, Česko-slovenská republika, Československá republika, Československá socialistická republika, Česko-slovenská federatívna republika, Česko-slovenská federativní republika, Česká a Slovenská Federatívna Republika, Česká a Slovenská Federativní Republika, a state that could not find its identity and also because of that did not even reach its eightieth birthday.

(Šútovec 1999: 7)

33 'Opinion polls conducted between 1990 and 1992 consistently showed that only 10–20 per cent of Slovak respondents were in favour of independence' (Hilde 1999: 651).

34 Many prominent Slovak politicians who were formerly close allies of Mečiar became frustrated with his authoritarian style and became some of his firmest opponents. The long list of 'traitors' includes among others: Milan Kňažko, the co-founder and former deputy leader of HZDS and foreign minister in the first (1990–1) and in the second (1992–3) Mečiar governments, who defected in March 1993 (subsequently he became minister of culture in 1998–2002); Jozef Moravčík, who headed the interim government, and Roman Kováč (unrelated to Michal Kováč) both held senior positions in the party before defecting in February 1994.

35 The fact that a similar law existed even in the Czechoslovak First Republic, where it was introduced at Masaryk's behest, did not diminish the fears of Mečiar's critics. Clearly, the law would have supplied an additional tool for the illiberal practices of Mečiar's administration, and hence could have caused

significantly more damage than a similar law administered in the Czechoslovak
First Republic.

36 Similarly, even the best legislation cannot secure fair treatment for minorities. An
instructive example was the ruling of a local court in Banská Bystrica which
dealt with a racially motivated assault on a Romany. While the court convicted
the culprit, eighteen-year-old skinhead Ján P., of damage to health, it 'refused to
apply penal code articles pertaining to racially motivated crime because,
according to the court, ethnic Slovaks and Roma are from the same race' (*Roma
Rights*, 2/1999). This is an example of how a seemingly anti-racist ruling in fact
misrepresented the purpose of the law, which was designed to accord additional
protection to racial minorities. Although the decision was overruled in April
2000 by a higher court (Vražda 2000), the original justification shows how pervasive anti-Romany sentiments are. (For a virtually identical court decision in the
Czech Republic, and a more theoretically based debate, see Chapter 2.)

6 Conclusions

1 Although my research only covers those three countries of Central Europe, I
believe that the same (or a similar) theoretical framework could bring highly
interesting insights also about Hungary. While Hungarian extreme nationalists
(e.g. István Csurka) have received ample publicity both in the popular media as
well as in the academic literature, the forces of liberal nationalism have been
largely ignored. Two recent studies, however, reversed this trend. First, László
Deme demonstrated that liberal nationalism 'vitally influenced politics, foreign
affairs and intellectual life in post-communist Hungary' (Deme 1998: 57).
Second, Eva Boka explored the Hungarian traditions of liberal nationalism by
focusing on the intellectual heritage of 'three initiators of cooperation in Central
Europe': József Eötvös, Oszkar Jaszi and István Bibó (Boka 1999: 435).

2 A telling example of such an approach was the study by Christian Boulanger
which argued that constitutionalism in Slovakia, which was an essential part of
liberal democratic order, had little chance of success because of the country's
unfavourable historical legacy. The pessimistic conclusion of this sophisticated
study was largely invalidated by the September 1998 elections, but the writer was
forced to ignore the outcome and stated that 'the paper had originally been
written before the Mečiar government was voted out of office...and does not
cover this and subsequent events' (Boulanger 1999: 1).

3 This is not to imply that Austria is not culturally and geographically a part of
Central Europe; the argument here rather seeks to utilize (and challenge) the old
conceptual division between well established Western democracies and the postcommunist societies of Central and Eastern Europe. One could also consider the
surprising success of Jean-Marie Le Pen in the first round of the French presidential elections of April 2002, when he defeated the socialist candidate Lionel
Jospin and won 17 per cent of the vote (only 3 per cent less than Jacques Chirac).
Hence, even in France, which is usually seen as a textbook example of a civic
nation, illiberal nationalism could make inroads into mainstream politics.

4 This is the title of a recently published collection of essays which attempt to
'compare and contrast the images which liberals in the West and social thinkers
of the same persuasion in the formerly communist-ruled countries currently
entertain about the working of pluralist systems and the conditions of their satisfactory performance' (Suda 2000: 1).

Bibliography

Ambrosewicz-Jacobs, Jolanta (2000) 'Attitudes of Young Poles Toward Jews in Post-1989 Poland', *East European Politics and Societies*, vol. 14, no. 3, fall, 565–96.

Ajnenkiel, Andrzej (1993) 'Nationality, Patriotism and Nationalism: The Polish Case from the Mid-Eastern European Perspective', in Roger Michener (ed.) *Nationality, Patriotism and Nationalism in Liberal Democratic Societies*, St Paul, Minnesota: Paragon Books, 107–37.

Anderson, Benedict (1983) *Imagined Communities*, London: Verso.

Anderson, Perry (1999) 'A Ripple of the Polonaise', *London Review of Books*, 25 November, 3–10.

Arendt, Hannah (1973) *On Revolution*, Harmondsworth: Penguin Books.

Bader, Veit (1998) 'Egalitarian Multiculturalism: Institutional Separation and Cultural Pluralism', in Rainer Bauböck and John Rundell (eds) *Blurred Boundaries: Migration, Ethnicity, Citizenship*, Aldershot: Ashgate, 185–222.

Banga, Dezider (1996) 'Three Dates with Roma Culture', *Slovensko*, 4, 24–30, http://www.matica.sk/cas_slovensko/c.4-96/.

Bannan, Alfred and Edelyeni, Achilles (1970) *A Documentary History of Eastern Europe*, New York: Twayne Publishers.

Barany, Zoltan (1995) 'Grim Realities in Eastern Europe', *Transition*, vol. 1, no. 4, 29 March, 3–6.

——(2002) *The East European Gypsies: Regime Change, Marginality and Ethnopolitics*, Cambridge: Cambridge University Press.

Barnard, F. M. (1965) *Herder's Social and Political Thought: From Enlightenment to Nationalism*, Oxford: Oxford University Press.

Barša, Pavel (1999) *Politická teorie multikulturalismu*, Brno: Centrum pro studium demokracie a kultury.

——(2001) 'Ethnocultural Justice in East European States and the Case of the Czech Roma', in Will Kymlicka and Magda Opalski (eds) *Can Liberal Pluralism be Exported? Western Political Theory and Ethnic Relations in Eastern Europe*, Oxford: Oxford University Press, 243–58.

Bauböck, Rainer (1998) 'The Crossing and Blurring of Boundaries in International Migration', in Rainer Bauböck and John Rundell (eds) *Blurred Boundaries: Migration, Ethnicity, Citizenship*, Aldershot: Ashgate, 17–52.

Bauerová, Ladka (1998) ' "Miracle" for Romany School', *The Prague Post Online*, 9 September.

Bednář, Miloslav (1998) *Spravedlnost, demokracie a česká filosofie politiky: Úvahy nad proměnou hodnot po roce 1989*, Olomouc: Votobia.

Beiner, Roland (ed.) (1995) *Theorizing Citizenship*, New York: State University of New York Press.

Beneš, Václav (1964) 'Background of Czechoslovak Democracy', in Miloslav Rechcigl (ed.) *The Czechoslovak Contribution to World Culture*, The Hague: Mouton, 267–76.

Berger, Tilman (2001) 'Sprache und Nation', in Walter Koschmal, Marek Nekula and Joachim Rogall (eds) *Deutsche und Tschechen: Geschichte, Kultur, Politik*, Munich: Beck, 186–91.

Berlin, Isaiah (1969) *Four Essays on Liberty*, Oxford: Oxford University Press.

——(1979) *Against the Current: Essays in the History of Ideas*, London: Hogarth Press.

Bernstein, Carl and Politi, Marco (1996) *His Holiness: John Paul the Second and the Hidden History of our Time*, New York: Doubleday.

Bertschi, C. Charles (1994) 'Lustration and the Transition to Democracy: The Cases of Poland and Bulgaria', *East European Quarterly*, vol. 28, no. 4, winter, 435–53.

Bingen, Dieter (1997) 'Kwaśniewskis Polen: Vorwärts und vergessen', in Hans-Hermann Höhman *et al.* (eds) *Der Osten Europas in Prozeß der Differenzierung*, Munich: Carl Hanser, 128–40.

——(1998) *Die Republik Polen*, Landsberg am Lech: Aktuell.

Biskupski, Mieczysław B. (2000) *The History of Poland*, Westport CT: Greenwood.

Błoński, Jan (1988) 'Poor Poles Look at the Ghetto', in Aharon Weiss (ed.) (1988) *Yad Vashem Studies XIX*, Jerusalem: Yad Vashem, 341–56.

Boka, Eva (1999) 'From National Toleration to National Liberation (Three Initiators of Cooperation in Central Europe)', *East European Politics and Societies*, vol. 13, no. 3, fall, 435–58.

Bollerup, Søren Rinder and Christensen, Christian Dons (1997) *Nationalism in Eastern Europe: Causes and Consequences of the National Revivals and Conflicts in Late-twentieth-century Eastern Europe*, New York: St Martin's Press.

Bombík, Svetoslav (1995) *Bližšie k Európe: Štúdie a články*, Bratislava: Slovenská nadácia pre európske štúdie.

Borsody, Stephen (1993) *The New Central Europe*, Boulder CO: East European Monographs.

Boulanger, Christian (1999) 'Constitutionalism in East Central Europe? The Case of Slovakia under Mečiar', *East European Quarterly*, vol. 33, no. 1, spring, 1–21.

Brown, J. F. (1994) *Hopes and Shadows*, Durham NC: Duke University Press.

Brubaker, Rogers (1998) 'Myths and Misconceptions in the Study of Nationalism', in John A. Hall (ed.) *The State of the Nation: Ernest Gellner and the Theory of Nationalism*, Cambridge: Cambridge University Press, 272–306.

——(1999) 'The Manichean Myth: Rethinking the Distinction Between "Civic" and "Ethnic" Nationalism', in Hanspeter Kriesi, Klaus Armingeon and Hannes Siegrist (eds) *Nation and National Identity: The European Experience in Perspective*, Zurich: Rüegger, 55–71.

Brusis, Martin (1997) 'Macht der Mythen. Geschichtsdeutungen im slowakisch-ungarischen Verhältnis', *Südosteuropa, Zeitschrift für Gegenwartsforschung*, vol. 46, nos. 9–10, 419–25.

Brzezinski, Mark (1998) *The Struggle for Constitutionalism in Poland*, New York: St Martin's Press.

Burgess, Adam (1997) *Divided Europe*, London and Chicago: Pluto Press.

Burke, Edmund (1968) *Reflections on the Revolution in France*, Harmondsworth: Penguin.

Bútora, Martin and Bútorová, Zora (1999) 'Slovakia's Democratic Awakening', *Journal of Democracy*, vol. 10, no. 1, 80–95.

Bútora, Martin and Skladony, Thomas (eds) (1998) *Slovakia 1996–1997: A Global Report on the State of Society*, Bratislava: Institute for Public Affairs.

Bútorová, Zora (ed.) (1998) *Slovensko pred voľbami*, Bratislava: Inštitút pre verejné otázky.

Bútorová, Zora, Gyárfášová, Oľga and Velšic, Marián (1999) 'Verejná mienka', in Mesežnikov, Grigorij and Ivantyšyn, Michal (eds) (1999) *Slovensko 1998–1999: Súhrnná správa o stave spoločnosti*, Bratislava: Inštitút pre verejné otázky, 233–72.

Cahn, Claude (2000) 'Doing Battle with Nationalism', *Transitions*, http://www.tol.cz/.

Cahn, Claude and Chirico, David (1999) *A Special Remedy: Roma and Schools for the Mentally Handicapped in the Czech Republic*, Budapest: European Roma Rights Centre.

Cahn, Claude and Trehan, Nidhi (1997) *Time of the Skinheads: Denial and Exclusion of Roma in Slovakia*, Budapest: European Roma Rights Centre.

Camrda, Jakub (1998) 'Co je a co není rasový motiv', *Lidové noviny*, 20 May, 11.

Čaněk, David (1996) *Národ, národnost, menšiny a rasismus*, Prague: Institut pro středoevropskou kulturu a politiku.

Canovan, Margaret (1999) 'Lasting Institutions: Arendtian Thoughts on Nations and Republics', *Graduate Faculty Philosophy Journal*, vol. 21, no. 2, 133–51.

Čarnogurský, Ján (1994) 'Identita Európy. Európske kultúrne tradície a nové geopolitické usporiadanie', *Literárny týždenník*, reprinted as 'European Cultural Traditions and New Geopolitical Arrangements', *Human Affairs*, 5/1995, 25–30.

——(1997) *Videné od Dunaja*, Bratislava: Kalligram.

Carpenter, Michael (1997) 'Slovakia and the Triumph of Nationalistic Populism', *Communist and Post-Communist Studies*, vol. 30, no. 2, 205–20.

Chirot, Daniel (1995) 'National Liberations and Nationalist Nightmares', in Beverly Crawford (ed.) *Markets, States, and Democracy*, Boulder CO: Westview, 43–68.

Chmel, Rudolf (1996) *Moja maďarská otázka*, Bratislava: Kalligram.

——(1999) 'Menšinový zákon pre väčšinu?', *OS: Fórum Občianskej spoločnosti*, August 1999, 3–4.

Chmel, Rudolf (ed.) (1997) *Slovenská otázka v 20. storočí*, Bratislava: Kalligram.

Chmelár, Eduard (2000) 'Uhorsko je naše', *Slovo*, 3/2000, http://www.noveslovo.sk/.

Churaň, Milan (2001) *Postupim a Československo: mýtus a skutečnost*, Prague: Libri.

Cibulka, Frank (1999) 'The Radical Right in Slovakia', in Sabrina P. Ramet (ed.) *The Radical Right in Central and Eastern Europe since 1989*, Pennsylvania: Pennsylvania State University Press, 109–32.

Cichocki, Marek A. (2000) 'Patriotyzm: kłopotliwe zobowiązanie', *Rzeczpospolita*, 18 December, www.rzeczpospolita.pl.

——(2002) 'Solidarystyczne podstawy patriotyzmu', *Znak*, April, www.znak.com.pl.

Cirtautas, Arista (1995) 'The Role of Nationalism in East European Latecomers to Democracy', in Stephen Hanson and Willfried Spohn (eds) *Can Europe Work? Germany and the Reconstruction of Postcommunist Societies*, Seattle and London: University of Washington Press, 24–46.

Cordell, Karl (ed.) (1999) *Ethnicity and Democratisation in the New Europe*, London: Routledge.

Coudenhove-Kalergi, Barbara and Rathkolb, Oliver (eds) (2002) *Die Beneš-Dekrete*, Vienna: Czernin Verlag.

Craig, Gordon A. (1984) *Geschichte Europas 1815–1980, Von Wiener Kongreß bis zur Gegenwart*, Munich: C. H. Beck.

Crawford, Keith (1996) *East Central European Politics Today*, Manchester: Manchester University Press.

Crowe, David M. (1994) *A History of the Gypsies of Eastern Europe and Russia*, New York: St Martin's Press.

Crystal, David (ed.) (1994) *The Cambridge Encyclopaedia*, Cambridge: Cambridge University Press.

Czarnota, Adam (1992) 'Constitutional Nationalism, Citizenship and Hope for Civil Society in Eastern Europe', in Alexandar Pavkovic, Halyna Koscharsky and Adam Czarnota (eds) *Nationalism and Postcommunism*, Aldershot: Darmouth, 83–100.

——(1998) 'Constitutionalism, Nationalism and Law', paper presented at the AASCPCS/ANZSA 1998 International Conference on Communist and Post-communist Societies, Melbourne, 7–10 July.

Dahrendorf, Ralf (1994) 'Die Zukunft des Nationalstaates', *Merkur*, 9/10, 751–61.

Davies, Norman (1981) *God's Playground: A History of Poland*, 2 vols, Oxford: Oxford University Press.

——(1996) *Europe, A History*, Oxford: Oxford University Press.

Dawisha, Karen and Parrot, Bruce (1997) *The Consolidation of Democracy in East-Central Europe*, Cambridge: Cambridge University Press.

Deak, Istvan (1979) *The Lawful Revolution: Louis Kossuth and the Hungarians, 1848–1849*, New York: Columbia University Press.

Deme, Laszlo (1998) 'Liberal Nationalism in Hungary, 1988–1990', *East European Quarterly*, vol. 32, no. 1, spring, 57–83.

Demetz, Peter (1997) *Prague in Black and Gold*, New York: Hill and Wang.

Dionne, E. J. Jr and Dilulio, John J. Jr (1999) 'What's God Got to Do with the American Experiment?', *Brookings Review*, spring, www.brookings.edu.

Djilas, Aleksa (1997) 'Democracy, Destiny, and the Clash of Civilizations', *Transition*, October, 33–41.

Djordjevich, Dušan (2000) 'The Spirit of Milošević Remains: The Case Against', *Central Europe Review*, http://www.ce-review.org/00/36/debate36con.html (accessed 17 January 2003).

Doležal, Bohumil (1998) 'Obraz nepřítele v české národní ideologii', *Střední Evropa*, 12/1998, 16–23.

——(1999) 'Česko: Na konci s dychom?', *Domino fórum*, 11–17 November, 2.

Dorinda, Outram (1995) *The Enlightenment*, Cambridge: Cambridge University Press.

Dostál, Ondrej (1998) 'Minorities', in Martin Bútora and Thomas Skladony (eds) *Slovakia 1996–1997: A Global Report on the State of Society*, Bratislava: Institute for Public Affairs, 39–45.

Dryzek, John S. and Holmes, Leslie (1998) 'The Real World of Civic Republicanism: Making Democracy Work in Poland and the Czech Republic', unpublished manuscript presented at the AASCPCS/ANZSA International Conference on

Communist and Post-Communist Societies, University of Melbourne, 7–10 July 1998.

——(2002) *Post-Communist Democratization: Political Discourses across Thirteen Countries*, Cambridge: Cambridge University Press.

Ďurica, Milan S. (1995) *Dejiny Slovenska a Slovákov*, Košice: Pressko.

Eatwell, Roger (1997) *European Political Cultures*, London: Routledge.

Eberts, Mirella W. (1998) 'The Roman Catholic Church and democracy in Poland', *Europe-Asia Studies*, 50, July, 817–42.

Eder, Jürgen (1999) 'Die Jahre mit Acht – 1918, 1938, 1948, 1968...Zum Historischen bei Libuše Moníková', in Delf Schmidt and Michael Schwidtal (eds) *Prag-Berlin: Libuše Moníková, Rowohlt Literaturmagazin*, no. 44, 87–99.

Elshtain, Jean Bethke (1999) 'The Bright Line: Liberalism and Religion', *New Criterion*, vol. 17, no. 7, March, 4–15.

Elster, Jon, Offe, Claus and Preuss, Ulrich, K. (1998) *Institutional Design in Postcommunist Societies*, Cambridge: Cambridge University Press.

Engels, Frederick (1970) 'The Magyar Struggle', in Karl Marx and Frederick Engels, *The Revolutions of 1848: Political Writings, Vol. I*, ed. David Fernbach, London: New Left Review.

Fawn, Rick (2001) 'Czech Attitudes Towards the Roma: Expecting More of Havel's Country?', *Europe-Asia Studies*, vol. 53, no. 8, 1193–219.

Fiala, Petr and Mikš, František (1998) *Úvahy o české politické krizi*, Brno: Centrum pro studium demokracie a kultury.

Findlay, Edward F. (1999) 'Classical Ethics and Postmodern Critique: Political Philosophy in Václav Havel and Jan Patočka', *The Review of Politics*, vol. 61, no. 3, 403–38.

Fischer-Galati, Stephen (ed.) (1970) *Man, State and Society in East European History*, New York: Praeger.

Fish, Steven F. (1999) 'The End of Mečiarism', *East European Constitutional Review*, winter/spring, 47–55.

Fisher, Sharon (1996a) 'Quotes from Slovak Ruling Party's Congress', *OMRI Analytical Brief*, vol. 1, no. 58, 9 April.

——(1996b) 'Slovak Parliament Approves Law on the Protection of the Republic...', *OMRI Analytical Brief*, vol. 1, no. 42, 27 March.

——(1996c) 'Making Slovakia More "Slovak"', *Transition*, 29 November, 14–17.

Fraser, Nancy (1997) *Justice Interruptus: Critical Reflections on the 'Postsocialist' Condition*, New York: Routledge.

Friszek Andrzej (1993) 'Pytania o polskim nationalizmie' [Questions about Polish Nationalism], *Więź*, November, 74–85, reprinted in *Osteuropa-Archiv*, A26–30.

Fukuyama, Francis (1989) 'The End of History?', *The National Interest*, summer, 3–18.

Gabal, Ivan (1999) 'Etnické klima české společnosti,' in Ivan Gabal *et al.*, *Etnické menšiny ve střední Evropě: konflikt nebo integrace*, Prague: G plus G, 70–96.

Gardels, Nathan (1991) 'Two Concepts of Nationalism: An Interview with Isaiah Berlin', *The New York Review of Books*, 21 November, 19–24.

Garton Ash, Timothy (1989) *The Uses of Adversity*, Cambridge: Granta.

——(1995) 'Prague: Intellectuals and Politicians', *The New York Review of Books*, 12 January, 34–41.

——(1999) 'Ten Years After', *The New York Review of Books*, 11 November, 16–19.

Gawin, Dariusz (1997) 'O kłopotach liberalnej demokracji z moralnością', *Znak*, July, 45–58.

Gellner, Ernest (1983) *Nations and Nationalism*, Oxford: Blackwell.

——(1987) 'Zeno of Cracow', in *Culture, Identity and Politics*, Cambridge: Cambridge University Press, 47–74.

——(1992) 'Nationalism reconsidered and E. H. Carr', *Review of International Studies*, 18, 285–93.

——(1993) 'The Forgotten Beginnings of the Czech National Revival', *Times Literary Supplement*, 14 May, 3–5.

——(1994) 'The Price of Velvet: Tomáš Masaryk and Václav Havel', in *Encounters with Nationalism*, Oxford: Blackwell.

——(1995) *Anthropology and Politics*, Oxford: Blackwell.

——(1997) *Nationalism*, London: Weidenfeld and Nicolson.

Glassheim, Eagle (2001) 'The Mechanics of Ethnic Cleansing: The Expulsion of Germans from Czechoslovakia, 1945–1947', in Philip Ther and Ana Siljak (eds) *Redrawing Nations: Ethnic Cleansing in East-Central Europe*, Lanham MD: Rowman and Littlefield, 197–219.

Głuchowski, Piotr (1999) 'Ave Radio Maryja', *Transitions*, March, 70–4.

Goble, Paul (1998) 'Poland: Facing The Past, Facing The Future', *RFE/RL*, 26 October.

Goldhagen, Daniel (1996) *Hitler's Willing Executioners: Ordinary Germans and the Holocaust*, New York: Knopf.

Gomułka, Stanisław and Polonsky, Antony (eds) (1990) *Polish Paradoxes*, London: Routledge.

Gowin, Jarosław (2001) 'Naród – ostatni węzeł', *Rzeczpospolita*, 18 January, http://www.rzeczpospolita.pl/.

Gray, John (1995) *Isaiah Berlin*, London: HarperCollins.

Greenawalt, Kent (1995) *Private Consciences and Public Reasons*, Oxford: Oxford University Press.

Greenfeld, Liah (1992) *Nationalism: Five Roads to Modernity*, Cambridge MA: Harvard University Press.

——(1995) 'Nationalism in Western and Eastern Europe Compared', in Stephen E. Hanson and Willfried Spohn (eds) *Can Europe Work? Germany and the Reconstruction of Postcommunist Societies*, Seattle: University of Washington Press, 15–23.

Grendel, Lájos (1997) 'Dilemy stredoeurópskeho občana', *OS: Fórum Občianskej spoločnosti*, June.

——(1998) *Moja vlasť, Absurdistan*, Bratislava: Kalligram.

Gross, Irena G. (1995) 'Adam Mickiewicz: A European from Nowogródek', *East European Politics and Societies*, vol. 9, no. 2, spring, 295–316.

Gross, Jan T. (2001) [2000] *Neighbors: The destruction of the Jewish community in Jedwabne*, Princeton: Princeton University Press (Polish original published in 2000 as *Sąsiedzi*).

Gyárfášová, Oľga (2001) 'Individuálna historická pamäť', in Oľga Gyárfášová, Vladimír Krivý and Marián Velšic (eds) *Krajina v pohybe*, Bratislava: Inštitút pre verejné otázky, 251–64.

Habermas, Jürgen (1990) 'Nochmals: Zur Identität der Deutschen, Ein einig Volk von aufgebrachten Wirtschaftsbürgern?', in *Die Nachholende Revolution*, Frankfurt a. M.: Suhrkamp, 205–24.

——(1995) 'Citizenship and National Identity: Some Reflections on the Future of Europe', in Ronald Beiner (ed.) *Theorizing Citizenship*, New York: State University of New York Press, 255–82.

Hahn, Fred (1990) 'Masaryk and the Germans', in Harry Hanak (ed.) *T. G. Masaryk (1850–1937) Vol. 3: Statesman and Cultural Force*, Basingstoke: Macmillan, 99–124.

Hahnová, Eva (1995) 'To, co vítězí, nemusí být vždy pravda: O Arnoštu Gellnerovi, bílém koni a moderním světu', *Lidové noviny*, 26 August, 2.

Hampshire, Stuart (1989) *Innocence and Experience*, Cambridge MA: Harvard University Press.

Hancock, Ian (1997) 'The Struggle for the Control of Identity', *Transitions*, September, 36–44.

——(2002) *We are the Romani people*, Hatfield: University of Hertfordshire Press.

Hardin, Russell (1995) *One for All*, Princeton: Princeton University Press.

Havel, Václav (1990a) *O lidskou identitu*, Prague: Rozmluvy.

——(1990b) *Disturbing the Peace*, New York: Alfred A. Knopf.

——(1991) *Letní přemítaní*, Prague: Odeon.

——(1994) 'The New Measure of Man', *New York Times*, 8 July, A27.

——(1995a) *Toward a Civil Society: Selected Speeches and Writings, 1990–1994*, Prague: Lidové noviny.

——(1995b) 'The Responsibility of Intellectuals', *The New York Review of Books*, 22 June, 36–7.

——(1997a) 'Pozdrav prezidenta České republiky Václava Havla účastníkum konference Sto let Masarykovy České otázky', in Eva Broklová (ed.) *Sto let Masarykovy České otázky*, Prague: Ústav T. G. Masaryka, 7–8.

——(1997b) *The Art of the Impossible – Politics as Morality in Practice: Speeches and Writings, 1990–1996*, New York: Alfred A. Knopf.

——(1999a) 'Kosovo and the End of the Nation-State', *The New York Review of Books*, 10 June, 4–6.

——(1999b) 'Iron Curtain's Silver Lining', *The Australian's Review of Books*, November, 4.

——(1999c) 'Nepropást duležité okamžiky historických rozcestí', *Lidové noviny*, 29 October, 11.

——(1999d) 'Address in Acceptance of "Open Society Prize" in Budapest, June 24, 1999', *The New Presence*, 29 June, http://www.new-presence.cz.

——(2002) 'Beneš und das "tschechische Dilemma": Das Drama eines europäischen Politikers', in Barbara Coudenhove-Kalergi and Oliver Rathkolb (eds) *Die Beneš-Dekrete*, Vienna: Czernin Verlag, 33–7.

Held, Joseph (ed.) (1992) *The Columbia History of Eastern Europe in the Twentieth Century*, New York: Columbia University Press.

Henry, Marilyn (1998) 'Polish Catholic Clergy Crowd Warsaw's Nozyk Synagogue', *Jerusalem Post*, http://www.megsinet.com/mikerose/clergy.html, 18 January.

Herder, Johann Gottfried (1994) *Schriften zu Philosophie, Literatur, Kunst und Altertum 1774–1787*, Frankfurt a. M.: Deutscher Klassiker Verlag.

Herer, Wiktor and Sadowski, Władysław (1990): 'The Incompatibility of System and Culture and the Polish Crisis', in Stanisław Gomułka and Antony Polonsky (eds) *Polish Paradoxes*, London: Routledge.

Hilde, Paal Sigurd (1999) 'Slovak Nationalism and the Breakup of Czechoslovakia', *Europe-Asia Studies*, vol. 51, no. 4, 647–65.

Hirst, John (1991) 'Australia's Absurd History: A Critique of Multiculturalism', *Quadrant*, March, 20–7.

——(1994) 'National Pride and Multiculturalism', *Quadrant*, November, 29–34.

Hobsbawm, Eric (1990) *Nations and Nationalism since 1780: Programme, Myth, Reality*, Cambridge: Cambridge University Press.

——(1997) *On History*, London: Weidenfeld and Nicolson.

Hodža, Milan (1942) *Federation in Central Europe*, London: Jarrold.

——(1997) *Federácia v strednej Európe a iné štúdie*, Bratislava: Kalligram.

Holmes, Leslie (1999) 'Exclusion and Inclusion in Central and Eastern Europe', in Leslie Holmes and Philomena Murray (eds) *Citizenship and Identity in Europe*, Aldershot: Ashgate, 121–46.

Holmes, Steven (1993) *The Anatomy of Antiliberalism*, Cambridge MA: Harvard University Press.

——(1996) 'Cultural Legacies or State Collapse? Probing the Postcommunist Dilemma', in Michael Mandelbaum (ed.) *Postcommunism: Four Perspectives*, New York: Council on Foreign Relations, 22–76.

——(1997) 'In Search of New Enemies', *London Review of Books*, 24 April, 3–10.

Holomek, Karel (1999) 'Romská menšina v České republice', in Ivan Gabal *et al.*, *Etnické menšiny ve střední Evropě: konflikt nebo integrace*, Prague: G plus G, 153–71.

Holy, Ladislav (1996) *The Little Czech and The Great Czech Nation*, Cambridge: Cambridge University Press.

Hood, Adam (1998) 'Gabčíkovo-Nagymaros and Postcommunist Legitimacy: Are Hungary and Slovakia Building Dams or Nations?', paper presented at the AACPCS/ANZSA International Conference on Communist and Postcommunist Societies, Melbourne, 7–10 July.

Horvath, Robert (1999) 'The Impossible Dream: Dissidents, Democratisation, and Radical Nationalism in Russia', Ph.D. thesis, Department of History, University of Melbourne.

Hrabal, Bohumil (1990) *Closely Observed Trains*, London: Sphere Books.

Hroch, Miroslav (1995) 'National Self-Determination from a Historical Perspective,' in Sukumar Periwal (ed.) *Notions of Nationalism*, Budapest: Central European University Press, 65–82.

Huntington, Samuel (1996) *The Clash of Civilizations and the Remaking of World Order*, New York: Simon and Schuster.

Hyde-Price, Adrian (1996) *The International Politics of East Central Europe*, Manchester: Manchester University Press.

Ignatieff, Michael (1993) 'Strange Attachments', *The New Republic*, 29 March, 42–6.

Jasiak, Marek (2001) 'Overcoming Ukrainian Resistance: The Deportation of Ukrainians within Poland in 1947', in Philip Ther and Ana Siljak (eds) *Redrawing Nations: Ethnic Cleansing in East-Central Europe*, Lanham MD: Rowman and Littlefield, 173–94.

Jászi, Oscar (1929) *The Dissolution of the Habsburg Monarchy*, Chicago: University of Chicago Press.

Jedlicki, Jerzy (1990) 'The Revolution of 1989: The Unbearable Burden of History', *Problems of Communism*, July-August, 39–45.

——(1999) 'Historical Memory as a Source of Conflicts in Eastern Europe', *Communist and Post-Communist Studies*, 32, 225–32.

Johnson, Lonnie R. (1996) *Central Europe: Enemies, Neighbours, Friends*, Oxford: Oxford University Press.

Jurík, Ľuboš (1998) 'Čo chceme s novinami našimi?', *EuroReport*, 16–30 April, 1.

Kaczorowska, Małgorzata (2003) 'Copenhagen Summit: The Afterglow', *The Warsaw Voice News*, 3 January, http://www.warsawvoice.com.pl/.

Kaldor, Mary and Velvoda, Ivan (1997) 'Democratization in Central and East European Countries', *International Affairs*, vol. 73, no. 1, 59–82.

Kalvoda, Josef (1991) 'The Gypsies of Czechoslovakia', *Nationalities Papers*, vol. 19, no. 3.

Kamenec, Ivan (1998a) 'Stereotypy v slovenských dejinách a v slovenskej historiografii', *OS: Fórum Občianskej spoločnosti*, March, 3–5.

——(1998b) *Tragédia politika, kňaza a človeka (Dr Jozef Tiso 1887–1947)*, Bratislava: Archa.

Kant, Immanuel (1983) *Perpetual Peace and Other Essays*, Indianapolis and Cambridge: Hackett.

——(1986) *Philosophical Writings*, New York: Continuum.

Keane, John (1999) *Václav Havel: A Political Tragedy in Six Acts*, London: Bloomsbury.

Kedourie, Elie (1966) *Nationalism*, London: Hutchinson.

Kemp, Walter A. (1999) *Nationalism and Communism in Eastern Europe and the Soviet Union: A Basic Contradiction?*, New York: St Martin's Press.

Kersten, Krystyna (2001) 'Forced Migration and the Transformation of Polish Society in the Postwar Period', in Philip Ther and Ana Siljak (eds) *Redrawing Nations: Ethnic Cleansing in East-Central Europe*, Lanham MD: Rowman and Littlefield, 75–86.

Kirschbaum, Stanislav J. (1995) *A History of Slovakia: The Struggle for Survival*, New York: St Martin's Press.

——(1999a) 'The First Slovak Republic (1939–1945)', unpublished manuscript, 1–36; forthcoming in *Österreichische Osthefte*, vol. 41, nos. 3/4, 405–25.

——(1999b) 'Slovakia: The End to a Confused Sense of Direction?', *International Journal*, vol. 54, no. 4, autumn, 582–602.

Kis, János (1996) 'Beyond the Nation State', *Social Research*, spring, 191–245.

Klaus, Václav (1997) *Renaissance: The Rebirth of Liberty in the Heart of Europe*, Washington: Cato Institute.

Koepke, Wulf (1987) *Johann Gottfried Herder*, Boston MA: Twayne Publishers.

Kohák, Erazim (1989) *Jan Patočka: Philosophy and Selected Writings*, Chicago: University of Chicago Press.

Kohn, Hans (1944) *The Idea of Nationalism: A Study of its Origin and Background*, New York: Macmillan.

Kołakowski, Leszek (1996) 'Laienpredigt über christliche Werke', *Transit*, 12, winter, 205–13 (reprinted from *Gazeta Wyborcza*, 20, 21 January).

Konkoly, Peter (1986) *Reminiscencie*, Košice: Gabriel Bielek.

Konrád, György (1995) *The Melancholy of Rebirth*, New York: Harcourt Brace.

Kořalka, Jiří (1994) 'Hans Kohns Dichotomie und die neuzeitliche Nationsbildung der Tschechen', in Eva Schmidt-Hartmann, *Formen des nationalen Bewußtseins im Lichte zeitgenössischer Nationalismustheorien*, Munich: R. Oldenburg Verlag, 263–75.

Korbonski, Andrzej (2000) 'Poland Ten Years after: The Church', *Communist and Post-communist Studies*, vol. 33, no. 1, March, 123–46.

Kosc, Wojtek (2001) 'Poland: Not Such Good Neighbors', *Transitions Online*, 5–11 March, http://www.tol.cz/index.html.

Kováč, Dušan (1993) 'Philosophie und Mythologisierung der slowakischen Geschichte', *Österreichische Osthefte*, vol. 35, no. 4, 517–36.

——(1997) *Slováci a Česi: Dejiny*, Bratislava: Academic Electronic Press.

——(1999) 'Vyústenie slovenských dejín?', *Plus 7 dní*, March 1999.

Kováč, Dušan and Lipták, L'ubomír (1997) 'Slovenskí historici o knihe', *Práca*, 19 April, reprinted in *Kritika & kontext*, nos. 2–3, 34–40.

Kováč, Dušan, Suppan, Arnold and Hrabovec, Emilia (eds) *Die Habsburger Monarchie und die Slowaken 1849–1867*, Bratislava: Academic Electronic Press.

Kováč, Ladislav (1989) 'Premýšl'anie o vede a našich dejinách', *Slovenské pohl'ady*, no. 3, reprinted in Rudolf Chmel (1997) *Slovenská otázka v 20. storočí*, Bratislava: Kalligram, 500–16.

Kovtun, George J. (ed.) (1990) *The Spirit of Thomas G. Masaryk: An Anthology*, Basingstoke: Macmillan.

Kowalski, Artur J. and Stanclik, Katarzyna (1998) 'The New Constitution of the Polish Republic', *Pigulky*, no. 24, 31 March, http://www.pdi.lodz.pl/Pigulki/.

Kramer, Mark (2001) 'Introduction', in Philip Ther and Ana Siljak (eds) *Redrawing Nations: Ethnic Cleansing in East-Central Europe*, Lanham MD: Rowman and Littlefield, 1–42.

Krasnodębski, Zdzisław (1995) 'Der Nationalismus in Ostmitteleuropa', *Leviathan*, 15, 235–53.

——(1997) 'Polityka i moralność – w ogóle, u nas i gdzie indziej', *Znak*, July, 4–19.

——(2001) 'Der Pöbel in Jedwabne', *Znak*, February, reprinted in German translation in *Transodra-online*, 23 December, http://www.dpg-brandenburg.de/text/nr23.htm.

——(2002) 'Wyschły owoc: O czasach postpatriotycznych', *Znak*, April, 77–92.

——(2003) 'Re: Liberal Nationalism in Central Europe', e-mail, 11 March 2003.

Krejčí, Jaroslav and Machonin, Pavel (1996) *Czechoslovakia, 1918–92: A Laboratory for Social Change*, New York: St Martin's Press.

Krekovič, Eduard (1998) 'Etnogenéza, archeológia a nacionalizmus', *OS: Fórum Občianskej spoločnosti*, January, 5–6.

Krekovicová, Eva (1999) *Medzi toleranciou a bariérami: Obraz Rómov a židov v slovenskom folklóre*, Bratislava: Academic Electronic Press.

Kriseová, Eda (1991) *Václav Havel. Životopis*, Brno.

Król, Marcin (1997) 'Narodowy albo liberalny?', *Znak*, March, 62–8.

——(1998) 'Integracja Europejska: Za jaką cenę', *Rzeczpospolita*, 14 November, http://www.rzeczpospolita.pl/.

——(1999) *Liberalizmus strachu a liberalizmus odvahy*, Bratislava: Kalligram [translated from the 1996 Polish original *Liberalizm strachu czy liberalizm odwagi*].

Krygier, Martin (1997a) 'Is there Constitutionalism after Communism? Institutional Optimism, Cultural Pessimism and the Rule of Law', *International Journal of Sociology*, vol. 26, no. 4, winter 1996–7, 17–47.

——(1997b) 'Virtuous Circles: Antipodean Reflections on Power, Institutions and Civil Society', *East European Politics and Societies*, vol. 11, no. 1, 36–88.

Krzemiński, Adam (2003) 'Hauptsache nach Europa: Polnische Modernisierungsschübe', *Merkur*, vol. 57, no. 1, January, 36–46.

Kučera, Rudolf (1998a) 'Totalitní demokracie v Československu 1945–1948', *Střední Evropa*, December, 72–81.

——(1998b) 'Opoziční smlouva – Předmět politického zápasu', *Střední Evropa*, December, 4–7.

Kukathas, Chandran (1995) 'Are There Any Cultural Rights?', in Will Kymlicka (ed.) *The Rights of Minority Cultures*, Oxford: Oxford University Press, 228–55.

——(1997) 'Liberalism, Multiculturalism and Oppression', in Andrew Vincent (ed.) *Political Theory*, Cambridge: Cambridge University Press, 132–53.

——(1998) 'Liberalism and Multiculturalism: The Politics of Indifference', *Political Theory*, vol. 26, no. 5, October, 686–99.

Kukral, Michael (1997) *Prague 1989: Theater of Revolution*, Boulder CO/New York: East European Monographs/Columbia University Press.

Kundera, Milan (1984) 'The Tragedy of Central Europe', *New York Review of Books*, 26 April, 33–6.

Kuroń, Jacek and Lipski, Jan T. (2001) 'Nienawiść do ofiary. O zbrodni w Jedwabnem mówi Jacek Kuroń', *Gazeta Wyborcza*, 16 February, http://www.gazeta.pl/.

Kuroń, Jacek and Żakowski, Jacek (1997) *Siedmiolatka czyli kto ukradł Polskę?*, Wrocław: Wydawnictwo Dolnośląskie.

Kusý, Miroslav (1995) 'Slovak Exceptionalism', in Jiří Musil (ed.) *The End of Czechoslovakia*, Budapest: Central European University Press, 139–55.

Kusý, Miroslav (1997) 'Slovenský fenomén', in Rudolf Chmel (ed.) *Slovenská otázka v 20. storočí*, Bratislava: Kalligram, 460–81.

——(1998) *Čo s našimi Maďarmi?*, Bratislava: Kalligram.

——(1999) 'Ľudské a menšinové práva', in Mesežnikov, Grigorij and Ivantyšyn, Michal (eds) (1999) *Slovensko 1998–1999: Súhrnná správa o stave spoločnosti*, Bratislava: Inštitút pre verejné otázky, 173–90.

Kymlicka, Will (1990) *Contemporary Political Philosophy*, Oxford: Clarendon Press.

——(1995a) *Multicultural Citizenship*, Oxford: Clarendon Press.

——(1997) 'The Sources of Nationalism', in Robert McKim and Jeff McMaham (eds) *The Morality of Nationalism*, Oxford: Oxford University Press.

——(1998) 'Ethnic Relations and Western Political Theory', in Magda Opalski (ed.) *Managing Diversity in Plural Societies: Minorities, Migration and Nation-Building in Post-Communist Europe Forum Eastern Europe*, Ottawa, 275–322.

——(2001a) *Politics in the Vernacular: Nationalism, Multiculturalism and Citizenship*, Oxford: Oxford University Press.

——(2001b) 'Western Political Theory and Ethnic Relations in Eastern Europe', in Will Kymlicka and Magda Opalski (eds) *Can Liberal Pluralism be Exported? Western Political Theory and Ethnic Relations in Eastern Europe*, Oxford: Oxford University Press, 13–105.

Kymlicka, Will (ed.) (1995b) *The Rights of Minority Cultures*, Oxford: Oxford University Press.

Kymlicka, Will and Norman, Wayne (1995) 'Return of the Citizen: A Survey of Recent Work on Citizenship Theory', in Ronald Beiner (ed.) *Theorizing Citizenship*, New York: State University of New York Press, 283–322.

Laffan, Brigid, O'Donnel, Rory and Smith, Michael (2000) *Europe's Experimental Union*, London: Routledge.

Laitin, David (1998) 'Liberal Theory and the Nation', *Political Theory*, vol. 26, no. 2, April, 221–36.

Leff, Carol Skalnik (1995) 'Czech and Slovak Nationalism in the Twentieth Century', in Peter F. Sugar, *Eastern European Nationalism in the Twentieth Century*, Washington: American University Press, 103–61.

——(1997) *The Czech and Slovak Republics: Nation versus State*, Boulder CO: Westview.

Leško, Marián (1996) *Mečiar a mečiarizmus: Politik bez škrupúl', politika bez zábran*, Bratislava: VMV.

Letz, Róbert (1996) 'Milan S. Ďurica: Dejiny Slovenska a Slovákov', *Proglas*, June, reprinted in *Kritika & kontext*, 2–3 (1997) 41–3.

Lewy, Guenter (1999) 'The Travail of the Gypsies', *The National Interest*, no. 57, fall, 78–86.

Lichtenberg, Judith (1997) 'How Liberal Can Nationalism Be?', *The Philosophical Forum*, vol. XXVIII, nos. 1–2, fall-winter 1996–7, 53–72.

Liebich, André (1996) 'Getting Better, Getting Worse: Minorities in East Central Europe', *Dissent*, summer, 84–9.

Linek, Bernard (2001) '"De-Germanization" and "Re-Polonization" in Upper Silesia, 1945–1950', in Philip Ther and Ana Siljak (eds) *Redrawing Nations: Ethnic Cleansing in East-Central Europe*, Lanham MD: Rowman and Littlefield, 121–34.

Linz, Juan J. and Stepan, Alfred E. (1996) *Problems of Democratic Transition and Consolidation: Southern Europe, South America, and Post-Communist Europe*, Baltimore: Johns Hopkins University Press.

Lipski, Jan Józef (1995) 'Dvě vlasti – dvě vlastenectví', *Střední Evropa*, 53, 10–32.

Lipták, L'ubomír (1994) *Die Geschichte der Slowakei und der Slowaken*, Bratislava: Ministry for Foreign Affairs.

——(1999) *Storočie dlhšie ako sto rokov*, Bratislava: Kalligram.

Lom, Petr (1999) 'East Meets West – Jan Patočka and Richard Rorty on Freedom: A Czech Philosopher Brought into Dialogue with American Postmodernism', *Political Theory*, vol. 27, no. 4, August, 447–59.

Lukáč, Pavol (1996) 'Milan Hodža: Federácia v strednej Európe', *Kritika & kontext*, 1/1996, 70–2.

Lukowski, Jerzy and Zawadzki, Hubert (2001) *A Concise History of Poland*, Cambridge: Cambridge University Press.

Macedo, Stephen (1995) 'Multiculturalism for the Religious Right? Defending Liberal Civic Education', *Journal of the Philosophy of Education*, vol. 29, no. 2, 223–38.

Macháček, Jan (1997) 'Papírové hlavy: V české justici vládne forma nad obsahem', *Respekt*, no. 48, 24–30 November.

Macura, Vladimír (2001) 'Die Wahrheit siegt', in Walter Koschmal, Marek Nekula and Joachim Rogall (eds) *Deutsche und Tschechen: Geschichte, Kultur, Politik*, Munich: Beck, 542–7.

Madison, James, Hamilton, Alexander and Jay, John (1987) *The Federalist Papers*, ed. Isaac Kramnick, Harmondsworth: Penguin.

Majman, Slawomir (1999) 'Andrzej Lepper: Close to Jesus', *Warsaw Voice News*, no. 22, 30 May, http://www.warsawvoice.com.pl/.

Mandelbaum, Michael (1996) (ed.) *Postcommunism: Four Perspectives*, New York: Council on Foreign Relations.

Mandler, Emanuel (1999a) 'Evropanství, nacionalismus a národní stát', *Lidové noviny*, 19 June, 11.

——(1999b) 'Jak vysoký je plot v Matiční ulici', *Lidové noviny*, 12 October, 10.

——(2001) *Češi i Němci: legendy, spory, realita*, Prague: Libri.

Mann, Arne B. (1992) 'The Formation of the Ethnic Identity of Romany in Slovakia', in Plichtová, Jana (ed.) *Minorities Politics*, Bratislava: Czechoslovak Committee of the European Cultural Foundation, 260–5.

Masaryk, T. G. (2000) [1895] *Česká otázka, Naše nynejší krize, Jan Hus*, Prague: Masarykuv ústav AV ČR.

Matuška, Alexander (1946) 'My sme Slováci', *Národná obroda*, 83/1946, reprinted in Rudolf Chmel (1997) *Slovenská otázka v 20. storočí*, Bratislava: Kalligram, 321–2.

Mazower, Mark (1998) *Dark Continent: Europe's Twentieth Century*, London: Penguin.

Mečiar, Vladimír (1994) 'Krajine pokoj, občanovi úctu', published on the official home page of HZDS, http://www.hzds.sk/spravy/15%5F99/kra1502.html.

Mesežnikov, Grigorij (1998) 'Domestic Politics', in Martin Bútora and Thomas Skladony (eds) *Slovakia 1996–1997: A Global Report on the State of Society*, Bratislava: Institute for Public Affairs, 11–25.

——(2000) 'Vládna koalícia: prevládne snaha o reformy alebo stranícky egoizmus?', *Mosty*, 4 April, 14.

——(2002) 'Domestic Politics', in Grigorij Mesežnikov, Miroslav Kollár and Tom Nicholson (eds) *Slovakia 2001: A Global Report on the State of Society*, Bratislava: Institute for Public Affairs, 21–92.

Mesežnikov, Grigorij and Ivantyšyn, Michal (eds) (1999) *Slovensko 1998–1999: Súhrnná správa o stave spoločnosti*, Bratislava: Inštitút pre verejné otázky.

Michnik, Adam (1985) *Letters from Prison*, Berkeley: University of California Press.

——(1993) *The Church and the Left*, Chicago: University of Chicago Press.

——(1995) 'Jakiego prezydenta Polska potrzebuje?', *Gazeta Wyborcza*, 16–17 September, 6–8.

——(1997) 'Grey is Beautiful: Thoughts on Democracy in Central Europe', *Dissent*, spring, 14–19.

——(1998a) 'The Clean Conscience Trap', *East European Constitutional Review*, vol. 7, no. 2, spring, 67–74.

——(1998b) 'Hero or Traitor: A Former Spy's Return Home Kindles Controversy', *Transitions*, vol. 5, no. 9, September, 26–33.

——(2002) 'Michnik pyta o Europe', *Gazeta Wyborcza*, 27 December, http://www.gazeta.pl/.

Michnik, Adam and Cimoszewicz, Włodzimierz (1995) 'O prawdę i pojednanie', *Gazeta Wyborcza*, 9–10 September, 6–7.

Mickiewicz, Adam (1944) 'The Books of the Polish Nation, from the Beginning of the World to the Martyrdom of the Polish Nation', in Adam Mickiewicz, *Poems*, New York: Polish Institute of Arts and Sciences in America.

Miháliková, Silvia (1996) 'The Painful Birth of Slovak Democratic Political Culture', *Slovak Sociological Review*, vol. 1, spring, 51–68.

Mill, John Stuart (1991) *On Liberty and Other Essays*, Oxford: Oxford University Press.

Millard, Frances (1995) 'Nationalism in Poland', in Paul Latawski (ed.) *Contemporary Nationalism in East Central Europe*, London: St Martin's Press.

——(1996) 'The Failure of Nationalism in Post-Communist Poland', in Brian Jenkins and Spyros A. Sofos (eds) *Nation and Identity in Contemporary Europe*, London: Routledge, 201–22.

Miller, David (1993) 'In Defence of Nationality', *Journal of Applied Philosophy*, vol. 10, no. 1, 3–16.

——(1995) *On Nationality*, Oxford: Clarendon.

Miłosz, Czesław (1962) *The Captive Mind*, London: Mercury.

Mináč, Vladimír (1965) 'Tu žije národ', *Kultúrny život*, nos. 44–5, reprinted in Rudolf Chmel (ed.) (1997) *Slovenská otázka v 20. storočí*, Bratislava: Kalligram, 342–68.

Mommsen, Wolfgang (1993): 'Nationality, Patriotism, Nationalism', in Roger Michener (ed.) *Nationality, Patriotism and Nationalism in Liberal Democratic Societies*, St Paul: Paragon House, 1–18.

Moore, Barrington (1966) *Social Origins of Dictatorship and Democracy*, Harmondsworth: Penguin.

Morawska, Ewa (1995) 'The Polish Roman Catholic Church Unbound: Change of Face or Change of Context?', in Stephen Hanson and Willfried Spohn (eds) *Can Europe Work? Germany and the Reconstruction of Postcommunist Societies*, Seattle and London: University of Washington Press, 47–78.

Mušinka, Mykola (1992) 'The Rusyne-Ukrainian National Minority in Slovakia', in Jana Plichtová (ed.) *Minorities in Politics*, Bratislava: Czechoslovak Committee of the European Cultural Foundation, 224–8.

Naimark, Norman M. (2001) *Fires of Hatred: Ethnic Cleansing in Twentieth Century Europe*, Cambridge MA: Harvard University Press.

Namier, Lewis B. (1942) *The Czecho-Slovaks: An Oppressed Nationality*, London: Hodder and Stoughton.

Naughton, James (2001) 'Background Notes on Czech and Slovak Literature: Literature up to the Husite Wars', http://users.ox.ac.uk/~tayl0010/czech.html (accessed 13 April 2003).

Němeček, Tomáš (2003) 'Čestný předseda ODS už nemusí "klamat rozhodčího" – je v cíli', *Respekt*, 10/03, http://respekt.inway.cz/.

Neudorfl, Marie L. (1999) 'Václav Havel and the Ideal of Democracy', in Stanislav J. Kirschbaum (ed.) *Historical Reflections on Central Europe*, New York: St Martin's Press, 116–37.

Nielsen, Kai (1997) 'Cultural Nationalism, neither Ethnic nor Civic', *The Philosophical Forum*, vol. 28, nos. 1–2, fall-winter 1996–7, 42–52.

Niżnik, Józef and Sanders, T. John (1996) (eds) *Debating the State of Philosophy: Habermas, Rorty, and Kolakowski*, London: Praeger.

Nowak-Jeziorański, Jan (2001) 'Potrzeba zadośćuczynienia', *Rzeczpospolita*, 26 January, http://www.rzeczpospolita.pl/.

Nussbaum, Martha (1996) *For Love of Country: Debating the Limits of Patriotism*, Boston MA: Beacon Press.

O'Brien, Conor Cruise (1988) *God Land*, Cambridge MA: Harvard University Press.

——(1992) *Great Melody: A Thematic Biography and Commented Anthology of Edmund Burke*, London: Sinclair-Stevenson.

——(1995) *On the Eve of the Millennium: The Future of Democracy through an Age of Unreason*, New York: The Free Press.

O'Neill, Onora (1986) 'The Public Use of Reason', *Political Theory*, vol. 14, no. 4, November, 523–51.

Obrman, Jan (1993) 'Havel Challenges Czech Historical Taboos', *RFE/RL Research Report*, vol. 2, no. 24, 11 June, 44–51.

——(1994) 'Sudeten Germans Controversy in the Czech Republic', *RFE/RL Research Report*, vol. 3, no. 2, 14 January, 9–16.

Offe, Claus (1992) 'Strong Causes, Weak Cures', *East European Constitutional Review*, vol. 1, no. 1, spring, 21–3.

——(1996) *Varieties of Transition: The East European and East German Experience*, Cambridge: Polity Press.

Opat, Jaroslav (1999) *T. G. Masaryk: Evropan, světoobčan*, Prague: Ústav T. G. Masaryka.

Osa, Maryjane (1997) 'Creating Solidarity: The Religious Foundations of the Polish Social Movement', *East European Politics and Societies*, vol. 11, no. 2, spring, 339–65.

Osiatynski, Wiktor (1992) 'The American and Polish Constitution', in Kenneth W. Thompson (ed.) *Poland in a World in Change: Constitutions, Presidents and Politics*, Maryland: University Press of America, 3–26.

——(1997) 'A Brief History of the Constitution', *East European Constitutional Review*, vol. 6, nos. 2–3, spring, www.law.nyu.edu/eecr.

Ossipov, Alexander (2001) 'Some Doubts about "Ethnocultural Justice"', in Will Kymlicka and Magda Opalski (eds) *Can Liberal Pluralism be Exported? Western Political Theory and Ethnic Relations in Eastern Europe*, Oxford: Oxford University Press, 171–85.

Palacký, František (1939) *Dějiny národu českého v Čechách a v Moravě I–VI*, 6 vols, Prague: Mazáč.

Palacky, Franz (1844) *Geschichte von Böhmen*, 6 vols, Prague: Kronberger und Řiwnač.

Patočka, Jan (2002) *Plato and Europe*, Stanford: Stanford University Press.

——(1990) *Náš národní program*, Prague: Evropský kulturní klub.

Pauer, Jan (1999) 'Tschechische Republik und das tschechoslowakische Erbe', in Leonid Luks and Donal O'Sullivan, *Die Rückkehr der Geschichte*, Cologne: Böhlau, 9–30.

Pawlikowski, John T. (1996) 'Křesťanská víra bez antisemitizmu', *Střední Evropa*, vol. 12, no. 1, 122–7.

Pekník, Miroslav *et al.* (eds) (2002) *Milan Hodža – štátnik a politik*, Bratislava: VEDA 2002.

Pešková, Jaroslava (1997) *Role vědomí v dějinách*, Prague: Lidové noviny.

Petráň, Josef and Petráňová, Lydia (1998) 'The White Mountain as a Symbol in Modern Czech History', in Mikuláš Teich (ed.) *Bohemia in History*, Cambridge: Cambridge University Press, 143–63.

Pichler, Tibor (1998) *Národovci a občania: O slovenskom politickom myslení v 19. storočí*, Bratislava: VEDA, Vydavateľstvo Slovenskej akadémie vied.

Pithart, Petr (1993) 'Národní, nebo občanský?', *Lidové noviny*, 5 January, 8.

——(1998) *Po devětaosmdesátém: Kdo jsme?*, Bratislava: Kalligram.

Plamenatz, John (1973) 'Two Types of Nationalism', in Eugene Kamenka (ed.) *Nationalism*, Canberra: Australian National University Press, 22–37.

Plichtová, Jana and Erös, Ferenc (1997) 'The Meaning of Some Political and Economic Terms in Relation to Experience of Two Slovak and Hungarian Generations', *Sociológia*, vol. 29, no. 6, 723–37.

Poole, Ross (1999) *Nation and Identity*, London: Routledge.

Popper, Karl (1945) *The Open Society and Its Enemies*, London: Routledge.

Porter, Brian A. (1992) 'Who Is a Pole and Where is Poland? Territory and Nation in the Rhetoric of Polish National Democracy before 1905', *Slavic Review*, vol. 51, no. 4, winter, 639–53.

——(1996) 'The Social Nation and its Futures: English Liberalism and Polish Nationalism in late 19th-century Warsaw', *American Historical Review*, vol. 101, no. 5, December, 1470–92.

——(2000) *When Nationalism Began to Hate: Imagining Modern Politics in Nineteenth Century Poland*, New York and Oxford: Oxford University Press.

——(2003a) 'Re: Liberal Nationalism in Central Europe', e-mail, 24 March.

——(2003b) 'The People of God: Poland, Catholicism, and History', paper presented at the University of Wisconsin, 1 April, 1–18.

Poulter, Sebastian (1987) 'Ethnic Minority Customs: English Law and Human Rights', *International and Comparative Law Quarterly*, vol. 36, July, 589–615.

Prazmowska, Anita J. (1995) 'The New Right in Poland: Nationalism, Anti-Semitism and Parliamentarism', in Luciano Cheles (ed.) *The Far Right in Western and Eastern Europe*, London: Longman.

Pynsent, Robert B. (1994) *Questions of Identity: Czech and Slovak Ideas of Nationality and Personality*, Budapest: Central European University Press.

——(1997) 'Národ, nic a láska (Pokus o Masaryka)', in Eva Broklová (ed.) *Sto let Masarykovy České otázky*, Prague: Ústav T. G. Masaryka, 326–42.

——(1998) 'Tinkering with the Ferkos: A Kind of Slovakness', *Slavonic and East European Review*, vol. 76, no. 2, April, 279–95.

——(1999) 'Die Dalimil-Chronik als polymythischer Text (Dalimil-Fichte-Havel)', in Eva Behring, Ludwig Richter and Wolfgang F. Schwarz (eds) *Geschichtliche Mythen in den Literaturen und Kulturen Ostmittel- und Südosteuropas*, Stuttgart: Steiner, 199–231.

——(2000) 'Tolerance and the Karel Čapek Myth', *The Slavonic and East European Review*, vol. 78, no. 2, April, 331–53.

——(2002) 'Západno-východné zovretie – dve východiská: Ľudovít Štúr (1815–1856) a Štěpan Launer (1821–1851)', translated from the German by Patrícia Elexová, *RAK*, VII, 8–21.

Rapant, Daniel (1968) 'Logika dejín', *Kultúrny život*, 33, 8–9.

Rawls, John (1971) *A Theory of Justice*, Cambridge MA: Harvard University Press.

——(1996) *Political Liberalism*, New York: Columbia University Press.

Raz, Joseph (1998) 'Multiculturalism', *Ratio Juris*, vol. 11, no. 3, September, 193–205.

Rorty, Richard (1989) *Contingency, Irony and Solidarity*, Cambridge: Cambridge University Press.

——(1991) 'The Seer of Prague', *The New Republic*, 1 July, 35–40.

——(1994) 'The Unpatriotic Academy', *The New York Times*, 13 February, E15.

——(1998) *Achieving Our Country*, Cambridge MA: Harvard University Press.

Rosenblum, Nancy L. (1998) *Membership and Morals*, Princeton: Princeton University Press.

Roszkowski, Wojciech (2002) 'After *Neighbors*: Seeking Universal Standards', *Slavic Review*, vol. 61, no. 3, fall, 460–5.

Ruane, Kevin (2002) *Reasons of State: To Kill a Polish Priest*, Sydney: Harper-Collins.

Ruml, Jan (1999) 'Myšlence národního státu už odzvonilo', *Lidové noviny*, 10 June, 11.

Sadowski, Michał (2001) 'Prawdy niewygodne. Jacek Kuroń: Kształtowaliśmy się sami jako naród męczenników', *Rzeczpospolita*, 26 May, www.rzeczpospolita.pl.

Sakwa, Richard (1999a) 'Postcommunist Studies: Once again through the Looking Glass (Darkly)?', *Review of International Studies*, 25, 709–19.

——(1999b) *Post-communism*, Buckingham: Open University Press.

Sandel, Michael J. (1996) *Democracy's Discontent: America in Search of a Public Philosophy*, Cambridge MA: Harvard University Press.

Sayer, Derek (1998) *The Coasts of Bohemia: A Czech History*, Princeton: Princeton University Press.

Schmögnerová, Brigita (1997) *Cúvanie napred*, Bratislava: Nadácia Ladislava Novomeského.

Schöpflin, George (1995) 'Nationalism and Ethnicity in Europe, East and West', in Charles A. Kupchan (ed.) *Nationalism and Nationalities in the New Europe*, Ithaca NY: Cornell University Press, 37–65.

——(2000) *Nations, Identity, Power*, New York: New York University Press.

——(2002) 'Identities, Politics and Post-Communism in Central Europe', the Eighth Annual Ernest Gellner Nationalism Lecture, 25 April, University College London, e-mail (19 September).

Schutz, Peter (2000a) 'Sme pekní, škaredá je otázka', *Domino fórum*, 2/2000.

——(2000b) 'Playing the Numbers Game', *Transitions online*, 9 February, http://www.tol.cz/index.html.

Schwarz, Karl-Peter (1993) *Tschechen und Slowaken: Der lange Weg zur friedlichen Trennung*, Vienna and Zurich: Europaverlag.

Scruton, Roger (1990a) *The Philosopher on Dover Beach*, Manchester: Carcanet.

——(1990b) 'Masaryk, Kant and the Czech Experience', in Stanley B. Winters (ed.) *T. G. Masaryk (1850–1937), Vol. 1: Thinker and Politician*, Basingstoke: Macmillan, 44–59.

——(1996) *Modern Philosophy: An Introduction and Survey*, London: Mandarin.

Sedová, Tatiana (1999) 'Od včerajška k dnešku a späť', *OS: Fórum Občianskej spoločnosti*, March, 89–90.

Segert, Dieter (2002) 'Viel weniger Rechtsradikalismus, als zu erwarten wäre', *Osteuropa*, vol. 52, no. 5, May, 621–5.

Seton-Watson, R. W. (1965) *A History of the Czechs and the Slovaks*, Hamden CT: Archon.

Šimečka, Martin (1997) 'Slovakia's Lonely Independence', *Transitions*, August, 14–21.

——(1998) 'The Importance of Reading Maps', *Partisan Review*, summer, 344–8.

Šimečka, Milan (1990) *Konec nehybnosti*, Prague: Lidové noviny.

Skilling, Gordon H. (1989) *Samizdat and an Independent Society in Central and Eastern Europe*, Basingstoke: Macmillan.

Sláma, Jiří (1998) 'Boiohaemum-Čechy', in Mikuláš Teich (ed.) *Bohemia in History*, Cambridge: Cambridge University Press, 23–38.

Slobodník, Dušan (1998) 'Kto túžil a túži po pokorenom Slovensku', published on the official home page of HZDS, http://www.hzds.sk/spravy/51/scen5101.html (accessed 9 January 1998).

Smith, Anthony D. (1991) *National Identity*, Harmondsworth: Penguin.

——(1993) 'A Europe of Nations – or the Nation of Europe?', *Journal of Peace Research*, vol. 30, no. 2, 129–35.

——(1995a) *Nations and Nationalisms in a Global Era*, Cambridge: Polity.

(1995b) 'The Dark Side of Nationalism: The Revival of Nationalism in Late Twentieth Century Europe', in Luciano Cheles (ed.) *The Far Right in Western and Eastern Europe*, London: Longman, 13–19.

Snyder, Jack (2001) *From Voting to Violence: Democratization and Nationalist Conflict*, New York: Norton.

Snyder, Louis L. (1990) *Encyclopedia of Nationalism*, New York: Paragon House.

Snyder, Tim (1998) 'Poland's Hot Summer of De-communization', *Transitions*, http://www.ijt.cz/transitions/toppolan.html.

Spousta, Jan (2002) 'Co všechno vyčteme ze sčítání lidu', *MF Dnes*, 17 July, B/6.

Stankiewicz, Katharina (2002) 'Die "neuen Dmowskis": eine alte Ideologie im neuen Gewand?', *Osteuropa*, vol. 52, no. 3, March, 263–79.

Stehle, Hansjakob (1991) 'Ein Nationalstaat von Hitlers Gnaden', *Die Zeit*, 19 September, 57–8.

Stevenson, Charles L. (1944) *Ethics and Language*, New Haven: Yale University Press.

Stoker, Bram (2002) *Dracula*, ed. John Paul Riquelme, Boston/New York: Bedford/St Martin's Press.

Stone, Daniel Z. (1990) 'Democratic Thought in Eighteenth Century Poland', in M. B. Biskupski and James S. Pula (eds) *Polish Democratic Tradition from the Renaissance to the Great Emigration: Essays and Documents*, New York: Columbia University Press, 55–72.

Štrasser, Ján (1996) 'Minulosť podl'a Štrelingera', *Domino Efekt*, 22/1996.

Strzeszewski, Michał (2002) 'Polska między Niemcami, Rosją i Ukrainą', Warsaw: Centrum Badania Opinii Społecznej.

——(2003) 'Czy Polacy lubią inne narody?', Warsaw: Centrum Badania Opinii Społecznej.

Suda, Zdeněk (2000) 'By Way of Introduction', in Jiří Musil and Zdeněk Suda (eds) *The Meaning of Liberalism – East and West*, Budapest: Central European University Press, 1–29.

Sugar, Peter F. (1997) *Nationality and Society in Habsburg and Ottoman Europe*, Aldershot: Variorum.

Sugar, Peter F. (ed.) (1995) *Eastern European Nationalism in the Twentieth Century*, Washington: American University Press.

Šulc, František (1998) 'Kotel plný hruzy', *Lidové noviny*, 22 May, 10.

Sunley, Johnathan (1996) 'Post-Communism: An Infantile Disorder', *The National Interest*, 44, summer, 3–15.

Šustrová, Petruška (1998) 'Prezident a státotvornost', *Lidové noviny*, 14 May, 10.

Šútovec, Milan (1999) *Semióza ako politikum alebo 'pomlčková vojna'*, Bratislava: Kalligram.

Svora, Přemysl (1998) *Sedm týdnu, které otřásly Hradem*, Prague: Svora.

Szacki, Jerzy (1995) *Liberalism after Communism*, Budapest: Central European University Press.

——(2002) 'O potrzebie patriotyzmu', *Znak*, April, www.znak.com.pl.

Szajkowski, Bogdan (1997) 'Poland', in Roger Eatwell (ed.) *European Political Cultures: Conflict or Convergence?*, London: Routledge, 157–71.

Szczypiorski, Andrzej (1998) 'Der März 1968 und die Polen', originally in *Gazeta Wyborcza*, 28/29 March, reprinted in German translation in *Transodra-online*, 18, October, http://www.dpg-brandenburg.de/text/nr18.htm.

Szomolányi, Soňa (1997) *Slovakia: Problems of Democratic Consolidation and the Struggle for the Rules of the Game*, Bratislava: Slovak Political Science Association and Friedrich Ebert Foundation.

Tamir, Yael (1993) *Liberal Nationalism*, Princeton: Princeton University Press.

——(1995) 'The Enigma of Nationalism', *World Politics*, 47, April, 418–40.

Taras, Ray (1998) 'Redefining National Identity After Communism: A Preliminary Comparison of Ukraine and Poland', in Ray Taras (ed.) *National Identities and Ethnic Minorities in Eastern Europe*, New York: St Martin's Press, 84–112.

——(1999) 'Politics in Poland', in Gabriel A. Almond, Russell J. Dalton and G. Bingham Powell Jr (eds) *European Politics Today*, New York: Longman, 364–420.

——(2002) *Liberal and Illiberal Nationalisms*, Basingstoke: Palgrave Macmillan.

Taylor, Charles (1992) *Multiculturalism and 'The Politics of Recognition'*, Princeton: Princeton University Press.

Tétreault, Mary Ann and Teske, Robin, L. (1997) 'The Struggle to Democratize the Slovak Republic', *Current History*, March, 135–9.

Ther, Philip (2001) 'A Century of Forced Migration: The Origins and Consequences of Ethnic Cleansing', in Philip Ther and Ana Siljak (eds) *Redrawing Nations: Ethnic Cleansing in East-Central Europe*, Lanham MD: Rowman and Littlefield, 43–72.

Thierse, Wolfgang (2000) 'Deutschland muss seine Tradition der kulturellen Integration fortsetzen', *Die Welt*, 30 December, http://www.welt.de/ (accessed 30 December 2000).

Tighe, Carl (1997) 'Adam Michnik: A Life in Opposition', *Journal of European Studies*, vol. 27, no. 3, September, 323–67.

Tischner, Józef (1998) *Etika solidarity*, Bratislava: Kalligram.

Tismaneanu, Vladimir (1998) *Fantasies of Salvation*, Princeton: Princeton University Press.

Tocqueville, Alexis de (1994) *Democracy in America*, New York: Alfred A. Knopf.

Todorova, Maria (1997) *Imagining the Balkans*, Oxford: Oxford University Press.

Tomčík, Miloš (1992) 'Masarykov podiel na aktivizácii slovenskej literatúry 19. a 20. storočia', in Jaroslav Opat, Miloš Tomčík and Zdeněk Urban, *T. G. Masaryk a Slovensko*, Prague: Masarykova společnost, 22–67.

Třeštík, Dušan (1998) 'Je český národ xenofobní?', in Petr Žantovský (ed.) *Česká xenofobie*, Prague: Votobia, 141–6.

Tucker, Aviezer (1996) 'Shipwrecked: Patočka's philosophy of Czech history', *History and Theory*, vol. 35, no. 2, May, 196–217.

——(1999) 'The Politics of Conviction: The Rise and Fall of Czech Intellectual-Politicians', in András Bozóki (ed.) *Intellectuals and Politics in Central Europe*, Budapest: Central European University Press, 185–206

——(2000) *The Philosophy and Politics of Czech Dissidence from Patočka to Havel*, Pittsburgh: University of Pittsburgh Press.

Tymowski, Andrzej W. (2002) 'Apologies for Jedwabne and Modernity', *East European Politics and Societies*, vol. 16, no. 1, winter, 291–306.

Uhde, Milan (1995) *Česká republiko, dobrý den*, Prague: Atlantis.

Ulc, Otto (1996) 'Czechoslovakia's Velvet Divorce', *East European Quarterly*, vol. 30, no. 3, fall, 331–50.

Urbinati, Nadia (1996) 'A common Law of Nations: Giuseppe Mazzini's democratic nationality', *Journal of Modern Italian Studies*, spring, 197–222.

Vachudová, Milada and Snyder, Tim (1997) 'Are Transitions Transitory? Two Types of Political Change in Eastern Europe Since 1989', *East European Politics and Societies*, vol. 11, no. 1, 1–35.

Vašečka, Michal (2002) 'Roma', in Grigorij Mesežnikov, Miroslav Kollár and Tom Nicholson (eds) *Slovakia 2001: A Global Report on the State of Society*, Bratislava: Institute for Public Affairs, 149–65.

Vetter, Reinhold (1998) 'März 1968 im Jahre 1998', *Transodra-online*, 18, October, http://www.dpg-brandenburg.de/text/nr18.htm.

Vilikovský, Pavel (1989) *Večne je zelený...*, Bratislava: Slovenský spisovateľ'.

——(1998) *Okrídlená klietka alebo zo života mladého Slovenska a starých Slovákov*, Levice: Vydavateľstvo LCA.

Vincent, Andrew (2002) *Nationalism and Particularity*, Cambridge: Cambridge University Press.

Vodička, Karel (2003) 'Rómovia na Slovensku: Prekážka na ceste do Európskej únie?', *OS: Fórum Občianskej spoločnosti*, April 2002, 13–18.

Votruba, Martin (1998) 'Linguistic Minorities in Slovakia', in Christina B. Paulston and Donald Peckham (eds) *Linguistic Minorities in Central and Eastern Europe*, Clevedon: Multilingual Matters, 255–79.

Vražda, Daniel (2000) 'Útok na Róma prvýkrát uznali za rasový', *Sme*, 28 April.

Waldron, Jeremy (1995) 'Minority Cultures and the Cosmopolitan Alternative', in Will Kymlicka (ed.) *The Rights of Minority Cultures*, Oxford: Oxford University Press, 93–122.

Walicki, Andrzej (1982) *Philosophy and Romantic Nationalism: The Case of Poland*, Oxford: Oxford University Press.

——(1989) *The Enlightenment and the Birth of Modern Nationhood*, Notre Dame IN: University of Notre Dame Press.

——(1990) 'The Three Traditions in Polish Patriotism', in Stanisław Gomułka and Antony Polonsky (eds) *Polish Paradoxes*, London: Routledge, 21–39.

——(1995) *Marxism and the Leap to the Kingdom of Freedom: The Rise and Fall of the Communist Utopia*, Stanford: Stanford University Press.

——(1997a) 'Intellectual Elites and the Vicissitudes of "Imagined Nation" in Poland', *East European Politics and Societies*, vol. 11, no. 2, 227–53.

——(1997b) 'Czy możliwy jest nacjonalizm liberalny?', *Znak*, March, 32–50.

——(1997c) 'Moralność polityczna liberalizmu, narodowa moralistyka i idee kolektywistycznej prawicy', *Znak*, July, 21–37.

——(2000) 'The Troubling Legacy of Roman Dmowski', *East European Politics and Societies*, vol. 14, no. 1, 12–46.

Warmińska, Katarzyna (1997) 'Polish Tartars: Ethnic Ideology and State Policy', in Cora Govers and Hans Vermeulen (eds) *The Politics of Ethnic Consciousness*, Basingstoke: Macmillan, 343–66.

Weidenhofferová, Iva (ed.) (1996) *Konfliktní společenství, katastrofa, uvolnění: Náčrt výkladu česko-německých dějin od 19. století*, Prague: Ústav mezinárodních vztahu.

Weiss, Aharon (ed.) (1988) *Yad Vashem Studies XIX*, Jerusalem: Yad Vashem.

Whitefield, Stephen and Evans, Geoffrey (1999) 'Political Culture Versus Rational Choice: Explaining Responses to Transition in the Czech Republic and Slovakia', *British Journal of Political Science*, 29, 129–55.

Willems, Wim (1997) *In Search of a True Gypsy*, London: Frank Cass.

Williams, Kieran (1997) 'National Myths in the New Czech Liberalism', in Geoffrey Hosking and George Schöpflin (eds) *Myth and Nationhood*, London: Hurst and Company, 132–40.

Winczorek, Piotr (1997a) 'Konstytucyjny sukces opozycji', *Rzeczpospolita*, 24 March, http://www.rzeczpospolita.pl/.

——(1997b) 'Konstytucja weszła w życie', *Rzeczpospolita*, 17 October, http://www.rzeczpospolita.pl/.

——(1998) 'The Political Circumstances of the Drafting of the Constitution of the Republic of Poland of 2 April 1997', unpublished manuscript presented at the AASCPCS/ANZSA International Conference on Communist and Post-communist Societies, University of Melbourne, 7–10 July.

——(2002) 'Pięć lat konstytucji', *Res Publica Nowa*, March, http://respublica.onet.pl/.

Winters, Stanley B. (ed.) (1990) *T. G. Masaryk (1850–1937): Thinker and Politician*, Basingstoke: Macmillan.

Wolchik, Sharon L. (1992) 'Czechoslovakia', in Joseph Held (ed.) *The Columbia History of Eastern Europe in the Twentieth Century*, New York: Columbia University Press, 119–63.

——(1997) 'Democratization and Political Participation in Slovakia', in Karen Dawisha and Bruce Parrott (eds) *The Consolidation of Democracy in East-Central Europe*, Cambridge: Cambridge University Press, 197–244.

——(1998) 'Czech and Slovak Popular Attitudes towards Politics', paper presented at the AASCPCS/ANZSA International Conference on Communist and Post-communist Societies, University of Melbourne, 7–10 July.

Woolf, Stuart (ed.) (1996) *Nationalism in Europe, 1815 to the Present: A Reader*, London: Routledge.

Young, Iris Marion (1990) *Justice and the Politics of Difference*, Princeton: Princeton University Press.

Zahradil, Jan, Plecitý, Petr, Adrián, Petr and Bednář, Miloslav (2001) 'Manifest českého eurorealismu', *OS: Fórum Občianskej spoločnosti*, May, 45–8.

Zajac, Peter (1996) *Sen o krajine*, Bratislava: Kalligram.

Žák, Václav (1999) 'Nebezpečné hry s národní kartou', *Lidové noviny*, 22 June, 9.

Zakaria, Fareed (1997) 'The Rise of Illiberal Democracy', *Foreign Affairs*, November/December, 22–43.

Żakowski, Jacek (2000) 'Czy Polacy mają czuć się winni zbrodni w Jedwabnem', *Gazeta Wyborcza*, 18 November, http://www.gazeta.pl/.

Zaremba, Marcin (2001) *Komunizm, legitymizacja, nacjonalizm: Nacjonalistyczna legitymizacja władzy komunistycznej w Polsce*, Warsaw: Wydawnictwo Trio.

Zdort, Marcin and Janowski, Michał (1997) 'Marsz tolerancji czy obłudy', *Rzeczpospolita*, 28 November, http://www.rzeczpospolita.pl/.

Zeman, Zbyněk and Klimek, Antonín (1997) *The Life of Edvard Beneš 1884–1948: Czechoslovakia in Peace and War*, Oxford: Clarendon Press.

Žiak, Miloš (1996) *Slovensko: Od komunizmu kam?*, Bratislava: Archa.

Žižek, Slavoj (1999) 'Attempts to Escape the Logic of Capitalism', *London Review of Books*, 28 October, 2–6.

Znoj, Milan (1997) 'Zpusoby tolerance jako typy demokracie', *Filosofický časopis*, vol. 45, no. 3, 497–505.

——(1999) 'Czech Attitudes Toward the War', *East European Constitutional Review*, vol. 8, no. 3, summer, 47–50.

Znoj, Milan, Havránek, Jan and Sekera, Martin (eds) (1995) *Český liberalismus: texty a osobnosti*, Prague: Torst.

Zumr, Josef (1997) 'Prof. Pekař opravdu o historickém vývoji nemá potuchy', in Eva Broklová (ed.) *Sto let Masarykovy České otázky*, Prague: Ústav T. G. Masaryka, 59–65.

Zygulski, Witold (1997) 'Muffled for the Good of the Fatherland', *Warsaw Voice News*, 9 November, no. 45, http://www.warsawvoice.com.pl/.

Reports

OSCE Report (1997) 'Human Rights and Democratization In Slovakia', in *Commission on Security and Cooperation in Europe*, September 1997.

Roma Rights (1999) 'Snapshots from around Europe', *European Roma Rights Center*, report no. 2/1999, and no. 4/1999, http://errc.org.

EIU Country Profile, Slovakia 1998–99.

EIU Country Report, Slovakia, 4th quarter, 1998.

Eurobarometer, March 2002.

Encyclopaedias and dictionaries

Academia (1972) *Malý encyklopedický slovník A–Ž*, Prague: Academia, Nakladatelství Československé akademie věd.

Encyclopaedia Britannica (1999) standard edition on CD-ROM.

EU-SAV (1993) *Malá slovenská encyklopédia*, Bratislava: Encyklopedický ústav SAV and Goldpress Publishers.

Malá encyklopédia Slovenska (1987) Bratislava: Vydavateľstvo SAV.

The New Shorter Oxford English Dictionary (1993) Oxford: Clarendon Press.

Slovak, Czech and Polish newspapers and periodicals

Domino fórum
Gazeta Wyborcza
Kritika & kontext
Lidové noviny
Literárny týždenník
Mladá fronta Dnes
OS: Fórum Občianskej spoločnosti
Plus 7 dní
Pravda
Respekt
Rzeczpospolita
Slovenská republika
Sme
Střední Evropa
Warsaw Voice News
Więź
Znak

Index